CRITICAL PERSPECTIVES ON APPLIED THEATR

As the twenty-first century moves towards its third decade, applied theatre is being shaped by contemporary economic and environmental concerns and is contributing to new conceptual paradigms that influence the ways in which socially engaged art is produced and understood. This collection offers fresh perspectives on the aesthetics, politics and histories of applied theatre. With contributions from leading scholars in the field, the book illuminates theatre in a diverse range of global contexts and regions. Divided into three parts: histories and cultural memories; place, community and environment; and poetics and participation – the chapters interweave cutting-edge theoretical insights with examples of innovative creative practice that traverse different places, spaces and times. Essential reading for researchers and artists working within applied theatre, this collection will also be of interest to those in theatre and performance studies, education, cultural policy, social history and cultural geography.

JENNY HUGHES is Senior Lecturer in Drama at the University of Manchester. Her publications include a monograph, *Performance in a Time of Terror* (2011), which was joint winner of the Theatre and Performance Research Association (TaPRA) New Career Research prize, and a co-authored book with James Thompson and Michael Balfour, *Performance in Place of War* (2009).

HELEN NICHOLSON is Professor of Theatre and Performance at Royal Holloway, University of London, where she is also Associate Dean (Research) for the Faculty of Arts and Social Sciences. Helen has been co-editor of *RiDE: The Journal of Applied Theatre and Performance* since 2004, and author of several books in the field, including *Applied Drama: The Gift of Theatre* (2005, second edition 2014), *Theatre & Education* (2009) and *Theatre, Education and Performance* (2011), for which she was awarded the Distinguished Book Award by the American Alliance for Theatre and Education in 2012.

CRITICAL PERSPECTIVES ON APPLIED THEATRE

EDITED BY

JENNY HUGHES

University of Manchester

HELEN NICHOLSON

University of London

CAMBRIDGE
UNIVERSITY PRESS

University Printing House, Cambridge CB2 8BS, United Kingdom

Cambridge University Press is part of the University of Cambridge.

It furthers the University's mission by disseminating knowledge in the pursuit of education, learning and research at the highest international levels of excellence.

www.cambridge.org
Information on this title: www.cambridge.org/9781107065048

First published 2016

Printed in the United States of America by Sheridan Books, Inc.

A catalogue record for this publication is available from the British Library

Library of Congress Cataloguing in Publication data
Hughes, Jenny, 1971– editor. | Nicholson, Helen, 1958– editor.
Critical perspectives on applied theatre / edited by Jenny Hughes and Helen Nicholson.
Cambridge ; New York : Cambridge University Press, 2016. | Includes bibliographical references and index.
LCCN 2015046466 | ISBN 9781107065048 (alk. paper)
LCSH: Theater and society. | Community theater.
LCC PN2049 .C75 2016 | DDC 792–dc23
LC record available at http://lccn.loc.gov/2015046466

ISBN 978-1-107-06504-8 Hardback

Contents

v

Figures

vii

Contributors

SYED JAMIL AHMED is a theatre director and Professor at the Department of Theatre and Performance Studies, University of Dhaka. He trained at the National School of Drama (India), obtained his MA at the University of Warwick (UK), and his PhD at the University of Dhaka (Bangladesh). He founded the Department of Theatre and Music (now Department of Theatre and Performance Studies) at the University of Dhaka in 1994, and served as its Chair till 1997. He has directed plays in Bangladesh, Pakistan, India and the USA, and has over 60 research articles to his credit (in English and Bengali, as well as translations in Korean, Chinese, French and Norwegian). He has received two Fulbright fellowships, and has served as a visiting faculty at the Antioch College (USA), King Alfred's University of Winchester (UK), San Francisco City College (USA), and Jadavpur University (India). His book-length publications in English are *Acinpakhi Infinity: Indigenous Theatre in Bangladesh* (2000), *In Praise of Niranjan: Islam Theatre, and Bangladesh* (2001), *Reading Against the Orientalist Grain: Performance and Politics Entwined with a Buddhist Strain* (2008), and *Applied Theatricks: Essays in Refusal* (2013). His major areas of interest are Indigenous Theatre of South Asia, and Applied Theatre.

PAUL DWYER is a Senior Lecturer in the Department of Theatre and Performance Studies at the University of Sydney. He has published widely on applied theatre, in particular the work of Augusto Boal, and is currently completing a monograph on discourse and performance in restorative justice conferencing. Paul is also a performance maker with extensive professional experience in documentary theatre, including The Bougainville Photoplay Project, which toured throughout Australia and won a Melbourne Green Room Award, and Beautiful One Day, a collaboration with Ilbijerri Theatre, Belvoir St Theatre, version 1.0 and members of the Aboriginal and Torres Strait Islander communities of Palm Island.

MARK FLEISHMAN is Professor in the Department of Drama at the University of Cape Town and co-artistic director of Magnet Theatre. His articles have appeared in the *South African Theatre Journal, Contemporary Theatre Review* and *Theatre Research International* as well as in numerous edited collections, most recently in Anthony Jackson and Jenny Kidd (eds.) *Performing Heritage* (2011) and Nicolas Whybrow (ed.) *Performing Cities* (2014). He is editor of *Performing Migrancy and Mobility in Africa: Cape of Flows* in the Studies in International Performance series at Palgrave (2015). He has directed many performance works performed nationally and internationally, and is involved in development projects in urban townships and rural communities using theatre as a tool for social justice and transformation. His major research areas are dramaturgy, performing the archive, migration and contemporary South African theatre.

KATHLEEN GALLAGHER is Distinguished Professor in Theatre, Youth, and Research in Urban Schools at the University of Toronto. Kathleen Gallagher's books include, *Why Theatre Matters: Urban Youth, Engagement, and a Pedagogy of the real* (2014); *The Theatre of Urban: Youth and Schooling in Dangerous Times* (2007) *Drama Education in the Lives of Girls: Imagining Possibilities* (2000). Her edited collections include: *Why Theatre Now: On the virtue and value of Canadian theatre in the new millennium* (forthcoming with Barry Freeman); *Drama and Theatre in Urban Contexts.* (with Jonothan Neelands, 2013); *How Theatre Educates: Convergences and Counterpoints with Artists, Scholars, and Advocates* (with David Booth, 2003), *The Methodological Dilemma: Creative, Critical and Collaborative Approaches to Qualitative Research* (2008). Kathleen Gallagher has published many articles on theatre, youth, pedagogy, methodology and gender and travels widely giving international addresses and workshops for practitioners. Her research continues to focus on questions of youth civic engagement and artistic practice, and the pedagogical and methodological possibilities of theatre.

PAUL HERITAGE is Professor of Drama and Performance, Queen Mary University of London where he set up People's Palace Projects (www .peoplespalaceprojects.org.uk) as a research centre that advances practice and understanding of art for social justice. Heritage directed a series of award-winning arts-based human rights projects in prisons across Brazil (1992–2005) and established long-standing partnerships between UK arts institutions and cultural organizations from Brazil's diverse peripheries (e.g. Barbican/AfroReggae; RSC/Nós do Morro). As International Associate at the Young Vic, Heritage created Festa| Amazônia (2008): a year-long performance project involving thousands of participants and spectators in London and the Amazon region. Other UK/Brazil cultural exchanges and research projects include Fórum Shakespeare (1995-present), Encounters Beyond Text: Art Transforming Lives (2009–10), Points of Contact (2010–13), RioOccupationLondon (London 2012 Festival) and The Art of Cultural Exchange (2014–16). In 2004 Heritage was made a Knight of the Order of Rio Branco by the Brazilian government.

JENNY HUGHES is Senior Lecturer in Drama at the University of Manchester (UK). Her research interests include: theatre, performance and poverty; protest performance and theatre activism; theatre, performance and war; aspects of applied theatre and performance, especially theatre and performance practices with young people living with risk. Publications include a monograph, *Performance in a time of terror* (2011), which was joint winner of the Theatre and Performance Research Association (TaPRA) New Career Research prize, and a co-authored book (with James Thompson and Michael Balfour), *Performance in place of war* (2009). At the time of writing, she is working on a research project called 'Poor theatres: a critical exploration of theatre, performance and economic precarity', funded by an Arts and Humanities Research Council Early Career Research Fellowship (www.manchester .ac.uk/poortheatres).

BAZ KERSHAW is Emeritus Professor in theatre and performance at University of Warwick and former Foundation Chair of Drama, Bristol University. Originally an engineer, he has degrees from Manchester, Hawaii and Exeter Universities, been keynote at many international conferences and visiting researcher at lead institutions on several continents. He was also principal researcher with PARIP (2000–06) investigating practice-as-research, co-founder of IFTR Performance as Research Working Group and UK's TaPRA. Work in experimental/community/radical performance includes shows at the legendary London Drury Lane Arts Lab, co-founding the first rural community arts team then reminiscence theatre company, plus frequent projects with Welfare State International. Publications include *Politics of Performance* (1992), *Radical in Performance* (1999), *Theatre Ecology* (2007) and, as editor/author, *Cambridge History of British Theatre Vol III* (2004), *Research Methods in Theatre and Performance* (with Helen Nicholson – 2011).

Since 2000 he has created eco-specific events in southwest England and an Earthrise Repair Shop for mending broken imaginings of Earth.

SALLY MACKEY is Professor of Applied Theatre and Performance and Pro-Dean at The Royal Central School of Speech and Drama, University of London. She is on the editorial board of *RiDE: the Journal of Applied Performance and Theatre*, started the first UK undergraduate degree in applied theatre and developed Central's research centre Theatre Applied: the Centre for Research in Performance and Social Practice. She was a member of the UK Arts and Humanities Research Council (AHRC) commissioning panels for the major themes of 'Landscape and Environment' and 'Living with Environmental Change'. She publishes on performance, place, community and the environment, co-editing two themed editions in RiDE 'On Site and Place' and 'Environmentalism'. Together with Deirdre Heddon, she is co-editing the new Palgrave series on Performing Landscapes; her own contribution will be *Performing Landscapes: Homes*. Recently, she has worked on outputs from two AHRC grants: Challenging Place and Performing Abergavenny (an AHRC Connected Communities award).

D. SOYINI MADISON, a Professor of Performance Studies at Northwestern University (USA), focuses on political economy of human rights and indigenous performance tactics. Her book, *Acts of Activism: Human Rights and Radical Performance,* is based on how local activists in Ghana, West Africa, employ performance, as tactical interventions, in their quotidian struggles for women's rights, water democracy, and economic justice. Madison adapts and directs her ethnographic data for the public stage. Her recent book, *African Dress: Fashion, Agency, and Performance,* co-edited with Karen Tranberg Hansen, is a collection of essays on the dressed body, in specific sites, throughout Africa and the Black Diaspora. Madison is now working on the 3rd edition of *Critical Ethnography: Methods, Ethics and Performance.* She is also writing a monograph on the politics of beauty as a performance tactic across the transnational and racial contexts of Black is Beautiful and Black Lives Matter.

HELEN NICHOLSON is Professor of Theatre and Performance at Royal Holloway, University of London where she is also Associate Dean (Research) for the Faculty of Arts and Social Sciences. Helen has been co-editor of *RiDE: The Journal of Applied Theatre and Performance* since 2004, and author of several books in the field, including *Applied Drama:*

The Gift of Theatre (2005, second edition 2014), *Theatre & Education* (2009), and *Theatre, Education and Performance: The Map and the Story* (2011), for which she was awarded the Distinguished Book Award by the American Alliance for Theatre and Education in 2012. Helen continues maintain a long-term interest in researching theatre education with young people, and arts practices in residential care homes for older adults living with dementia. At the time of writing, she was leading the first major research project on amateur theatre, funded by the Arts and Humanities Research Council.

PETER O'CONNOR is Professor of Education and Director of the Critical Research Unit in Applied Theatre at the University of Auckland. He established the Teaspoon of Light Theatre Company in Christchurch post the earthquakes, and his work in Christchurch following led to UNESCO funded research and programme development. His research has focused primarily on using applied theatre as a public education medium to address major social issues including public health, gender equity in schools and the development of inclusive, empathetic and critical school cultures. Recent research includes national programmes on preventing family violence and child abuse and parenting programmes in Youth Justice Facilities. He is currently engaged in the ongoing debates about charter schools and the nature of quality public education. Peter was previously the National Education Manager for the Race Relations Office and the National Project manager for the Like Minds campaign with the Mental Health Foundation. His 2003 PhD on his work in forensic psychiatric units won the 2006 AATE Distinguished Dissertation Award in Washington DC, and in 2012 he was named Griffith University School of Education and Professional Studies Alumnus of the Year for his contribution to applied theatre and social justice.

SILVIA RAMOS is a social scientist with a doctorate in Public Health and Violence from the Fundação Oswaldo Cruz (Fiocruz), and currently one of the Coordinators of the Centre for the Study of Security and Citizenship at the University Candido Mendes, Rio de Janeiro (http://www.ucamce sec.com.br). Her research focuses on youth, violence, the police, media and sexual rights. Ramos has developed projects in partnership with groups such as AfroReggae and worked alongside young activists from the *favela* complexes of Alemão and Maré, where she is currently studying the trajectories of young people who leave the drug trade. She was State Sub-Secretary of Security for Rio de Janeiro (1999–2000), creating the social programme that accompanied the Pacifying Police Units/UPPs in Rio's *favelas* (2010). A founder of the Brazilian Forum of Public Security, Ramos has published books on the police and racial discrimination, media and violence, Lesbian, Gay, Bi-sexual and Transgender rights.

WAN-JUNG WANG received her PhD from Royal Holloway, University of London in applied drama and theatre in 2007. She is currently Professor at Department of Drama Creation and Application at National University of Tainan (Taiwan) and is an active director, playwright, teacher, writer and researcher in the field of applied drama and theatre. She has written seven books in Chinese on theatre studies, including: *Light and Sight on Stage* (2003), *On Wings We Fly across the Darkness* (2002), *Country Farmer Enters into the City of God* (2009), *The Legend of King Da Du* 2009). She has also written academic articles published in international and local journals in both English and Chinese, including in *RIDE: The Journal of Applied Theatre and Performance*.

CHAPTER I

Applied theatre
Ecology of practices

Jenny Hughes and Helen Nicholson

At high tide on the Thames on 13 June 2015 at 11.53 am a group of art activists began an unsanctioned twenty-five hour durational performance in the expansive Turbine Hall at Tate Modern, a large art gallery on the gentrified South Bank in London. Entitled *Time Piece*, this was the latest in a series of interventions by Liberate Tate, an art collective who stage performative protests against the oil industry's sponsorship of cultural organisations. Described as a 'textual intervention', seventy-five performers used charcoal to inscribe the concrete floor with passages and quotations from dystopian novels, environmental reports, slogans and non-fictional works about art, climate change and fossil fuel. Each performer scribbled silently, veiled and dressed in black, and when the gallery closed at 10 pm, twenty activists continued their carefully choreographed work through the night, unimpeded by security guards or the police. By morning, when Tate Modern re-opened its doors, the Turbine Hall remained closed to visitors. When the tide turned at 12.55 pm on 14 June, the performers left and the cleaning staff moved in.

We begin with this performative protest not because it is representative of all applied theatre, but because its concerns resonate with many of the ideas explored in this book. As a piece of activist art, *Time Piece* both invokes a long history of performative protest and also captures contemporary anxieties about the relationship between climate change, global capitalism, neoliberalism and the arts, all of which are debated by authors in this book. Beyond the substance of its environmental message, the performance illuminates deeper cultural responses to the contemporary landscape that are also articulated in this collection of essays. *Time Piece* re-imagined synergies between time and the material world, recognising that temporality is experienced in multiple ways. Liberate Tate capture this impulse on their website, describing how *Time Piece* draws attention to the different temporal registers that affect lives as 'lunar time, tidal time, ecological time, geological time and all the ways in which we are running out of time'.[1] The hunched figures dressed in black veils, quietly creating a rising tide of words on the floor, were like mourners marking a space by inscribing its relationship to lost time, a performative memorialisation of material life destroyed by practices of industrial excavation and economic exploitation driven by fossil fuel economies. Echoing many of the examples explored in this book, the performance drew attention to the geopolitics of place and was underscored by an impetus to re-make relationships between the human and non-human world. In the final moments of the short film of *Time Piece*, an applauding audience watch a gallery cleaner with his mop and bucket wash away the text, emphasising the impermanence of performance. Given that Liberate Tate habitually use social media to promote their vision for social change and to document their artistic interventions, it is significant that the last words to be wiped clear carry the hashtag, #TimePiece.

Critical Perspectives on Applied Theatre arises from our shared perception that, as the twenty-first century moves into its third decade, applied theatre is shaping and is shaped by new conceptual paradigms that are not only responsive to contemporary concerns but are also influencing the ways in which socially engaged art and art-making are produced and understood. Gathered together in this collection are debates about theatre's relationship to temporality and cultural memory, the politics of place, environment and attachment, and the material and relational dimensions of human and non-human agency. Applied theatre emerges as a creative force that responds imaginatively to the ways in which the loci of power have become diffuse and fragmented in the twenty-first century, and to new questions about how increasingly nuanced ideas of authority can be harnessed for social change. As Liberate Tate testify, the Anthropocene has, if anything, made the political imperatives of applied theatre even more pressing. This book responds critically to these twenty-first century challenges, setting out fresh agendas by analysing creative forms of compassionate art-making that engage with post-humanist perceptions of a material world.

By connecting with a contemporary set of political vocabularies in this book, our ambition is not to set up a new orthodoxy, but to capture and interrogate some of the divergent practices that constitute applied theatre. Isabelle Stengers' idea of an 'ecology of practices' is particularly pertinent in this context, offering what she describes as 'tools for thinking':

> An ecology of practices does not have any ambition to describe practices 'as they are'; it resists the master word of a progress that would justify their destruction.

It aims at the construction of new 'practical identities' for practices, that is, new possibilities for them to be present, or in other words to connect. (2005, 186)

An ecology of practices promises to hold divergent and critical perspectives in conversation, enabling connections to be found. Crucially, Stengers suggests, there is 'no identity of a practice independent of its environment', and this implies that all practices are contingent on place and time. She suggests that a sense of belonging is integral to a researcher's toolkit, and it is significant that all authors represented in this book have chosen to write about contexts they know well, and in places to which they have attachment. The affective registers and intimacy of scale that this inspires lends the writing an autobiographical quality, perhaps particularly when the researchers are also working as artists.

This book is presented as a set of debates and practices that can be read in dialogue with each other. We have grouped the chapters into three parts, each of which gather together chapters that explore specific aspects of applied theatre: Histories and cultural memories; Place, community and environment; Poetics and participation. Curating chapters in this way is designed to help readers navigate the territory in different ways, either reading sequentially through the book or, to adapt Stengers' words, finding new possibilities to be present and to connect. In this introduction, we begin by exploring the 'practical identities' of applied theatre, and asking why it is time to consider critical perspectives on applied theatre. Following that, rather than introducing each section in turn, we consider two broad conceptual challenges that have emerged as central debates in the book. First, we examine the ways in which a new attentiveness to the historical is evident across many of the essays collected here, which, taken together, offer readings of applied theatre's relationship to memory, history and historiography from a series of resonant intersections between place and time. Second, we investigate how materialities of place and the politics of attachment are inviting new social imaginaries. The ecologies of practices in this book, therefore, reflect the different temporal dimensions of applied theatre, reaching to the past to understand the present and the future, reflecting on the dynamic between place and community, and also recognising that social change is always enacted in the material present of the here and now.

Why critical perspectives?

'Applied theatre' is now an established term and is widely associated with creative practices that engage with the social, educational and political functions of theatrical processes. As an 'ecology of practices' applied theatre is continually shifting and developing, with the consequence that it has not one identity but many practical identities, differently and appropriately nuanced according to context. As part of its richness, applied theatre is associated with a body of experimental theatre-making rather than a set of toolkits, and in universities applied theatre is a field of teaching and research that can no longer be described as emergent. This institutional acceptance comes, however, with its own set of disciplinary challenges, and the impetus behind this edited collection is to respond to some of these. One such challenge is economic; funders in all sectors and settings expect to see outputs, outcomes and evidence of the work's impact and efficacy, and students also hope to increase their 'employability' as a result of their expensive university education. In part, this economic imperative has upheld an emphasis on applied theatre as a mode of personal and social problem-solving in which predetermined goals are realised, and this can mean that applied theatre is conceptualised in ways that serve neoliberalism well. This lack of criticality can sometimes be obscured by an apparently activist rhetoric: applied theatre transforms, promotes well-being, improves quality of life, and moves people on. Notably, writing about applied theatre has often been preoccupied with a central tension between understanding itself as a force for imaginative resistance and as problematically entwined with networks of power and exploitation. Our invitation to authors was to develop critical perspectives that would begin to re-balance this necessary tension. A critical perspective starts from a recognition that theatre-making is inevitably entwined in networks of power and exploitation, however, it also encourages artists and researchers to seek out a presence in those networks that complements the resistant practices that are immanent there rather than adopting more acquiescent relations that flatten out practice and reflection.

By critical perspectives, then, we mean to provide an intellectual mapping of key practices, questions and debates that have shaped applied theatre. We also want to trouble the markers of applied theatre as a disciplinary space, identifying emergent areas of research and practice that reflect the complexity and richness of contingent practices. We aim to name such markers in this introduction and in the collection as a whole — countering, on the one hand, too easy accounts of the transformational powers of theatre and, on the other, apologetic expressions of applied theatre's political engagements and its aesthetics. Following Stengers' analysis, there are three kinds of critical perspectives that run through the collection. First, rather than presenting applied theatre as a 'discipline' and working to preserve or develop particular orthodoxies, 'master words' or narratives of progression, we offer a framing of applied theatre as an ecology of practices that make pragmatic, imaginative and contingent relations, connections, attachments and belongings. Second, a search for critical kinds of reflection and practice is a long-standing feature of applied theatre, and we welcome the engaged and at times impassioned writing in this collection that indicates a revitalisation of these resistant relations. As part of both of these perspectives, it is also noticeable that the essays in this book provide critical interrogations of practices that feature a new appreciation of the historical experiences that have shaped the material and immaterial environments of communities and artists over time.

The collection is remarkably consistent in terms of the absence of grand claims for theatre's transformational powers, and in the authors' refusal to make sharp distinctions between the aesthetic and social discourses of the practices they explore. There are signs of a new, measured and confident voice for applied theatre that is politically aware and reflexive. Finally, then, it is clear that the kinds of criticality evident in this book are stimulating new thinking about efficacy and aesthetics. Importantly, these essays are not in defence of the practices they depict, and nor are their arguments overwhelmed or reduced by consideration of the complex networks of power that those practices are embedded in. They make neither grand nor small claims, and instead are characterised by a growing awareness that, following Stengers, it is the 'staking' of a claim that is the problem, as it fails to notice a 'gathering' that occurs via an ecological perspective on practices that 'makes present ... something which transforms their relation to the stakes they have put up' (2005: 195). As part of this, the essays exhibit appreciation of the relationship between the artist and process of art-making as engaged in a social and material network that is reproduced, disturbed and reinvented by each theatrical happening. This collection provides a platform for dialogue about applied theatre by asking the kind of productive questions that will keep its borders open, developing advanced debate and discourse that is necessary to support its complexity and reinforce its status as a fluid ecology of practices.

Histories and cultural memories

By opening this chapter with Liberate Tate's *Time Piece* we hope to draw attention to the ways in which environmental concerns create an imperative to reconsider human relationships to time and place. One book used as part of the rising tide of words charcoaled onto the floor of the Turbine Hall was marine biologist Rachel Carson's 1950 bestseller *The Sea Around Us*, and a citation on the floor reminded spectators that a wave carries messages from the landscapes of the deep ocean as well as changing surface environments met along its journey, messages that travel via the ominous and omniscient force of tidal time: '[T]here is no drop of water in the ocean, not even in the deepest parts of the abyss, that does not know and respond to the mysterious forces that create the tide' (1989 [1950]: 149). *Critical Perspectives on Applied Theatre* mirrors the concerns of environmental artists by evidencing a new attentiveness to the operations of time in creative practice and in the histories of practices. In some essays, this attentiveness to the historical is present in explorations of how artists and communities have drawn on experiences of remembering and forgetting, presence and absence, recovery and loss in the processes of making theatre. In others, there is a valuing of intimate moments of encounter in a creative process, moments that are framed in ways that evidence their richness as modes of engaging with questions that have broad significance for this ecology of practices, and for cultural practice more generally.

There are two key perspectives on the historical that are present in this book, and both connect to our discussion of applied theatre in this introduction. First, applied theatre is seen as dangerously forgetful of its histories, and there is a connected search for histories that have as yet not been written; and, second, there is a move to create history by standing still in one place and time, and noticing how landscapes intervene in a conversation about time, a process which might also involve encounters with ghosts present in such landscapes. Baz Kershaw's essay opens the collection, and he reflects on applied theatre's increasingly established status. He examines a series of well-known works as well as student textbooks on applied theatre, drawing attention to historiographical insights, absences and omissions in these sources. He notes the predominance of micro-accounts of theatre projects that populate the literature, and his provocation to the field is clear. There is a need for comparative microanalyses 'inflected with holistic analysis and ecological principles', so as to create metahistories of theatre's engagements with global issues of ecological threat, political and economic crisis, and their networks of causation. Amongst other examples, Kershaw looks to a theatre practice that made use of stories from a now extinct South African tribe, archived more than 100 years before, re-inserting those stories into landscapes marked by the present-absence of that tribe (drawing on work by Mark Fleishman, also present in the collection). This layering of story and landscape is evocative and Kershaw's essay provides a series of impressionistic glances towards a historiographical practice that acknowledges human agency as a non-determinant and relational feature of meaning-making. In this practice multiple temporalities are all engaged in a conversation about the shapes and forms of survival (or not), and ghostly presences – landscapes, forgotten people and extinct cultural practices – are invited into the conversation: 'the *past is incessantly accessibly alive* in some way or another and the *future is never wholly an absence* in histories of the present'. Here, to cite Prasenjit Duara, '[h]istory is the circulatory and dynamic repository of live possibilities for future actions' (2015: 9), a receptacle through which myths, narratives, memories, official and unofficial accounts are exchanged and reformulated.

The essays respond to this rich provocation by engaging with history in ways that are attentive to place, with historical reflections arising from particular landscapes and architectures important to applied theatre. Hughes' essay explores theatrical entertainments in a Victorian workhouse in Rochdale, United Kingdom, and she makes a case for the inclusion of theatrical forms of nineteenth century rational recreation, and temperance and Sunday School drama in the histories of applied theatre, complementing narratives that locate histories of applied theatre in modernist experimentation. Memories and archives are also used as creative sources for theatre projects, and Wan-Jung Wang's essay provides an engaging analysis of theatre performances in city spaces of Southeast Asia. Her work is inspired by the forgotten, destroyed, invisible and disappearing memories of inhabitants whose homes are under threat from development. Paul Heritage and Silvia Ramos' account of the occupation of two abandoned wards of a psychiatric hospital in Rio, Brazil, by young artists from the favelas looks to the countercultural movement of the 1950s as a source of inspiration. Their essay is written as a series of letters to Brazilian psychiatrist Nise de Silveira (1905–99), whose pioneering efforts to develop creative psychiatric care in Rio de Janeiro are being revitalised by the artistic occupation carried out in the contemporary moment.

Applied theatre is an ecology of practices made from encounters with borders, with those encounters characterised by openness and commitment to a *process* of making relations rather than staking out a secure or fixed position. Stengers proposes an approach to the historical that refuses to make destruction of an existing position a condition of the new:

> It is clearly hard to think without reference to a kind of progress that would justify its past as a path leading to our present and future. The ecology of practices has this ambition. (2005: 185)

Ecological *histories* of practices might be made, then, by witnessing, collecting and gathering rather than overturning and discarding what has gone before. An understanding of applied theatre as a practice of 'gathering' multiple temporalities together rather than working in linear time seems most relevant, and this approach features in the essays written by Wan-Jung Wang, Paul Dwyer and Helen Nicholson. It becomes clear how multiple temporalities – a shifting between and across, allowing meaning and identity to emerge from the gathering together of many experiences of time, and relations to time, in one place – are engaged in applied theatre practices to different ends in contingent settings. And that the contingency of *this time, this place* is of utmost significance (and a source of resistance) for people living in the contexts of precarity that host each of these practices. Here, the historical might be experienced as a burden that needs to be negotiated as much as a resource for figuring a response to the present, with the creative practice of theatre engaging with it in a variety of ways. Negotiating historical burdens might be attended to by remembering, as in the examples examined by Wang, or by focusing on the present rather than on personal history, as in the project with immigrants explored by Sally Mackey, or by memorialising, as in the account of theatrical practices of reconciliation in Bougainville, Papua New Guinea, by Dwyer. Alternatively, the historical might need to be re-imagined altogether, as described by Nicholson in her account of a one-to-one performance practice that emerged when helping an elderly neighbour prepare to move into a care home. Here, theatre played a role in refiguring history and time into an assortment of receptacles for gathering and carrying the identities of a person safely over a change in her everyday life.

Discussions of history and time in this collection demonstrate attentiveness to how experiences of time unfold in the *shaping* of theatre practice, and to allow the temporal its own agency as part of a creative process. It is perhaps Dwyer's provocation to move towards a 'slower' applied theatre practice that is most striking in this regard, by which he means a practice that builds from dialogues with people and place over time (over decades, in his case). A cautionary modality is introduced here, in that Dwyer questions his own presence in a country that has suffered from a history of exploitation connected to his home country. In response, Dwyer slowed down time – allowing his practice to unfold as a fluid set of cultural and economic exchanges that were entirely unknown at the outset and where power dynamics were continually acknowledged and nego tiated. This attention to the 'time' of time resists an urge to work towards the new and the utopic, and instead responds to how time, as an interrelation of human and non-human agency, shapes people and places. Time has an omniscience that influences the future of creative practice in unpredictable ways, and as such, demands to be included in the conversation.

New materialities of applied theatre

Woven through these essays is an interest in the productive relationship – and sometimes tension – between human agency and the agentic capacities of the material world. Historically, as we have suggested, applied theatre has been primarily concerned with human agency, with the consequence that theatre practice has been harnessed to various forms of individual improvement or societal action. What these histories share is a way of seeing the material world as an inert backdrop to a human-centred social drama rather than as significant and a presence. Perhaps for the first time in applied theatre this collection of essays shows an emergent engagement with both economic materialism and the inequitable distribution of wealth, and the political implications of understanding the material world as an active force in everyday life. This new attention to the materialist ontologies of applied theatre is noted by Kershaw, who observes that human memory is embodied as well as linguistic, and cites the political theorist Jane Bennett's concept of vital materialism (2010: 14–17), an idea that recognises that some forms of matter have their own agency and defy human will. Although not all authors gathered here would align themselves with new materialist theories, the book is marked by the attention paid to the sensory, embodied, affective and place-based qualities of applied theatre as one way to erode fixed binaries between the human and non-human world and to recognise their reciprocity.

Inevitably this emphasis on the materialities of applied theatre has involved challenging some familiar orthodoxies; the progressive spirit of the nineteenth and twentieth centuries was marked by the view that greater advancement in self-knowledge and rational understanding of the world would improve the human condition. This way of thinking led theatre-makers to develop practices designed to encourage rational debate, with the expectation that enacting solutions to shared social problems would enable participants to challenge or resist their oppressions. Although this approach remains one aspect of politically engaged theatre-making, it is noticeable that that this cause-and-effect linearity ignored or underplayed the aesthetics of duration, place and attachment explored by authors represented in this book. Sally Mackey's chapter marks such a shift in emphasis, where she instates place as a performative landscape that carries its own agency in a creative process and suggests how invitations to participants to attend to the quotidian and sensed environment in imaginative and playful ways 'thickens' places for new residents. Kathleen Gallagher shares Mackey's interest in the materialities of everyday life and the sensory qualities of theatre-making in her work with homeless youth in Toronto, Canada. Gallagher applied the 'aesthetic of talk' to this creative project, a process that recognised the limits of theatres of debate and acknowledges that the affective register has political force.

Many of the essays in the collection offer an analysis that is responsive to the politics of scale as well as to the affective, sensory and place-based dynamics of human and non-human interaction in creative practice. Gallagher investigates the relationship between applied theatre as a micro-political intervention and wider socio-structural analyses. She describes this relationship as a 'precarious dance between personal story and structural change', a phrase that scopes out a useful terrain for ongoing investigations of both the poetics of participation and the non-linearity of social change. From his position in South Africa, Mark Fleishman is similarly concerned with the material politics of scale, observing that the inequalities that continue to define everyday life in South Africa play a significant part in how questions of citizenship and authority are enacted and performed in the process of community-based theatre-making. By troubling hierarchical notions of authority, however, Fleishman suggests that the process of collaboration between participants and theatre-makers creates a temporary micro-community, fostering an active citizenship that is sited in the material practices of theatre-making and situated in the complexity of its political, social and cultural setting. In this configuration, and in the terms described by D. Soyini Madison in this collection, social justice becomes a form of labour, poetically and politically poised between the storied identities and micropolitics of everyday life, and the macro-structures of material inequalities. As such, each of these essays confirm Diana Coole and Samantha Frost's observation that new materialist thought 'compels us to think of causation in ... complex terms; to recognise that phenomena are caught in a multiple of interlocking systems and forces and to consider anew the location and nature of capacities for agency' (2010: 9).

Across the collection authors suggest that there is an urgent need to respond to the catastrophic ways in which the material world sometimes asserts itself into everyday life. The chapters written by Syed Jamil Ahmed and Peter O'Connor demonstrate how, in the face of environmental disasters, theatre-makers can respond in different ways. Both Ahmed and O'Connor debate the politics of neoliberalism, with O'Connor giving an account of the urgent attention to the present engendered by the earthquakes in Christchurch in 2010–11. His essay pays attention to the way a disaster – an eruption and disruption of the temporal – can become a focus for competing forms of theatrical narrative, and argues for the necessity of theatre projects that explicitly disrupt neoliberal disaster capitalism's territorialism and in ways that allow communities into decision-making processes about their futures. Writing about the devastating consequences of climate change on his home country of Bangladesh, Ahmed provides a searing critique of how some forms of applied theatre are, perhaps unwittingly, complicit in upholding neoliberalist politics of self-care and self-responsibility in the face of ecological disaster rather than addressing the materialist politics that is causing this crisis. Ahmed points out that the neoliberal *homo economicus* exists everywhere, and the outdated view that there are clear binaries between the privileged, colonising and capitalist West and the colonised, impoverished and subaltern 'Rest' fails to acknowledge how everyone is reciprocally implicated in neoliberalism, from Bangladeshi farmers seeking the best prices for their produce on their mobile phones to well-intentioned Western theatre practitioners wishing to work in impoverished countries. In offering an alternative to the interventionist practices he associates with applied theatre, Ahmed suggests that the neoliberal idea of self-care might be 're-visioned as social care' through storytelling. Ahmed's voice is passionate, polemical and persuasive, and his contribution to the ecology of practices offers a powerful tool not only to think further about responses to climate change but also to consider how theatre-makers are always and inevitably embroiled in the materialist politics that neoliberalist agendas appear to evade or ignore.

Throughout this collection of essays, authors articulate experiences of belonging and feelings of attachment to the contexts of practice in ways that are ethically sensitive. Applied theatre requires reciprocity, a process that is often politically complex and emotionally challenging. These relations of reciprocity are explored by Helen Nicholson in the final essay in this collection, where she argues for a new ontology of applied theatre as a practice of relation. A relational ontology of applied theatre opens questions about how future theatre-makers might attend to place and time, both contesting and problematising its limits as well as in ways that open up new social imaginaries. Her argument again draws attention to how theatre-making offers the possibility of figuring a relation to time and place that is in step with the multiple temporalities that shape material worlds, resisting separation into autonomous components that might be lifted out of context and reproduced elsewhere. In answer to pressures to describe applied theatre using the discourses of economic productivity noted earlier and contested throughout this collection, what emerges here is an understanding that a changed world is no longer solely an outcome of human action, if it ever was. Instead theatre-makers create worlds of shifting scales and measures – in which small objects sustain extraordinary resonances, unpolished and improvised artistic experiences make profound political statements, insignificant moments of encounter alter dimensions of place and time, and established forms and meanings are swept away in an instant. And in that spirit, we bring our own attempt to scale and measure the debates opened in this book to a close and offer it up to readers for consideration as an artefact that carries meaning only in relation to their own contingencies of time and place.

References

Bennett, J. 2010. *Vibrant Matter: A Political Ecology of Things.* London: Duke University Press.

Carson, R. 1989 [1950]. *The Sea Around Us.* Oxford: Oxford University Press.

Coole, D. and Frost, S. (eds.) 2010. *New Materialisms: Ontology, Agency, and Politics.* Durham and London: Duke University Press.

Duara, P. 2015. *The Crisis of Global Modernity: Asian Traditions and a Sustainable Future.* Cambridge: Cambridge University Press.

Liberate Tate. *Time Piece.* www.facebook.com/liberatetate/videos/1622725534633 402/. Last accessed 29 July 2015.

Stengers, I. 2005. 'Introductory notes on an ecology of practices'. *Cultural Studies Review* 11.1: 183–196.

PART I

Histories and cultural memories

CHAPTER 2

Toward a historiography of the absent
On the late pasts of applied theatre and community performance

Baz Kershaw

Preamble

For performing theatre practice everywhere 'history' has become an especially tricky realm since the Earth became threatened by a likely increase of
humankind reaching over ten billion individuals in the first half of the
twenty-first century (Emmott 2012). In such an environment, how might
any human art be 'applied' to the past so as to produce more hopeful
futures, let alone performances conventionally conceived as always already
disappearing into ephemerality? Thus in 2000, as a long-term performance
practitioner, I found myself searching for multi-perspective angles on time
passing under the rotting iron hull of a dry-docked nineteenth century
ocean liner that, arguably, had changed the world (Kershaw 2011). I was
testing how an imagined Last Mermaid Alive – encountered immediately
as from the past alive in the present – might automatically instill in the
bodies of spectators a resistance to what philosopher Paul Ricoeur identifies
as a widely assumed 'pathological deficiency' of memory (2004: 21). Five
years later I was in a small nineteen century urban zoo observing a pair of
environmental movement artists who were dancing an improvised trio
with a Latin American spider monkey (Kershaw 2012a). My research focus
there was on how the attention of visitors might be stretched via such rare
anthropocentric exceptions so that they might encounter a state which
Italian philosopher Giorgio Agamben calls 'bare life' (1995: 8). Perhaps,
I figured, that could be one historically temporal vector where an unendur-
able future might be directly engaged the better to forestall it. Might
dreams be made of such stuff that makes re-visioning 'histories' possible
through 'applying' performance to the pasts of the present – a rotting iron
ship, ancestral cousins of *Homo sapiens*, and so on – so as to make some
not-too-distant futures into durably hopeful times?

Introduction

Those attempts to take the past off guard, so to speak, were responding to a putative period in which postmodernism had rendered 'history without a subject' and 'erased the distinction between aesthetic and political modes of expression' (Ashley 1997: 7). Western cultures were experiencing 'the disappearance of a sense of history . . . in which our entire social system has little by little begun to loose a capacity to retain its own past' (Jameson 1985: 125). Scholars were radically divided on exactly when the past was thus denuded, but generally its heyday was allotted somewhere between the 1960s and the last decade of the twentieth century (Butler 2002: 12). Simultaneously there was a rapid and radical conversion of leading Western states into neoliberal monetarist economies, arguably creating a new 'logic of late-capitalism' (Jameson 1991: 48–49). From these perspectives, the mid- to late 1980s British emergence of socially engaged participatory performances called 'applied theatre' was, well, expectable.

A similar theatrical trend evolved in the United States, though it was most commonly called 'community performance'. However, any neat historicising transatlantic parallels are troubled by two curious nominative contrasts. First, the United States' 'community performance' largely was a replacement of 'grassroots theater' and Britain's 'applied theatre' generally displaced 'community theatre'. Second, both these substitutions occurred whilst the nature, idea and ideal of 'community' were subject increasingly to radical deconstructive doubts (Amit and Rapport 2002). Yet by the mid-2000s, on both sides of the Atlantic and elsewhere, these genres had flourished to become an international phenomenon, and often its individual artists and sometimes groups were associated with universities and colleges. However, despite this remarkably successful growth, applied theatre, community performance and related forms apparently have attracted few historians, and no significant histories of their collective practices have appeared.

My interest in this absence is less about *why* such histories are still largely waiting to be written. But more in *how* historiographies appropriate to these and related practices can be created. Especially as theatre and performance historiography more generally enjoyed an energetic and exciting turn-of-the-third-millennium renaissance that still continues. Was that conundrum simply the result of urgency in the need for creative innovation in times of profoundly destabilising change? Might it stem from a mainly localised response to the extraordinary globalising spread of neoliberal capitalism? Or even from a fixation on the present in a period when the planet increasingly was facing a future of human-produced environmental crisis?

Paradoxically, then, the two decades flanking the imaginary boundary of the third millennium were a heyday for applied theatre and its cognate genres. The name itself was still relatively new as the Berlin Wall fell and the Soviet Union started fragmenting in 1989 (*RiDE* Viewpoints 2006: 90–95). Yet not long after the global economy all but collapsed completely in 2008 a specialist market of practical guides, edited readers, key course texts, scholarly collections, specialist journals, DVDs, blogspots, apps and doubtless twitterings galore was flourishing in the British Isles and, to a lesser extent, in the United States. For students the panoramas of learning opportunities and career prospects had widened rapidly, especially in Britain, with qualifications from humble educational diplomas to the highest research degrees available from institutions spanning post-sixteen education colleges through to a significant batch of top-ranking universities. In 2014 a celebrated New York state graduate centre skipped the usual American 'community performance' tag and announced a Master of Arts in Applied Theatre (CUNY 2014). The significance of this proliferation can be gauged from the recruitment pitch of a modest London college recently granted degree-awarding powers.

> A degree in Drama and Applied Theatre will equip you with a range of transferable skills. As well as the wealth of opportunities within the theatre profession, students may wish to pursue a career within teaching, event management and promotion, diplomacy, politics, international development, youth work, arts therapy, workshop facilitation, social care, the health service or the criminal justice system. (St Mary 2015)

The age of a fully flexible creative industry 'grassroots' workforce labouring for the good of every citizen's well-being was nigh. So what better way for bright young Western people of conscience to ethically cover their backs against the crisis-strewn, cheek-by-jowl ravages of those astounding decades. Especially given the long turn-of-millennium slippage from communism's rapid collapse through an impetuous war on terror to massive State fiscal bailouts of class-A banks; including principally their production of a 'new world disorder' (Kershaw 1999: 5).

The gap between that macro-history and the many micro-accounts of particular applied theatre/community performance projects and/or creative methods is indeed curious, particularly given the sector's overall tendency to work with socially and politically disadvantaged groups and communities. There were signs of concern about this disconnect early in the new millennium. In 2005 an article in a leading journal sketched out elements of a historiography and called for attempts to create more

(McDonnell 2005). In 2009 a Sydney conference included 'Examining Our Past' as part of its agenda (Winston 2010: 145–146). But, despite subsequent appeals for responses in the same journal, that crucial component of history *per se* remained absent. In 2014 two American scholars published a proto-empirical study of the 'gaps, silences and comfort zones' of applied theatre/community performance research. Surveying almost 500 articles in the main journals they describe a 'field' focused largely on contemporary or recent events. Just 2 per cent of the total are classed as 'historical' and none of those included substantive macro-histories as such (Omasta and Snyder-Young 2014: 7). Might that absence simply result from the sector's speedy historical success? Could the many links with universities and colleges somehow have discouraged interest in its diverse precursor traditions? Had dissidence become an embarrassment as it became institutionally respectable? Or was some other dynamic of history preventing a reflexive take on its many pasts?

Key notes on methods and methodologies

Historiography is a principal concern of this enquiry as it can generate forms of critical reflexivity especially suited to particular histories of many kinds. Applied theatre and community performance – hereafter AT and CP – should be no exception to this, even though compared to the periods generally covered by earlier theatre/performance histories their short pasts equate the *present day*. Also by 2010 an impressive New Theatre Historiography movement was thriving internationally through innovative methodologies and methods, often deploying digital technologies (Postlewait and Michieli 2010). Yet still its success largely rested on a doubtful credo. Namely, the 'constitutive problem of performance history [is that] ... all writing about performance must face its own impossibility ... [as] the event eludes its capture' (Worthen with Holland 2003: 6), due always to its unavoidable ephemerality. Hence a performed event always already is gone for good in the moment of its doing.

However, this logocentric assumption has been challenged by ideas of human memory as constituted in part by embodiment, visceral experience and vitality, alongside linguistic discourses. Possibilities that philosopher Paul Ricoeur has explored with impressive thoroughness and political theorist Jane Bennett tested through the notion of 'vital materialities' (2010: x). It is also a prospect variously entertained by radical critical theorists such as Deleuze and Guattari, by quantum and mediation theories, by neuroscience, and by investigations of 'affect', all subsequently more or less incorporated in performance/theatre studies (Thrift 2008: 12–13). All fundamentally and diversely can imply that past human events potentially could be made alive in the present and might always already be configuring vectors of multiple futures.

This trend opens up holistic and ecologically inflected perspectives on the past-as-history. For AT/CP that could be an efficacious evolution especially as its practices often are shaped by the memories of participants. So designs of specific historiographical methods may need to *start with* the practices themselves. This then poses interesting preconditions for any historiography that aims to connect them to macro-histories with regional, national, international and/or global reach. In particular, those intent on including cultural, social, political, economic, environmental and other domains of human endeavour. However, to explore those prospects from the angle of current *absences* requires reflexive strategies that directly challenge normative perspectives on those domains, so the following notes suggest how that might be done.

- Privilege comparative micro-accounts of a wide range of particular practices.
- Compare examples cross culturally, focusing on established traditions and innovations.
- Analyse accounts from overlapping sources, for example monographs, edited collections, student readers, journal articles, in summary and in detail.
- Focus on historical interests/references, temporal reach/periodic terminology, implicit/tacit historiographical methods.
- Establish clear differences between 'history as such' (e.g. flows of events) and 'history *per se*' (e.g. accounts of past events).
- Examine interrelations between micro-accounts and macro-events, but inflect such binaries through holistic analyses and ecological principles.

In evolving these methods, this chapter primarily centres on practices in Britain and the United States because they were among the prime movers of global history as such during the past three centuries or so. But globalisation ensures that transatlantic choice cannot exclude other regions which, more or less explicitly, figure in this historiographical experiment; increasingly so when it considers AT/CP practices in war zones and at museums/heritage sites. Such spatial and temporal dimensions are critical to how macro-histories may impinge on, and be evoked by, locally focused projects which almost routinely – if often indirectly – engage with questions of equality, justice and freedom of expression and living. Hence democratic principles are rarely absent from the remarkable span of CP/AT creative methods, as was often the case in earlier cognate practices around the globe (van Erven 2001). So hovering in the ether of those methods, so to speak, often there is acute concern for modelling forms of radical dissident democracy with participants. Not surprisingly, then, the shadows of neoliberal democratic-capitalist globalisation and its historically disastrous affects and effects inevitably ghost that creativity (Klein, 2007). Any historiography for these practices therefore needs must take that into account by including a paradoxically imperative resistance. Paradoxical because it must somehow eschew a negative binary response, which automatically confirms what it resists. Hence my chief concern is to evolve ecologically holistic means for making performance/theatre history *per se* based on histories as such of the present day. Remembering hopefully that tomorrow never comes because it is indeed always before the times.

Segment 1: Reading Readers for nascent historiographies

Student Readers are useful to this task as they present structured surveys that constitute analyses of their subject and aim to become a representative 'snapshot' of a defined period. Of several AT/CP Readers published by 2015 the first two remain exemplary for how their structural designs drew attention to durable practices with substantive implications for historiographical methods. For example, *participation* and *intervention* constitute key critical aspects of CP/AT creative practices, especially through private remembrance and public display. But also both these processes meet their nemesis in everyday *forgetting* of the past. Which in turn substantially affects the complex business of forging connections between micro- and macro-histories *per se*. As histories of more or less wider events are downplayed, then surely critical analysis risks socio-political reduction of its relevance. Paul Ricoeur is helpfully challenging in this respect when, for example, he paradoxically calls the process of reminiscence 'the forgetting that preserves'. This then constitutes 'an immemorial resource and not an inexorable destruction', because it recognises the past specifically as always already 'having-been' and not just entirely lost forever (2004: 442). A fabulous insight – drawn partly from Heidegger – that positively chimes with a currency of 'degrees of ephemerality' and 'performance remains' that, as we shall see in concluding, can haunt performance *per se*. But because also 'inexorable destruction' is a crucial aspect of the 'dramaturgy of being' (2004: 443), we need further angles of critical analysis to create

AT/CP 'test cases' that can gauge their actual historic and historiographical valence. Ricoeur argues that such types of test may best be provided by a 'history of the present day' in which the 'testimony of witnesses . . . rubs up against writing [and] documentary traces' (2004: 449).

The Introduction to Tim Prentki and Sheila Preston's *The Applied Theatre Reader* (2009) presents a two-page 'history of applied theatre' that cites drama therapy, Bertolt Brecht and Augusto Boal as precursors, plus community theatre, Theatre in Education and Theatre for Development as AT's main subset. Its fifty-one chapters divide broadly into brief editorial introductions/conclusions (2009: 8), key theoretical sources (2009: 17) and case studies/reports on individual practices/projects (2009: 26). None of the theoretical sources significantly engage with history as such, though most tend more or less to imply broader historical critiques. All the detailed accounts of practice naturally are part of particular histories but few explicitly offer fuller accounts of historical change as such. So identifying history *per se* in this collection requires an oblique methodological approach. A scholarly equivalent to finding needles in haystacks, such as scanning through its index with eyes half shut. Paradoxically, that simple filtering process might expose complex patterns of more expansive *historical interests*.

Applying that historiographical 'technique' for me revealed some suggestive temporally related couplings and thematic connections:

$$\begin{array}{ccc}
\text{traditional cultures} & + & \text{indigenous forms} \\
/ & | & \backslash \\
\text{autobiographical memory} & + & \text{community stories} \\
\backslash & | & / \\
\text{witness testimony} & + & \text{colonial eras}
\end{array}$$

Using index entry numbering to pursue the textual detail of each pairing produced hunches, possibly for making resonant historical hay. The following explores the results from this method in varied detail. For the first coupling in respect of its resonances with the third, before the second is briefly considered alone. Leaving increasing gaps in which readers might extend this analytical game of making AT/CP history *per se*.

First matter of note generated by the top–bottom linkage patently alludes to well-known 'world' or 'global' histories of colonialism and, simultaneously, of local and personal-private histories. Even without delving deeper into the ashy textual tangle of an imaginary rick, the macro-histories of colonialism and the micro ones of its witnesses indicate a symbiotic co-dependence that has been mightily agonistic. Also this

implies a *doubling up* of mutual antagonisms, *because* of the fact that –
whether witnesses were for, against or neutral regarding colonisation – the
hierarchies of power would tend to be operating normatively top down.
Therein lie many tales of privilege and persecution, exploitation and exile
internal and external. The unjust mega-nature of dominant historical
ideologies which moderate liberals loved to hate, at least until an entirely
other dominant breed of greed was spawned by late twentieth century
neoliberal capital.

Next comes a test of these speculations via the Reader's reports of actual
practices and its selected theories. In its accounts of *traditional cultures*
three examples provide especially dynamic contrasts. First, in South Africa
their diversity of playfulness in history as such was silenced by colonial
language (2009: 112). Second, internationally their uses in AT could be
pursued with the oppressors as well as the oppressed, and a paradigm for
this is cited in *Italy* (2009: 182). Third, theoretical analysis asserts an overall
depredation of historic non-Western cultures by mass media production of
new lifestyles (2009: 314–318). In contrast, *indigenous creative forms* are
practised with diversity as a *continuing* norm. For example, local home-
made culture in Malawi produces multi-layered performances (2009:
100–101); popular performance styles from Sierra Leone through Losotho
to Kenya and beyond provoke critical conscience and consciousness (2009:
193); in South Africa quality historical performance aesthetics foster contemporary Freireian 'conscientisation' (2009: 196); and Zimbabwean
native theatre provides a bottom-up radical resource of resistance to continuing cultural suppressions (2009: 345). So perhaps the steamroller
history of colonisation and its violent or otherwise oppressive aftermaths
never succeeded in completely squashing the performing spirit of indigenous cultural diversity. Which could imply that 'theatre for development' as
a forerunner subset of AT was possibly always primed for co-option to
postcolonial interests. There is not much new in this view, perhaps. But the
methodological route that led to it clearly could raise scepticism about
overt or implied *international* theatrical meta-histories of former colonies,
especially as a component for bringing justice to subaltern populations on
specific continents. Particularly in an era characterised by widening dis-
parities between the obscenely rich and massively burgeoning ranks of the
extremely poor. In other words, AT's conventional focus on local groups
may tend to block an affective address of the most obviously dangerous,
wider histories as such of the present day.

Outcomes of this kind for an emergent historiography can indicate the
high stakes created by the *lack* of meta-histories *per se* regarding AT/CP

and their predecessor genres in the twentieth century and earlier. So a focus on the close coupling of community stories and autobiographical memory *within* particular diversities of practice and theory could reveal how disparate methods can coalesce to produce coherent overlapping histories *per se* of specific trends in the past. Prentki and Preston provide examples for analyse to test that through their different emphases on memory and storytelling. Thus bell hooks' 'space of radical opening' (2009: 82), John Somers' rural community plays (2009: 208), Penny Bundy's trauma as witness (2009: 235) and Helen Nicholson's 'intergenerational reminiscence' (2009: 268) clearly exemplify creative uses of *personal* memory for more or less dissident public purposes; meanwhile the community storytelling reported by Sarah Thornton from Liverpool, UK (2009: 165), Marina Coutinho and Marcia Nogueira from Rio de Janeiro (2009: 163), John Somers again from Devon's Payhembury (2009: 208) and L. Dale Byam's from various parts of Zimbabwe (2009: 346) strongly suggest how *collective* witnessing can productively extend the limits of community in individualising democracies. The overlaps and tensions between these two sets of AT emerge through a subdued urgency that focuses on immediacy of action in the everyday. So even this small sample of micro-histories might be combined holistically to create selective accounts of varied radical theatre and performance pasts ripe for recycling via custom-made historiographies. But AT's routine postmodernist-inflected focus on everyday practices seems to prevent such historical-ecological common sense.

Overall, though, the need to draw differences between such globally and locally oriented theatre histories is moot. Because performance ecologies as such produce complex interrelations founded on relatively simple 'evolutionary' principles (Kershaw 2007: 18–20). So the task for AT/CP-oriented theatre/performance historiography is to invent methods for creative inquiries into their epistemological and ontological processes in appropriate time frames. Edited Readers are a bonus source for this as their editors must aim somehow to be comprehensive whilst being condemned always to fall short of that ideal. Though the advantage of that latter absence for AT/CP history *per se* is yet to emerge. Hence to explore this prospect further I cross the ocean sky of an Atlantis now mostly devoid of iceberg clouds, to consider new new-world types of community performance in and beyond the States that invented a war on globalised terror.

Petra Kuppers and Gwen Robertson's introduction to *The Community Performance Reader* suggests that such volumes could create 'a history for an idea or practice' (2007: 1). It indicates a range of other publications from the United States, Britain and elsewhere dealing with social, political and

aesthetic aspects of CP. Its six principal theoretical chapters avoid history
per se. Those and its twenty-nine case studies are grouped in five Parts:
Pedagogical Communities; Relations; Environments; Rituals, embodiment, challenge; and Practices. So the hypothetical hayrick here has an
implied structure, and that rules out anything like an ash metaphor.
The Reader's index consists primarily of proper names – people, places,
groups and so on – plus a small selection of key topic words spread
variously across the five Parts. Could this distribution indicate a meta-
history of 'an idea or practice' for CP? If their page numberings were iron
filings would a scan with eyes magnetically wide open reveal some pattern
of historical attractors? Doubtless there may be better ways to conjure up
historiographies, but the refined panorama of specific practices in this
Reader's collection invites an unconventional gaze.

Such a scan reveals that 'capitalism' and 'modernity' – with twelve
entries in total – appear *only* in the theoretical chapters, while 'myth' and
'storytelling' – with twenty entries – are found exclusively in the practical
case studies. This stark contrast indicates different perspectives on history
as such are in play. And the divide, not surprisingly perhaps, is as between
macro- and micro-oriented versions of histories *per se.* For the former,
modernity and capitalism are the current context within which the
theory chapters pursue critical analyses of particular and wide-ranging
socio-political concerns. For example, Augusto Boal on oppression,
Paulo Freire on pedagogy, Gerald Delanty – via Habermas, Touraine,
Bauman – on critiques of community, Dwight Conquergood on ethical
ethnography, and so on. So history *per se* and therefore explicit historiographies are largely absent from theory, maybe due to the present-day/
everyday urgency of those concerns. Yet twelve case studies share seven-
teen index entries for 'myth' and 'storytelling' where these forms variously stand in as aspects of history as such, and all principally focus on
their participants' present-day conditions. Given this distribution of
terms, the almost equal division of 'identity' between theory (7 chapters)
and practice (6) likely reflects the importance of identity politics in the
period when most of the volume's projects took place. From this perspective, the indexical absence of 'history' could imply the culturally
continuing influence of postmodernism (two entries) and its negative
impact on 'community'.

However, although this Reader hardly engages with history *per se,* its
case studies often invoke historical tendencies and themes relevant to their
particular time and location. But what criterion could most usefully
indicate   appropriate   historiographical   methods   for   community

performance histories-as-such to gain greater historicising traction? To resolve that question the simplifying micro/macro binary must be collapsed and, given the complex diversity of the micro-case-studies, their macro-context could well provide a source for that. Hence any indications of *non*-theatre/performance histories might turn the historiographical trick of uniting what theory/practice has separated. Two chapters in particular are possibly paradigmatic of this. Because the historical-contextual conditions for their case studies are presented with terrific economy. Yet also they evoke profound questions of human survival that, tellingly, are directly engaged by two further chapters in the Reader's Part on Environment. My hunch is that this doubling of contrasting interests might illustrate how historiographies can be generated for *multiple* AT/CP theatre/performance histories of the present day.

American Cedar Nordbye is one of several visual artists featured in the Reader. He specialises in social sculpture and public arena interventions. His case study project focused on the Empire State Building's 86th floor observation deck where, in 1997, the Palestinian immigrant Ali Abu Kamal had shot several tourists before killing himself. On the attack's third anniversary Nordbye visited the deck with a bag holding a self-made wooden ball, a 'sheaf of silk-screen prints ... depicting a gun', and a 'handful of lottery tickets' (2007: 133). He begins kicking the ball gently towards unsuspecting visitors gazing out at New York. Reactions range from aggressive to playful. But some accept his offer of free lottery tickets, listen to the Kamal story and learn that he had no record as a terrorist. Nordbye asks them, if the ticket is a winner, to donate a third of its value to the Israeli–Palestine peace process. Finally he floats a gun print off the deck and invites them to follow suite, which they did. The performance was repeated in 2001 followed by a toned-down adaptation in 2002 when, under threat of arrest, he signed a statement promising not to return. 9/11 had taken another kind of toll. However, Nordbye's technically simple event *implicitly* engaged historically with the American and British attacks on Iraq, the Twin Towers falling, the so-called war on terror and subsequent social, economic, environmental and other repercussions. In contrast, the delicacy, subtlety, sensitivity and remarkably tactful negotiations of his artwork were profound. Deeply entwined with the history it critiques, yet also involving strangers in performing actions that strongly challenge the period's ultra-violent ethos. Its participants' commitment creates an inescapably fragile virtual 'community' of memory traces from that very particular present day. Who can say for certain that these shadowy refractions together will *not* somehow produce dissident affects?

Nordbye suggests such 'community' performances might constitute venues for 'democratic writing of history "from the street"' (2007: 138). Creating a playfully minimalist less-is-more distributed community-making aesthetic rich with the highly intense irony of his event's title: 'Empire Project'.

Reporting as a disabled person, Petra Kuppers in 2004 initiated a two-year-long CP project in a Welsh village with users of its mental health self-help centre. Their focus was site specific and concentrated on two features of the nearby Brecon Beacons National Park moorland. The group made digital videos using footage of their work on the moors, which included soundtracks of poetry written by them. These events were exceptional because, due to the participants' mental health conditions, the moorlands were formerly inaccessible. Kuppers points up the democratic ethic arising from this 'inscription of difference into sedimented patterns of naturalized "law" on the moorland' (2007: 36). That rather abstract formulation was made particularly concrete in their second project, Sleeping Giants, which focused on a massive moorland feature whose outline looks like a man lying on his back. But this can only be seen by travelling the route of a disused nineteenth century canal that carried coal from local mines to the ironworks of southern Wales. Hence the resultant video-poem's back-story was the 'weight of history, the lost grandeur of Welsh economic power' (2007: 44). Which, for the group of 'ex-miners, factory workers, one teacher, homemakers' and others was ultimately the complex source of their health problems (2004: 38). From this perspective, their self-filmed video-poem responses to improvisations on the moor become a creatively reflexive deconstruction of that history as such which, Kuppers suggests, enables a 'new community to come into being' (2007: 44). An enthusiastic public reception of the project's two videos locally, plus at London and other 'international film festivals, conferences, and disability culture meet-ings' (2007: 45), appears to support her interpretation. So it could well be true that through such historicised 'political labor' (2007: 36) the 'impossible goal of community emerges as a provisional place from which to speak' (2007: 46).

That observation has profound significance for histories of the first two decades of the twenty-first century, when the twinned threats of terrorism and viral pandemics *together* tended to rank higher than climate change in global political systems. So it is curious that projects in the Reader's section on Environment mostly exclude history as such. Yet still the two that engage the natural environment provide telling historiographical data, but almost by default. Hence Theresa May's analysis of her CP practice with the 'tribal people' fishing communities of the northern Californian Kalamath River understandably focuses on their predicament in September 2002, when 60,000 salmon died from low water levels caused by upstream industrial-scale farming. The disaster is treated as part of a 'history of . . . issues' (2007: 154), in which indigenous history as such is an absence because a 'Salmon Ceremony' was 'lost' following 'contact with whites' around 1850 (2007: 153). Yet the present-day community's tribal elders cannily used historic myths as rhetoric, claiming that the 'salmon were angry', while others argued that the 'fish-kill was another buffalo-kill . . . intended to annihilate Indian peoples' (ibid.). These reactions informed a theatrical performance acted by university students and tribal members. Deep ironies ensued, as the imagined substitution of native Indians for buffalo was shadowed by the apocalyptic horror of the parallel disaster some 3,000 miles to the East.

Meanwhile in Nigeria, Ubong Nda initiated an environmental sustainability project at Ikot Ayan Itam, a village of around 13,000 people located on land with a 'problematic topography' (2007: 166). His report adopts a typical 'Theatre for Development' format, so its historiographical interest is neatly, but rather abstractly, summarised under 'Community research'. This includes a 'background' study of 'their beliefs, value systems, traditions, taboos, general world-view, relationship with neighbors (sic), social, political, religious and economic activities [plus] technological development'. It also notes with ethical exactitude that 'taboos [were] taken seriously . . . as wrong handling . . . could create mistrust, alienation and even outright ejection . . . from the community' (2007: 166). Nda's reward for this informed sensitivity was a three-part performance involving primary school pupil folk-chorals, a local university student dance-drama, and a forty-minute community-acted drama, all received with 'rapt attention' and followed by a collective resolution to 'forestall the environmental drift of Ikot Ayam Itam' (2007: 174). He describes the planned follow-up public results prompted by the show's success as materially practical and politically astute. So apparently this was a community creatively renewing its *own history as such* in light of fresh environmental imperatives informed by a workable historiography. Maybe just an infinitesimal adjustment to the continuing global hierarchy of risk distribution, but still it serves a useful reminder that histories as such generally benefit from carefully crafted creative openings. Thus these African/American/Welsh couplings of acutely contrasting projects might serve to show how CP and AT aesthetics can produce cognate historical purposes of social/political/environmental kinds *because* of their extraordinary differences.

Of course the two Readers themselves can be submitted to that creativity test, so exactly how the editors define the subject of their titles is not insignificant. Kuppers and Robertson are productively evasive as they contest and qualify established terminologies before offering 'a collaborative search for an expressive relation to the world that celebrates and critiques *both* difference and cohesion' (2007: 2). Prentki and Preston adopt a lexical angle to propose 'umbrella', beneath which they include sixteen forms/genres/practices ranging from 'community theatre' to 'reminiscence theatre, and so on' (2009: 10). The OED has ten definitions of 'umbrella', the last one being 'covering a number of meanings or associated terms' (OED online). So 'community performance' could be under it as well. But OED definition nine also lists a 'controlling or unifying agency' (OED online), which hardly matches the democratic spirit of many practices featured in both Readers.

Segment 2: Interregnum as a quartet of bright instruments

That textual mimicking of colonialism may be little more than a rhetorical flourish when set against the actual histories of modernism. However, it does signal how anything 'applied' might require careful qualification to gain affective traction on the past through history *per se*. Because it implicitly favours cohesion over diversity even through a 'history of the present day', thus refracting the macro-histories of global neoliberalism. Which invites back tracking to earlier and influential sole-authored texts on CP/AT, four from 2003 and 2005 and one from 2009. These fit my British/American comparator purposes, but the fourth also reports on projects done elsewhere. So the following presents an exercise in geographical and historical reflexivity while reaching into decidedly dangerous regions. It risks a highly condensed 'thumbnail sketch' of the texts to provide focus on one key idea in each of their takes on AT/CP, especially regarding history as such, with the last raising two key questions about the historiographical implications of those ideas. Thus possibly forging methodological hinges on analytical doors that open onto *non-reductive* liberal perspectives for identifying the historically radical in more recent CP/AT practices.

Applied theatre specialist James Thompson hangs his faith in its practices on their powers to produce 'bewilderment' among all its participants (2003: xxii–xxiv). He sees this as a wild card in AT's pack of processes and principles, including scepticism regarding history as settled ground rather than forever shifting sands (2003: 16). Bewilderment is Thompson's performative parallel to radical uncertainties that positively haunt advanced research in the wake of modernity's quantum and critical theories, though a *provisional* 'certainty' can be achieved by AT practices. A singular prop for that could be its commitment to 'justice, human rights and equality' (2003: 2). This acute flexibility arises through openness about all AT genres, because they offer a 'practice that has many different histories and varied rationales depending on where it is happening' (xix). From this radically liberal perspective how then might *its* collective history *per se* be understood and described?

Helen Nicholson avoids directly addressing the question of histories in her analysis of AT, focusing on how its 'interdisciplinary and hybrid practices' engage contemporary politics and ethics (2005: 2). This perspective clearly implies historical interests, so she sketches out a twentieth century genealogy of 'political, radical and alternative theatres' stretching from the 1920s international Worker's Theatre Movement to 1980s community theatres around the world (2005: 8–10). She shares Thompson's view of AT's dynamic diversity, describing it as 'continually on the move and always negotiated', so it is best 'conceptualised as a diasporan (sic) rather than a disciplinary space' (2005:159). That 'space' metaphor matches the scattering of people, culture and language that defines diaspora somewhat obliquely, as the term implies no limit and opens up a lively dynamic indeterminacy of politics and ethics for AP. Nicholson proposes the mutual drama of 'gifting' between practitioners and participants as source of temporal resolutions (2005: 165–166): an intriguing principle for histories of AP yet to be written, especially regarding diaspora gifting.

Jan Cohen-Cruz identifies American CP as possessing 'a boundary-jumping quality: is it art or ritual, therapy or politics?' (2005: 2). Thus implying a close-on-infinite reach for ways of making theatre with communities. She also calls it 'a field' (2005: 2), opening a difference to *amateurs* of old-style United States 'community theatre' within 'an entertainment frame' (7). That separation facilitates 'tracing historical sources' of CP (2005: 9), from 1912 pageantry to 1970s avant-gardes, plus nine 'case studies' of *professional* companies circa 1979–1999 (2005: 60–78). From those studies her key boundary-leaping trajectory deduces 'core principles' and 'critical tools' for CP (2005: 9). A roster of performance theorists is springboard for this scale-shift, implying symbiosis between analysis and creativity. Her account closes with a 2003 Washington DC ceremonial: 400 congregants performed short dance-phrases in unison aimed to expatiate recent 'sins' (2005: 181). Devised and led by a prominent CP choreographer, hieratically echoing Laban's historic community mass-dance events. Yet more radically, another 'boundary-jump' suggests bringing 'people of wealth and social status' into the ambit of CP 'local acts': an acute levelling of sorts (2005: 182).

Sonja Kuftinec gained extensive experience as practitioner–scholar dramaturge to a leading United States CP company. From 1995 to 2008 she pursued projects that 'modelled various forms of reconciliation' (2009: xiii) with war-damaged youth in the Balkan States and Israel. Workshops and performances took in places that were war zones in all but name. Yet likely the riskiest of her 'Between the Lines' CP events happened in Berlin. A gallery-based installation-exhibition had youth from seven Balkan regions symbolically re-animating their wartime experiences in a deliberately fragmented event. Visitors encountered solo performers in separate spaces then an ensemble denouement that collaged together moments of war-raw youthful *disconnection*. Situated near the German Reichstag building, the venue implied geo-historical links *between* the new Balkan and older Israeli states, rendering the performers as ghostly remnants of regimes with extremely opposed ideologies. For Kuftinec, the performers' histories communicated 'what it felt to be viscerally impacted but to have no say in those revisions' (2009: 94). That description's coolness subtly hints at still-present horrors. So the event's implied historiography has profound relevance for future global histories.

Could that 'visceral impact' vector produce fresh types of geo-political CP/AT that incorporate and significantly qualify Cohen-Cruz's 'boundary-jumping', substantively fulfil Nicholson's 'diaspora-gifting' and augment in actuality Thompson's 'many different histories'? Drawing out those four vectors thus poses a crucial conundrum for histories of CP/AT. Given that they could be combined in variable constellations for different types of practice, how might they inform particular historiographical principles and procedures for future preview histories stemming from present day ones? More colloquially, what critical sense could they make of the complex wider histories of today viewed through shadows currently cast by the future?

These questions are posed partly in response to Sonja Kuftinec's *Staging America* (2003), because it is probably singular among AT/CP books in explicitly highlighting *historiography* as a main concern. So next a clarification of how Kuftinec uses the term in light of its two principal definitions according to OED. First coined in mid-sixteenth century, it signifies 'The writing of history; written history' (OED online). Then in the late eighteenth century a second inflexion emerges: 'The study of history-writing, esp. as an academic discipline' (OED online). So the initial usage references the *crafting* of 'history', while the later signifies that crafting's *methods*. Kuftinec inclines strongly towards the first, ontological, usage as she evolves 'historiographic perspectives' (2003: 23) that produce a straightforward 'genealogy' of 'historical moments' of CP in America, namely: '(1) progressivism and pageantry; (2) representation and grassroots theater; (3) socialism, identity politics, and community specific theaters; and (4) radical coalition building and the American Festival Project' (2003: 26). These are framed usefully and interestingly by theoretical reflections on those specific histories. But substantive epistemological description of historiographical matters remains absent, though *neither is it needed* given the main focus of her study on contemporary practices. However, that absence usefully raises the stakes for AT/CP overall on the creation of historiographies which are responsive to the always shifting scenes of time, endurance, remembrance, forgetting, pasts, presents, futures. Especially regarding further kinds of history-making *per se* that the new world disorder might demand.

Those particular histories-in-potential were an implicit target of this vector-framing exercise, which now behoves an example. So, with respect to Sonja Kuftinec, I venture a fairly modest proposal: if the remarkable Berlin project was interpreted in terms of 'diaspora-gifting', how might its 'visceral impact' on participants have produced 'boundary-leaping' to radically 'different histories' *for* and even *of* the future? My hunch is that this approach to AT/CP historiography-making may be well suited to their practices and actual affects and effects over time. And that in turn might generate valuable understandings of broader social, political, economic, environmental and other pasts, presents and futures.

Segment 3: Performing remains through future ecologies

So having trawled through the literature and its environment for emergent CP/AT histories and nascent historiographies we return to Ricoeur's 'history of the present day' (2004: 449) through its war zones and museum/heritage sites. The monograph *Performance in Place of War* (Thompson et al. 2009) and essay collection *Performing Heritage* (Jackson and Kidd 2011) both report projects from Britain, the United States and elsewhere. Both stem from large-scale funded projects and create useful historical perspectives achieved through, respectively, co-authorship dealing with consistently violent presents and coordinated multiple authoring of increasingly accessible pasts. Inevitably they were responding more or less directly to the evolution of an expanding and crisis-ridden globalisation of neoliberalist capitalism. Could these broadly focused accounts of many projects in the early twenty-first century foster advanced AT and CP historiographies? More specifically, might their inevitable engagement in the globally unprecedented twenty-first century compulsive politico-economic mash-up somehow produce nostalgia for the future of *tomorrows'* present days? This final segment briefly explores the production of violence as a spectral shadow of disappearing histories as such, before investigating *how* such nostalgia could become antidote to the de-historicising phantasm of inevitable ephemerality. And thus perhaps short-circuit neoliberal future-shock catastrophism (Klein 2007) via a creative performance pragmatics of *historico-archival resurgence* in present-day histories to come.

It is a commonplace that the United States' declaration of a 'war on terror' following the 9/11 Twin Tower atrocities globalised deadly human conflict as an anywhere anytime event. Thereafter, extreme violence haunts every ordinary everyday as never before: a ubiquitously imminent, deeply dark spectre of history's disappearance. A spectre that out-modernises postmodernism with a vengeance. From this perspective, the concluding chapter of *Performance in Place of War* appropriately engages a future of 'collapsing ... space and time' (2009: 279) through the trope of *shadows of war* as coined by anthropologist Carolyn Nordstrom (2004). Appropriate because that *shadow* metaphor presumes the now 'standard' conditions of globalisation: space–time collapse, ceaseless mobility of markets, forever-shifting contours of power, always already unstable identities, a growing climate of fear, and so on. Hence it manifests many fierce aporia forever opening up via burgeoning miasmas of divisive change. All of which, argue Thompson et al., pose a 'challenge ... to trace the less evident, shadowy relationships between economic, military, social and cultural forces and practices reported here' (2009: 285). They also recognise the paradoxically ambivalent potential of technologies, especially digital ones, both to naturalise 'images of terror' (2009: 287) and/or to create 'new networks across the "shadows of war" ... redefine social relationships ... bring about a more hopeful politics' (ibid.).

This possibility is exemplified by three AT/CP projects: a 2001 streetwise re-enactment of Guantanamo Bay that 'implicated' Manchester passers-by in human rights issues by estranging them (2009: 299); the United States-initiated multiple public readings of Aristophanes *Lysistrata* in many towns and cities globally as a 'theatrical act of dissent' protesting the 2003 American/British invasion of Iraq (2009: 293); a 2005 anti-war play in Kalutara, Sri Lanka, created by women students who used Internet 'accounts of war' to defuse government censorship only to be thwarted by threats of violence from local extremists (2009: 290). Remarkably, in a highly connected biosphere the acute differences between these creative critiques appear as collective strength. Yet here a historiographical conundrum kicks in. Almost with another vengeance, so to speak, for the projects are described as evoking fragmented genealogies: youthful artists in Sri Lanka are linked to Brecht's *Mother Courage* through temporal and geographic 'alienation'; Guantanamo's reconstruction echoes war memorial commemorations of local soldiers lost in action; distributed *Lysistrata* readings attach to Ancient Greek theatre via historical continuities in artists' critiques of war (2009: 300). These historicising refractions are no doubt legitimate socio-aesthetic hallmarks of the past. But they seem oddly out of kilter with their contemporary environment of neoliberal capitalist globalisation and its endemic injustices. Especially given recent histories of, for example, the post-1989 quasi-closure of the Cold War, the 'triumph' of fiscally driven liberal democracy, and even a fantasy totalising 'end of history' (Fukuyama 1992). So what constructions of the *absent* from these near-ubiquitous conditions generating 'shadows of war' could become potential source of optimistic principles of AT/CP historiographies for these endgame times?

One more brief return to Ricoeur's 'history of the present day' as divination is required for this necromantic task. He considers how evidence can re-implicate witnesses as party to painful events, particularly as spoken testimony 'rubs up against writing' when simultaneous documentary traces are gathered (2009: 449). In their dangerous field work the *Performance in Place of War* authors could well have faced this dilemma alongside their local participants, highlighting ethical complexities for AT/CT creative research methods, performance histories *per se* and their historiographies (Thompson et al. 2009: 15). Ricoeur addresses the historical problems of such processes by analysing histories of memory itself (2009: 385–389), from which he derives a primary methodological feature through 'the ancient tradition of reflexivity' (2004: 95, cf. 36–38). So a critical question for potential histories of CP/AT becomes: how can 'histories of the present day' draw on longer-term multiple pasts to build reflexive connections between current memories and tomorrow's *futures*? Or more ambitiously, where on Earth can performance and theatre best evolve present day history via nostalgia for the future of many diverse histories as such?

Maybe museums and heritage sites especially could turn the paradoxical trick of finding illumination among the many shadows of *Homo sapiens'* present-day predicaments. Which brings us, finally, to *Performing Heritage* and the optimism of an anonymous wit: if you turn on the light quickly enough you can see what the dark looks like. My methodological switches for this futuristic task are twinned. The first provides a temporal challenge by querying the idea of 'intangible heritage' as in some way detached from Earthly material futures. The second adds another spatial troubling of the British/American couplings mainly featured so far. My aim is to show that these slightly skew-whiff angles on *Homo sapiens*' current 'glocal' histories could produce a strong historiographical gleam to the imminent futures of AT and CP. But to achieve that demands recognition of the everyday denial of human *compulsive performances* fostered by globalised neoliberalism. In particular, common automatic denials creating *lacunae* that disconnect culture from nature to create the endgames of an overheating planet (Kershaw 2012b). So to conclude I consider two AT/CP projects that challenge normative views of 'heritage' – and potentially other *historicising* traditions – which exemplify that process, but in acutely contradictory ways. My final hunch is that the profundity of the differences between them will produce clues for how best to begin creating the absent histories of radically resistant CP/AT practices.

Australian heritage studies researcher Laurajane Smith argues that 'heritage *is* a cultural performance' (my emphasis) and thus it is *not* 'things or spaces that are themselves "heritage" [but] the uses [they] are put to that makes them "heritage"' (2011: 69). Her *bête noir* for this view is an '"Authorised Heritage Discourse" (AHD)' (2011: 71) fixated on 'materiality', 'innate value', 'national narratives' and 'heritage experts' all 'institutionalised within public policy' (2011: 70). In countering this fixation she argues that heritage performance is 'based on the premise that *all* heritage is intangible' (ibid.) and 'that these performances ... will *always* be contested' (ibid. my emphases). To support these claims Smith presents findings from her 2003–2007 British research projects, which involved two classic heritage institutions: 'country houses/stately homes' and 'social history museums', the latter including Beamish open-air museum (based on a Northern mining village) and Liverpool's International Slavery Museum. Interviews showed visitors to the former primarily holding to traditional values of nation state-hood, while at the latter they favoured local/regional traditions and class critique (2011: 72–78). Hence Smith's key terms 'intangible' and 'contested' imply clear-cut antonyms – tangible and uncontested – resting on straightforward binary divisions in both theory and practice. But what are the consequences of defining heritage and its ethics in these ways?

The 'intangible heritage' concept became a key component of a safeguarding convention of UNESCO in 2003 (2003: 77), primarily including practices such as music, folklore, festivals and so on, and initially exemplified by a list of Masterpieces of Intangible Heritage (UNESCO 2003). An approach that soon attracted criticism for reinforcing the power of national States over communities and artist practitioners, including its potential for suppressing politically dissident groups (Kirshenblatt-Gimblett 2004). Later debates led to more liberal interpretations. But the crucial problematic is that 'intangible' is always already shadowed by its antonym, just as 'ephemeral' is by 'durable' and 'material' by 'immaterial', plus their many cognates. These and other binaries of course characterise the global performance of modernism, a.k.a. the Enlightenment, industry, colonialism, Empire and so on. Also, according to leading environmental historians, climate change/global warming (McNeill 2001). *Plus* contestation as inherent to those systemic states, whether through, say, wars on terror or transactions in capitalist fiscal regimes.

However, as my opening notes on method indicated, a wholesale stress on performance ephemerality has been challenged increasingly, because memory is constituted at least as much by embodiment, visceral experience and vital matter as by linguistic factors. This implies that ephemerality and materiality, for example, are concurrent vectors in the everyday performance of life processes. But that decisively does not imply binary formulations are best avoided, because they are essential to reflexive engagement with, and perception of, those processes. This is especially so for the ecologies of interaction between the micro-processes of actual performances and the macro-environments of an unprecedented new world disorder, plus many other points in the excluded middle of those binaries. In this regard the crucial vector for CP/AT continues to be the qualities of performance *remains* and their strategic striations between the pasts, presents and futures (Schneider 2011). So that prospective *degrees of ephemerality* could arise obliquely from my final project example (Kershaw 2007: 77–80). Suggesting that the trade between history as such and history *per se* always already has many roots, so to speak, in multiple futures.

Since 2002 performance director/scholar Mark Fleishman has been 'Remembering in the postcolony' of Cape Town and South Africa (2011: 234). Every spring he travels 200 plus kilometres with artist colleagues and students to Clanwilliam, a rural town of 7,500 people in the Western Cape. For eight days they run workshops with 500 'school learners' in a variety of arts to produce a spectacular lantern parade whose route transgresses the town's 'apartheid urban plan' (2011: 241). It culminates in an outdoor performance for several thousand residents based on a single story from the /Xam, a regional indigenous tribe that was sent extinct in the late nineteenth century. The story is presented 'not as the /Xam would have told it, but recast for our time' (ibid.). It is drawn from an oral tradition archive of 2,000 notebooks with 13,000 pages, compiled by German linguist Wilhelm Bleek in a caring act of conservation. Which, Fleishman wryly notes, constitutes 'another kind of death' (2011: 237). Hence this is a heritage project that would seem to depend on a process akin to necromancy. Because it aims holistically to revive a long-gone past into a present day history where the shadow of apartheid still haunts the rainbow communities of South Africa.

Even if that were just remotely achieved, the conditions it could create likely will carry potentially profound implications for the practices of CP/ AT and their historiographies. To grapple with that possibility therefore requires a reflexive method especially alert to how many contiguous histories might coexist and thrive in the passage of time. From this perspective, Fleishman's account of his project's core procedures is reveal-ing. He talks of 'gathering a story from the archive . . . inserting it into a . . . landscape from which it has been extracted . . . allowing the occupants . . . to play with that story in multiple ways' (2011: 244). Now the environs of Clanwilliam apparently provide an especially stimulating playground that is *reflexively structured* as, besides their stories, the /Xam left a widespread heritage of rock art that invites visceral responses to the landscapes it punctuates. Hence might this environment create a sense of long-gone histories-as-such which are still performing as present-day history towards multiple futures?

So now our journey through the varied texts of applied theatre and community performance in search of *their* histories-as-such has arrived at a surprising historiographical watershed. Where the timbre of long-past storytelling still speaks volumes for many futures. Because //Kabbo, the deceased linguist's principle informant, described the /Xam's biospheric creativity as follows: 'I do merely *listen watching* for a story . . . that it might float into my ear . . . [for] I feel that a story *is* the wind. . .' (2011: 238–239, my emphasis). To 'listen watching' intimates a kinaesthetic opening in a landscape that 'is' precociously alive, like the wind. Not only as story-provider, but also as an agency always already performing the listener watching. That is to say, the biosphere and its environs *perform the human subject* into life as such. Thus reflexivity is not solely a human quality. Because the health of all environments depends on feedback systems that monitor their performance, *including* how humans are performing as part of them. It follows that, even as humanity always performs alongside and with all living and inanimate things, *Homo sapiens* is always already *performed by Earth's ecologies* (Kershaw 2015). This then carries significant epistemological import for how present temporalities passing through to the future can be construed. It implies that time can never be just linear or space forever and everywhere bounded, because they have been always homologically interchangeable as space-time. Hence the *past incessantly is accessibly alive* in some way or another and the *future is never wholly an absence* in histories of the present. It is therefore very likely true that coming events cast their shadow before and thus the future indeed is always before its time.

Acknowledgements

Many thanks to Matt Omasta and Dani Snyder-Young for sharing the detail of their research data.

References

Agamben, G. 1995. (trans. D. Heller-Roazen). *Homo Sacer: Sovereign Power and Bare Life*. Stanford, CA: Stanford University Press.

Amit, V. and Rapport, N. 2002. *The Trouble with Community: Anthropological Reflections on Movement, Identity and Collectivity*. London: Pluto Press.

Ashley, D. 1997. *History Without a Subject: The Postmodern Condition*. Boulder and Oxford: Westview Press.

Bennett, J. 2010. *Vibrant Matter: A Political Ecology of Things*. Durham and London: Duke University Press.

Butler, C. 2002. *Postmodernism: A Very Short Introduction*. Oxford: Oxford University Press.

Cohen-Cruz, J. 2005. *Local Acts: Community-based Performance in the United States*. New Brunswick and London: Rutgers University Press.

CUNY. 2014. CUNY School of Professional Studies, Master's Degree in Applied Theatre, http://sps.cuny.edu/programs/ma_appliedtheatre. Last accessed 29 July 2015.

Emmott, S. 2012. *Ten Billion: An Exploration of the Future of Life on Earth*, www.royalcourttheatre.com/news/articles/ten-billion-an-exploration-of-the-future-of-life-o/. Last accessed 29 July 2015.

Fleishman, M. 2011. "'For a little road it is not. For it is a great road; it is long": performing heritage for development in the Cape' in Jackson and Kidd, pp. 234–248.

Fukuyama, F. 1992. *The End of History and the Last Man*. London: Penguin.

Jackson, A. and Kidd, J. (eds.) 2011. *Performing Heritage: Research, Practice and Innovation in Museum Theatre and Live Interpretation.* Manchester: Manchester University Press.

Jameson, F. 1985. 'Postmodernism and consumer society' in Foster, H. (ed.) *Postmodern Culture.* London: Pluto Press.

Jameson, F. 1991. *Postmodernism: Or, the Cultural Logic of Late Capitalism.* London and New York: Verso.

Kershaw, B. 1999. *The Radical in Performance: Between Brecht and Baudrillard.* London and New York: Routledge.

Kershaw, B. 2007. *Theatre Ecology: Environments and Performance Events.* Cambridge: Cambridge University Press.

Kershaw, B. 2011. 'Nostalgia for the future of the past: technological environments and the ecologies of heritage performance', in Jackson and Kidd, pp. 123–143.

Kershaw, B. 2012a. 'Dancing with monkeys? On performance commons and scientific experiments' in Wendy Arons and Theresa J. May (eds.) *Readings in Performance and Ecology.* Basingstoke: Palgrave Macmillan, pp. 59–76.

Kershaw, B. 2012b. '"This is the way the world ends, not. . .?" On performance compulsion and climate change'. *Performance Research* 17.4: 5–17.

Kershaw, B. 2015. 'Performed by ecology: how *Homo sapiens* could subvert present day futures'. *Performing Ethos; An International Journal of Ethics in Theatre & Performance.* 4:2: 113–134.

Kirshenblatt-Gimblett, B. 2004. 'Intangible Heritage as Metacultural Production', www.nyu.edu/classes/bkg/web/heritage_MI.pdf Last accessed 29 July 2015.

Klein, N. 2007. *The Shock Doctrine: The Rise of Disaster Capitalism.* London: Penguin Books.

Kuftinec, S. 2003. *Staging America: Cornerstone and Community-Based Theatre.* Carbondale and Edwardsville: Southern Illinois University Press.

Kuftinec, S. 2009. *Theatre, Facilitation, and Nation Formation in the Balkans and Middle East.* Basingstoke: Palgrave Macmillan.

Kuppers, P. and Robertson, G. (eds.) 2007. *The Community Performance Reader.* Abingdon and New York: Routledge.

McDonnell, B. 2005. 'The politics of historiography – towards an ethics of representation'. *Research in Drama Education* 10.2: 127–138.

McNeill, J. 2001. *Something New Under the Sun: An Environmental History of the Twentieth Century.* London: Penguin.

Nicholson, H. 2005. *Applied Drama: The Gift of Theatre.* Basingstoke: Palgrave Macmillan.

Nordstrom, C. 2004. *Shadows of War: Violence, Power and International Profiteering in the Twenty-first Century.* Philadelphia: University of Pennsylvania Press.

OED: Oxford English Dictionary online: 'umbrella' and 'historiography'. Last accessed 29 July 2015.

Omasta, M. and Snyder-Young, D. 2014. 'Gaps, silences and comfort zones: dominant paradigms in educational drama and applied theatre discourse' *Research in Drama Education* 19.1: 7–22.

Postlewait, T. and Michieli, B.S. 2010. 'A transnational community of scholars: the theatre historiography working group of IFTR/FIRT'. *Theatre Research International* 35.3: 232–249.

Prentki, T. and Preston, S. (eds.) 2009. *The Applied Theatre Reader*. Abingdon and New York: Routledge.

Ricoeur, P. 2004. (trans. K. Blamey and D. Pellauer) *Memory, History, Forgetting*. Chicago: University of Chicago Press.

RiDE Viewpoints. 2006. 'Applied Theatre/Drama: an e-debate in 2004'. *Research in Drama Education* 11.1: 90–95.

St Mary University. 2015. www.stmarys.ac.uk/undergraduate/docs/leaflets-16-17/2015-may-drama-applied-theatre-2015-3-p3.pdf. Last accessed 30 July 2015.

Schneider, R. 2011. *Performing Remains: Art and War in Times of Theatrical Enactment*. Abingdon and New York: Routledge.

Smith, L. 2011. 'The "doing" of Heritage: Heritage as performance', in Jackson and Kidd, pp. 69–81.

Thompson, J. 2003. *Applied Theatre: Bewilderment and Beyond*. Peter Lang: Oxford.

Thompson, J., Hughes, J. and Balfour, M. 2009. *Performance in Place of War*. London, New York, Calcutta: Seagull.

Thrift, N. 2008. *Non-Representational Theory: Space|Politics|Affect*. London and New York: Routledge.

UNESCO. 2003. www.unesco.org/culture/ich/index.php?lg=en&pg=00002. Last accessed 29 July 2001.

van Erven, E. 2001. *Community Theatre: Global Perspectives*. London and New York: Routledge.

Winston, J. 2010. 'Editorial'. *Research in Drama Education* 15.2: 145–146.

Worthen, W.B. with Holland, P. 2003. *Theorizing Practice: Redefining Theatre History*. Basingstoke: Palgrave Macmillan.

CHAPTER 3

A pre-history of applied theatre
Work, house, perform

Jenny Hughes

This chapter explores an ambiguous precedent in the histories of applied theatre: theatrical entertainments in the Victorian workhouse in Britain. Historical conceptions of Victorian workhouses have characterised them as 'Poor Law Bastilles', imprisoning vulnerable populations in shaming and repressive regimes of discipline and punishment (Engels 1993 [1845]: 292). In the workhouse, the poor were categorised according to the extent to which they were deemed able to work, with a time and place regime crafted to condition the able-bodied poor into habits of work and good character by, for example, following a strict daily routine and performing monotonous forms of labour. However, the Victorian workhouse was also part of the first centrally and systematically administered welfare system, and it focused on improving the care and education of neglected and orphaned children, and providing comfort for elderly, ill and vulnerable adult members of society. On the one hand, the workhouse entertainments examined in this chapter were compliant with a disciplinary regime that recognised life as valuable only when it *works*, that is, when immersed in capitalist systems of productive labour. On close inspection, however, the permitted forms of sociality exemplified by visiting entertainers also show how the workhouse regime opened up to the economically excluded in ways that prefigure egalitarian and progressive forms of cultural practice.

Here, I examine three theatrical performances – a glee concert, temperance entertainment and Sunday School amusement – taking place in a workhouse in Rochdale (Lancashire, UK) between 1877 and 1887. As theatrical forms of rational recreation and missionary education, each is embedded in the Protestant religious culture predominant in Britain at the time which, as Max Weber famously asserted in his classic work *The Protestant Ethic and the Spirit of Capitalism*, accelerated the historical development of capitalism across Europe and its colonies (2002 [1905]). Although an exploration of the colonial trajectories of the theatrical encounters with the poor explored here cannot be the focus of this chapter, it is important to note that, as cultural practices embedded in discourses of workfulness, respectability and self-help associated with the development of capitalism, their significance extends far beyond the specific spatial and temporal context examined. It is also important to draw attention to the way each example exhibits what might seem surprisingly imaginative and social modes of religiosity concomitant with Protestant religious culture. As such, each entertainment provides a perspective on what I am calling the fledgling social theatres of the nineteenth century, and taken together, they present a counter-perspective to narratives of applied theatre history founded on assumptions about the mutually exclusive nature of Protestant, utilitarian and Romantic mobilisations of culture. They also invite a reconsideration of normative understandings of organised religion as a repressive and pacifying force. Each of the entertainments examined here works in coalition with a disciplinary regime infused with religious feeling as well as economically driven imperatives to make life work, but they also display a peculiar mixture of coercive and emancipatory rhetoric. So for example, they extol hierarchically framed moral perspectives but also, in their affective resonances and practices of association, figure creative responses that celebrate potential and minister to threatened, excluded and abandoned forms of life. Workhouse entertainments, then, represent a problematic material and affective architecture that haunts applied theatre's pasts and presents. A critical examination of the imaginative and social modes of religiosity immanent to workhouse entertainments contributes to ongoing debates about the economic, political and aesthetic relations of applied theatre, as well as extends existing historical accounts of the field.

This investigation of entertainments in a Rochdale workhouse was triggered by my participation as a researcher in a contemporary project in Rochdale with tenants of social housing described as 'workless', 'vulnerable' and 'complex-needs clients'. I turned to history as a resource to explore how theatre projects like this might work both with and against (neo)liberal welfare regimes that require individuals to take responsibility for lifting themselves out of pernicious networks of economic inequality. Twenty-first century welfare reform in the United Kingdom has featured examples of performative 'welfare-speak' that encapsulate this demand: 'our economy depends more than ever before on our people ... we need a welfare system that enables people to become authors of their lives' (Department for Work and Pensions 2008: 11). This statement has uncanny resonance with Foucault's oft-cited comment that neoliberalism is a context in which 'self' becomes 'the *homo œconomicus* as entrepreneur of himself, being for himself his own capital, being for himself his own producer' (2008: 226). Unsurprisingly, reports from participants of theatre projects often conflict with such discourses and stress social as opposed to individual outcomes. Participants of the project in Rochdale, for example, reported positive impacts that were inseparable from the opportunity to meet twice a week over a period of six months, which created a supportive social network for a group of people, many of whom were extraordinarily isolated, in turn inspiring in them the confidence and energy to leave the house, and discover interests that they had either forgotten or had not had the opportunity to develop before.

The tension between theatre as a means of disciplining the self and theatre as a world-making project that mobilises diverse figurations of the social is core to the discussion that follows. To explore this tension, I draw on the motif of *chora*, an idea developed by ancient Greek philosopher Plato to account for the processes by which the universe is made. Plato describes *chora* as a 'receptacle' – a strangely characterless time, place and process where amorphous materials are shaped into the orderly and legible forms that populate the universe (2008). As *chora*, life remains impossible to apprehend and appears instead as disordered combinations of limbs, bodies and energies. Judith Butler explores Plato's *chora* as a performative process of sifting such peculiar combinations into recognisable forms, and this sorting, not least in the gender discriminations reproduced by Plato in his description, appropriates the potency of the female body and marginalises other bodies. For Butler, then, *chora* is a disciplinary force underpinning the performative processes of speech and discourse by which some bodies come to matter and others are excluded from systems of intelligibility (1993: 53–54). Whilst accepting Butler's account, I am also drawn to understanding *chora* as a disruption that unsettles any process of forming, in which life is encountered in unfathomable variety, and where the disciplinary energies released are amenable to redirections. Jacques Derrida's account of *chora* as something that 'lets itself be called or causes itself to be named without answering, without giving itself to be seen, conceived, determined' is helpful here (1995: 97). For Derrida, *chora* calls attention to 'the fold of an immense difficulty: the relationship, so ancient, so traditional, so determinant, between the question of sense and the sensible and that of receptivity in general' (ibid.: 110). Notably, the complexities of reception revealed by Derrida's understanding of *chora*, and the idea that any form is sculpted in perpetual proximity to a promise of its undoing, are features of the workhouse entertainments examined here.

The 'proto-drama' in applied theatre history

Anthony Jackson's location of the history of theatre education in modernist drama of the fin de siècle and the workers theatre movement of the 1930s, and Helen Nicholson's explorations of the creative social work of reformers and progressive educationalists of the late nineteenth and early twentieth centuries have provided springboards for my investigation here (Jackson 2007; Nicholson 2010). However, the research of a single institution – a workhouse – in one time and place has also revealed the existence of a wealth of social and educational theatre activity that preceded both modernist experiment and progressive educationalists' embrace of the arts. This body of activity has been overlooked and has even been assumed not to exist. Gavin Bolton, for example, comments that Puritan forms of Protestantism that predominated in the nineteenth century led to the relative absence of school drama in this period (2007: 47). This assumed lack of compatibility between Protestantism and theatre perhaps explains the neglect of the contexts of theatrical activity explored in this chapter, all of which evolved in a social and cultural milieu dominated by Protestantism. Theatrical activity associated with the rational recreation, temperance and missionary education movements throughout the nineteenth century engaged large numbers of people and were infused with the liberal ideals and self-help imperatives of Protestant culture. Interestingly, this culture, especially in its nonconformist varieties, is sometimes disparaged by thinkers influencing movements associated with applied theatre history, such as poet and schools inspector Matthew Arnold, who is rudely dismissive of the vernacular and utilitarian modes of nonconformist sociality that mobilised missionary cultural practice (1869: 29–30).

Exploring the antecedents of the workers' theatre movement, Raphael Samuel identifies a lack of a 'continuous history' of socialist theatre during the nineteenth century (Samuel et al. 1985: xx). In place of a linear tradition, he describes a series of disparate contexts of theatrical activity, including the Socialist Sunday Schools of the Owenite and Chartist movements of the 1830s and 1840s, noting the prevalence of reading and recitation, as well as musical performance in these contexts. He concludes that these proto-dramatic activities – unlike the proletarian aesthetics of workers' theatre – were adjuncts to the main activity of politics, morally improving and entertaining rather than critically focused (1985: 13–15). Significantly, the performance forms identified by Samuel – reading, recitation, musical performance – replicate theatrical modes of 'rational recreation' that emerged in response to public concern about the social and

cultural habits of the mass of urban poor concomitant with industrialisa-
tion. My contention here is that an analysis of these forms and their
contexts provides a view of applied theatre history that is as historically
important as the socialist lineage excavated by Samuel. Cultural historian
Peter Bailey describes how rational recreation activities, often supported by
social élites, materialised a 'play discipline to complement the work discipline that was the principal means of social control' under industrial
capitalism (1978: 5). Sanctioned modes of rational recreation countered the
attractions of an emergent and 'degenerate' culture industry, providing
respectable entertainment that included opportunities for cross-class
encounters and worked to 'sugar the pill' of moral instruction (1978: 54).

Bailey opens up a new way of thinking about the social significance of
popular cultural activity and also provides a nuanced reading of the extent
to which these sanctioned cultural activities can be understood as disciplinary impositions of middle-class respectability on the poor. Part of the
challenge here is to understand the complex nature of class in the nineteenth century. For Brian Harrison, the distinction between the 'respectable' and 'rough' poor was more significant than that between working and
middle classes, with the 'respectable classes' in nineteenth century society
identifying themselves 'by culture and conduct rather than by occupation
and income' (1994: 28). Importantly, members of the respectable classes,
particularly following the economic depression of the early 1870s, became
increasingly conscious of the fragility of their place in the economic order
(Shiman 1988: 93). Here, the performance of self as respectable represented
a practical defence against the threats of poverty and unemployment and
participation in improving cultural activity helped to hold the social world
open during moments of economic precariousness. Interestingly, Bailey
describes the transactions of rational recreation as often characterised by
ambivalence, with the unease of bourgeois gentlemen participating in
cultural activities with working men, for example, arising from suspicion
of 'deferential mimesis' and a 'vague perception of the latter's capacity for
dissembling' (1978: 178).

The uncertain nature of this transaction evokes Derrida's identification of the choric nature of reception noted above, of course, and also
relevant here is Jacques Rancière's argument that theatre accrues political potency by producing moments of 'dissensus'. In *The Philosopher
and His Poor* (2003 [1983]), Rancière links the production of dissensus
to the dissimulating capacities of theatre, which – drawing on Bailey's
comment about deferential mimesis above – can be understood to
emerge within performances of a respectable self in sanctioned cultural

environments. Rancière explores how political philosophers such as Plato and Marx perform 'exclusion by homage' to the poor by providing critical schemas that deny the poor a capacity to be, and think themselves to be, more than one thing at a time. For Rancière, workers enjoying melodrama in nineteenth century Paris, in their imitation of the bourgeois habit of attending the theatre, have a dissensual potency that eludes such categorisations, and one that Rancière aligns with the political: they are engaged in 'the production, within a determined, sensible world, of a given that is heterogeneous to it' (2003: 226; also see 2011: 175–232). For my investigation, it is important to emphasise that the production of dissensus can happen as part of nuanced coalitions with the forces of order as much as in oppositional or agitational contexts. Here, dissensus can be manifested as an orderly appropriation of experience, and an appropriation that insists on a place for all forms of life (rather than one that ends in a sense of alienation or displacement). In addition, disciplinary structures of all kinds – punitive and benevolent – can be affirmed by such transactions.

Anne Varty's study of children and theatre in Victorian Britain provides a link between this notion of dissensus and theatrical activity with children in the nineteenth century, also highlighting the double – coercive and emancipatory – potential of a theatrical transaction. Influenced by Romantic discourses of the child's closeness to nature and imitative capacities, the child became symbolised in Victorian Britain as 'janus-faced . . . the anarchic-arcadian primitive to be accommodated within civilised society' (2008: 234). Representing a form of 'savage innocence', Varty argues that the child performer was released from antitheatrical prejudices of the Victorian period, which, as Jonas Barish notes, were expressed as suspicion of the mutable persona of the actor and a general perception of theatre as lacking in respectability (1981: 317). Instead, the child performing in public becomes a figure of fascination, providing a spectacle of 'controlled' and 'scrutinised' savagery which, for Varty, culminates in the child's assimilation into civilisation as well affirmation of the superiority of Victorian society (2008: 15). Read alongside Rancière's discussion of the critical mimesis of theatre, it becomes possible to argue that the performing child's position in a theatrical transaction – as a human form in the process of becoming orderly and legible – mobilises a potent sense of the fragilities of reception, and in turn reveals the insecure boundary between dissimulation and authenticity, discipline and revolt, fixity and adaptability. It also becomes possible to align public fascination for the figure of the performing child with the potency of transactions between performers and

paupers as part of workhouse entertainments, which similarly evoked
uncertain spectacles of transformation.

An elegy for association: the Orpheus Glee Club

> Human nature must be different in Rochdale ... There must have
> been a special creation of mechanics in this inexplicable district of
> Lancashire – in no other way can you account for the fact that they
> have mastered the art of acting together, and holding together, as no
> other set of workmen. (Holyoake 1900: 1)

'The hall appears to be an excellent one for singing' – this comment at
the end of an account of the opening of Dearnley workhouse in
Rochdale in 1877 refers to a performance in the workhouse dining
hall by the Orpheus Glee Club to a group of seventy 'rate-payers'
invited to inspect the new workhouse, built to accommodate 900
paupers (n.a. *Rochdale Observer*, 22 December 1877). A little more
than a week later, the Orpheus performed again, with the workhouse
now adorned with Christmas decorations 'but how different were the
guests!' Here, 300 paupers were treated to a Christmas dinner of 'good
old English fare ... which disappeared with marvellous rapidity',
followed by humorous songs, recitations and a violin solo from 'a
good muster of the members of the Orpheus'. Addresses from
Guardians of the poor rendered advice to the young and, once the
children had gone to bed, there was dancing (n.a. *Rochdale Observer*,
29 December 1877). The workhouse was described as a 'credit and an
ornament' to the town, 'designed in every detail to facilitate character'
by encouraging habits of work and frugality in the able-bodied poor
(n.a. *Rochdale Observer*, 22 December 1877). According to historian
David Vincent, during the nineteenth century, Rochdale became 'one
of the most alert and socially creative towns in England' (1976: 96) –
a renowned centre of working-class self-help, radical-liberal political
coalitions and nonconformist chapel society. Built in the same decade
as other public amenities – the town hall, a free library, a public
washhouse, the Lyceum, a new sewage system – Dearnley workhouse
was part of a municipal architecture that represented the culmination
of Chartist activity, the cooperative movement and poor law agitation
of previous decades (Cole 1994; Gowland 1979: 68–93).

The Orpheus Glee Club exemplified the new 'associational culture' of
the industrial midlands and north during this period, which, as historian
Simon Gunn comments, was noted for its musical societies (2000: 27–29;

134–56). The Orpheus consisted of twenty amateur performers working with a professional conductor, meeting weekly at the Lyceum in Rochdale. Interestingly, and to some extent countering Gunn's alignment of associational culture with middle-class public life, a reviewer of a concert performance by the Orpheus during this period noted that its members were 'principally, if not entirely, working men' who 'sing with much precision, and attention to light and shade, and are evidently thoroughly under command' (n.a. *Manchester Courier*, 12 November 1883). This difficulty in securely placing the Orpheus in relation to class reflects the complex intersection of class and respectability discussed above, which is in turn also reflected at the Lyceum itself. Lyceums were sites of rational recreation that supported the 'diffusion of useful knowledge' to the working classes and they benefited from middle-class patronage, with the Lyceum in Rochdale also receiving government aid, presumably in recognition of its contribution to the 'improvement' of working people (Robertson 1875: 191). Notwithstanding this public subsidy, as music historian Dave Russell comments in his social history of music, subscription fees and lack of access to suitable clothing would likely have barred the very poor from participating in such associations (Russell 1996: 43). All of which places the members of the Orpheus in an interesting position as regards their performances for both wealthy rate-payers and the poor in the workhouse: here, a group of workers modelling self-help, good habits and the profitable use of time offered a mimetic embodiment of the principles and practices of the workhouse.

'Self-help' is important to the history of Rochdale, but local meanings of this term did not carry the same associations as a more prominent notion of self-help outlined by Samuel Smiles in his best-seller *Self-Help* (1859). Smiles extols the virtues of self-reliance and self-government and urges men to become 'active agents in their own well-being and well-doing', demonstrating this with biographical sketches of individuals of 'good character' (1996: 16). In Rochdale, the term 'self-help' came from the cooperative movement, with the title of an early history of this movement, written by George Jacob Holyoake (who also claims that the cooperators were the first to use the term), illustrative of its distinctions from Smiles' individualism – *Self-Help By the People* (1900). Privileging the principle of cooperation over competition, radicals in the town engaged in an exercise of 'world-making', devising associational systems of manufacture, provision, democracy, education and welfare (1900: 11). For Peter Gurney, cooperative self-help represented a critical reworking of the values of thrift, work and frugality, which in turn became practical resources, put to use to build a morally-bound monetary economy. As part of this, as Gurney comments, 'it is important to remember that capital as well as labour was disciplined' (1996 16). Strains of this cooperative mode of sociality and its disciplining potency can be heard in the voices of working men joined together to perform glees in the opening week of the new workhouse.

Programmes for Orpheus concerts show that they conformed to the 'respectable' choral repertoire of this time – including Old English airs, songs from the golden age of gentlemen's glee, selections from Handel and Haydn, and hymns. Glees are complex constructions, challenging to sing, consisting of different parts and contrasting movements, with each voice (or group of voices) taking a different part. A contemporaneous source presents the history of glee as embedded in a folk tradition of travelling minstrels who, arriving at great houses in medieval times, mobilised customary obligations on the gentry to host their rowdy performances, also tracing the etymology of the word 'glee' to association and companionship (Barrett 1886: 70–80). Arguably, these convivial and carnivalesque echoes are spectrally present in the performances in the workhouse, camouflaged by the self-help mimesis perfected by the Orpheus. The respectability of choral culture, and the associations of glee with the moral obligations of the gentry, ensured the sanction of the Guardians, and created, to draw again on Rancière, a dissensual performance, not least in the way the singers' technical competence in performing a complex form of song associated with the elite enacted a claim for equality. The disciplinary energies of this performance are multi-directional, and whilst this dynamic is carefully controlled by the spatial and social transactions of performance, its associations cannot be fixed.

One song that the Orpheus may have sung at the workhouse was *A Fine Old English Gentlemen* – this old English glee was performed by the Orpheus Glee Club at the opening of a coffee house in 1880 and was a favourite of choirs at this time (n.a. *Rochdale Observer*, 18 December 1880). The song harks back to an idyllic past of fraternity between classes, telling of an English gentleman of 'the olden time' who, whilst living in the midst of plenty, 'kept up his old mansion at a bountiful old rate, with a good old porter to relieve the poor at his gate' and who, 'when winter's cold brought frost and snow ... open'd house to all'. The fine old English gentleman of the song gave a ball each year, and 'nor was the houseless wanderer e'er driven from his hall ... for while he feasted all the great, he ne'er forgot the small' (Carmen 1904: 256). The performance of these lyrics at the workhouse, arguably, reminds the Guardians of their age-old obligation to the poor, whilst also carrying an ironic critique of the thinness of association that opens up to the excluded once a year. This Old English glee had been much parodied, with its recycled versions likely to be known to listeners. Generally attributed to prominent song writer Henry Russell in 1835, Charles Dickens' *The Fine Old English Gentleman: New Version* (1841) drew on the irony implicit in the lyrics to satirise the recently elected Tory government – with Dickens' version later reproduced as part of socialist traditions of song (Rumens 2012). Its performance acknowledges, perhaps, the broader performances of inequality that all were participating in. This acknowledgement is most acutely present in the affective environments of the sung lyrics and their choric mnemonics, environments that become infused with the sense and sensibility of a social world available to all, founded upon an orderly mélange of those separated by wealth, rank and name.

Marching in time: the Band of Hope

> Here is a medium through which the child can be trained in a way that will never be forgotten. Whether he himself takes part in the play or whether he is part of the audience ... makes no difference. Truths will be etched on his mind that stay with him throughout his life. 'The drama in temperance work'. (Turner 1942: 48–49)

By the mid-1880s, theatrical entertainments in Dearnley workhouse were a regular occurrence and included performances by local choirs, Sunday Schools, temperance societies and other amateur performance groups. Entertainments in the workhouse were so frequent, in fact, that the Board of Guardians noted that they were becoming burdensome, expensive and 'were not always appreciated by the inmates themselves' (n.a. *Rochdale Observer*, 11 January 1888). Here, I focus on an entertainment given by the 'Temperance and Band of Hope Union' in 1887 (Rochdale Board of Guardians, 1887). Originating in Leeds in 1847, the Band of Hope was the first national organisation to provide social and recreational activity for children, and it engaged vast numbers of young people across Britain and its colonies.[1] A prototype applied performance network for children and young people, it generated an extensive archive of recitations, dialogues and short plays for performance by its members that, taken together, provide an extraordinary insight into the uses of theatre for personal, health and citizenship education in the nineteenth century. Brian Harrison shows how alcohol, which interfered with the work disciplines of industrial society, became constructed as a social problem in the Victorian period. The temperance movement that emerged in response reached a broad

section of the population, often directed at and sometimes driven by
working people (1994: 27–28). Providing a safe environment and entertaining diversion at a time of public concern about how children were using
their increasing leisure time, the Band of Hope had a large national
membership (Shiman 1973: 50) – by 1888, for example, the Rochdale
Band of Hope Union alone had forty-three separate societies and 7,248
members (Lancashire and Cheshire Band of Hope Union 1888).

For Robert Tyler, early historian of Band of Hope, the movement was
innovative in its commitment to develop young people as powerful presences in their communities. In a period when children were expected 'to
be seen and not heard ... the Band of Hope was allowing its young
members to express themselves audibly and often volubly' (1946: 39).
A typical Band of Hope would meet fortnightly or monthly, with the
meeting itself a performative event. An opening address, sometimes given
by a young person, would be followed by a hymn, and perhaps an input by
a visiting speaker. Young people would perform recitations, dialogues and
plays, and meetings ended with an invitation to new members to make
a solemn pledge of abstinence and wear a ribbon to publicly communicate
this commitment, facilitating 'emotional identification and a powerful
sense of belonging' (McAllister 2011: 10). Here, the creation of strong
characters, capable of taking leadership roles in the community, was an
explicit aim. As historian Stephanie Olsen comments, youth organisations
in this period incorporated a blend of Romantic and utilitarian discourse:
'a distinctly unromantic corruption of Wordsworth's "child as father of the
man"' (2014: 95). Here, there was a belief that 'the child exemplar, pure of
heart and noble of spirit, could shape not only his child peers, but also the
adults in his life' (2014: 4). For the Band of Hope, the 'child exemplar' was
a beacon for the 'human race', with the latter construction accruing
shifting nationalistic, Christian, communitarian and liberal emphases
across the different times and places of the movement. Importantly, the
'drunkard' is determinedly *included* in these social imaginaries, a subject of
compassion, never written off, capable of transformation and making
a positive contribution to the world. Band of Hope performances, therefore, tend to affirm Harrison's comment that the temperance movement
promoted an idea of an inclusive and equitable social order: 'haltingly,
sometimes inconsistently, but ultimately decisively, they were widening
the bounds of tolerance and understanding' (1994: 349). Like the Orpheus,
Band of Hope performances by young people opened up the social domain
at the same time as disciplined authority, often admonishing adults who
drink as well as authorities that license the sale of alcohol.

The Band of Hope entertainment at the workhouse is likely to have taken the shape of a typical meeting, with selections of songs, recitations and dialogues performed. The available repertoire was extensive and eclectic, with the recitations, dialogues and plays ranging from melodramatic pieces that depict scandalous downfalls and sensational rescues to declamatory agitprop pieces celebrating the healing powers of drinking water. There are plays that take the form of debates, pledges, lectures and direct appeals, depictions of emotional transformations, and also humorous pieces drama-tising trials – with 'drink' personified as a criminal – and battles – where young people plan and enact an attack on 'drink'. Here, I focus on three short plays published in *The Onward Reciter* in 1885 (Hallsworth 1885) – a monthly publication of the Lancashire and Cheshire Band of Hope Union providing, as its front matter states, 'a repository of appropriate recitations and dialogues' for Band of Hope meetings. *The Onward Reciter* was one of many Band of Hope penny and half-penny pamphlets distributed nationally and, in line with other juvenile literature of the time, exhibited a 'strong moralistic tone' (Shiman 1988: 143), advocating virtues such as effort, hard work, thrift, honesty, staying hopeful, working collectively, self-sacrifice, engaging in respectable pursuits, gaining useful knowledge, saving money, keeping the home tidy and leading by example.

The Band of Hope disciplined the young person by means of public rituals that segmented their leisure time into activities with profitable uses and affirmed their identities as community leaders. The three plays dis-cussed here focus on the issue of time in the formation of good character – a theme that maps directly onto the strict routines of the workhouse. In *Bad Habits*, for example, the audience meet seven young people about to go on a ramble (a rational recreation *par excellence*), who extend the performative motif of the teetotal pledge by committing to rid themselves of bad habits accrued from their past use of time. The entire piece is taken up with naming each other's bad habits – 'a hasty temper', a propensity for 'exaggeration' and 'unladylike exclamation', lateness, conceit, 'carelessness, both in attire and conversation', and the use of slang – culminating in a collective pledge to amend these habits and cultivate 'a forgiving and charitable disposition toward others'. The second example, *The Thief of Time*, a humorous performance given by three boys, also exhibits a concern for time, but attending to 'now' rather than making amends for past misuse of time. John Ray, Charley Cheerful and Ralph Ready are on their way to take part in a recitation competition. Charley and Ralph are prepared, but the best reciter among them, John – 'a terrible fellow for putting off study until the last moment' – has been boating, stealing melons and playing ball rather than rehearsing. John enters, hurriedly learning his recitation, and is interrupted by a series of comic characters, including an Irish farmhand, hunting for the young thief whose voice he heard in the melon patch the night before. His attention is drawn by the sound of John rehearsing, and here, John's voice, neglected and underprepared, performs its prescribed role as an asset to the community by becoming the means of his involuntary exposure as the thief, and – by the end of the play – providing John with an opportunity to express his intention to improve himself. My final example, *What We Mean to Do* is an energetic rhyming dialogue that extends the performative pledges of *Bad Habits* and *The Thief of Time* by focusing not on self-improvement, but hopes for the future. Here, five boys and five girls, a 'band of youthful pilgrims, just starting out in life' recite 'what we mean to do' in order 'to do our very best'. The first reciter, despite being 'such a little wee thing, it's scarcely fair to ask', pledges to search the town for 'all the hungry poor, the careworn and cast down' and feed, clothe, comfort and console them. Following this, the other children, in order of age and size, make pledges to find work for poor children in decent trades, minister to the sick, work for the temperance cause, train women in domestic skills, encourage men to be kind to their wives, develop public amenities, care for the elderly, protect animals and promote Christianity.

In each of these pieces, there is gendered construction of the social that is of course problematic, but there is also, especially evident in *What We Mean to Do*, a sculpting of time that projects a caring and compassionate social order. The cumulative rhythm created by a succession of voices that gradually increases in strength dynamises a set of statements that powerfully defines expectations for the welfare of self and other. The social themes of the plays are matched by the social energies of the performance event. Demonstrating 'character' is a key motif, but interestingly, in these and other examples, there are many 'larger than life' characters (often adults, and frequently gender, class and cultural stereotypes), who make mistakes and are naïve or silly, which must have provided moments of hilarity when performed by children for their peers. Working alongside other young people in a small group, with supportive adults, accessing opportunities for friendship, intellectual stimulation and light-heartedness after the monotony of the working day, adds up to an inhabitation of time that exhibits but is not reducible to its broader disciplinary scriptings. Here, the texts and their performance include the possibility of inhabiting time as a pleasure in itself and of expanding the uses to which time is put to include developing young people as critical agents, engaged in making tolerable worlds, characterised by self-respect and compassion for others.

The least may do something: Sunday School amusements

These young people are not empty vessels that you have to fill; they are living souls you have to develop ... Every little child is a little world, each soul a dominion in itself, where passions nestle, and feelings centre and affections throb and tendencies expand: and the great work that waits to be done all turns upon the right unfolding and right development and use of these tremendous forces.
'What is a Sunday School?' (Hopps 1885)

Performing in the workhouse in January 1888, a year after the Band of Hope, was Clover Street Sunday School, one of many Sunday Schools in Rochdale giving entertainments at the workhouse during this period (Rochdale Board of Guardians 1888). Annual tea party entertainments of Sunday Schools, reported in the *Rochdale Observer*, show that the performance of hymns, glees, instrumental solos, recitations and dialogues were common, as were, although more occasionally, the performance of plays. Scholarly discussions debate the extent to which Sunday Schools in this period can be understood as examples of radical education organised by and for the working class; however, all agree as to their prominence in everyday life during the nineteenth century. By the mid-nineteenth century, most people in Britain would have experienced Sunday School at some point in their childhood and they were a 'facilitating response' to the problem of child labour, offering an education that fitted to the working week (Snell 1999: 168). In line with this, Sunday Schools introduced 'a rigid discipline of time and place' that accorded with capitalist regimes, with rulebooks, timetables, expectations of cleanliness, methods of noise and movement control and a commitment to punctuality (Laqueur 1976: 222). E. P. Thompson, in *The Making of the English Working Class*, is famously scathing about Sunday Schools, accusing them of introducing forms of 'workful recreation' that reflected a repressive blend of Methodism and utilitarianism (1968: 412). However, he also draws attention to a *softer* phase of Sunday Schools that corresponds with the period of interest here, as sites that offered fellowship, mutual aid and a range of social activity (ibid.: 416–418), and the shift in Thompson's account draws attention to the possible existence of imaginative social practices inside the most apparently rigid regimes. As Thomas Laqueur notes, Thompson's reading also fails to acknowledge the importance of religion as a source of resilience for working children and adults in the nineteenth century (1976: 160–161; also see 187–189). In this context, the disciplinary contexts of Sunday Schools – like those of rational recreation and the Band of Hope – provided children with a protective environment in an uncertain world, affirming their good and respectable character and ensuring access to a network of social support.

Clover Street Sunday School in Rochdale was part of a Unitarian chapel strongly identified with the Chartist and cooperative movements (Cole 1944: 49). Unitarianism, prominent in the manufacturing districts of nineteenth century Lancashire, privileges a critical interpretation of faith rather than passive following of orthodoxy. Embedded in traditions of rational dissent, Unitarianism is founded on the 'assertion of the simple humanity of Christ as the supreme exemplar' rather than as the son of God, a position which supports the movement's 'fundamental optimism as to human powers of self-improvement' (Ditchfield 2007: 27–28). Unitarian commitment to education led to the development of an impressively broad Sunday School curricula and, interestingly, Sunday School teachers did not experience themselves as disseminators of charity, despite the local Sunday School often being the charity of choice for wealthy locals. Instead, teachers saw themselves as offering 'a kind of unpaid ministry' as part of a 'co-operative institution, by which children of the congregation find a means of kindly intercourse and mental improvement' (Manchester District Sunday School Association 1879). By the mid-1880s, Clover Street had twenty-seven teachers (fourteen men and thirteen women), and 265 children enrolled (Manchester District Sunday School Association 1886) and in line with chapel life in the industrial North at this time, it provided access to a rich social world (Gunn 2000: 125). Alongside religious instruction on Sundays, the school offered a varied evening programme of educational and cultural activity, including a Young Men's Union (with papers, magazines and games provided), a Dickens' Literary Society, a Saturday evening society (offering instruction in needlework, calisthenic exercises and writing classes to young women) and singing classes.

Following the Education Act (1870), which introduced compulsory elementary education, the Manchester Unitarians engaged in a long-term re-evaluation of Sunday Schools, and this included explicit advocacy of cultural activity to enhance the respectable character of working children. Thus Reverend Wright, giving a talk at a meeting in 1891, defends the embrace of recreational amusements in Sunday Schools as a means of developing 'moral character': '[u]se any books, any methods, you find most instrumental; be broad and varied as you please . . . The end – the unique purpose of all – is the shaping of character' (Wright 1891: 9). As with the Band of Hope, the aim was to develop young people as morally upright community leaders, but here the construction of moral character is infused with spiritual as well as theatrical energy. As Laqueur suggests, the methods developed by Sunday Schools provided a 'religious analogue' to Romantic discourses that 'regarded the child as especially capable of receiving god's grace and therefore able to teach and convert adults whose spiritual vision had become clouded' (Laqueur 1976: 10). As such, the performing child in Sunday School amusements may have carried an extraordinary potency, evoking but also reversing the direction of the disciplinary forces described by Varty, cited above. Whilst Varty describes theatrical performance by Victorian children as accruing power from witnessing the child in the process of becoming socialised, in Sunday School performance the child also presences God's grace, a force that overwhelms and regulates worldly authorities. This, again like the Band of Hope performances, promises to open rather than close the social domain to the figure of the child, as well as many other forms of life, as will become clear.

Theatrical activity played an important role in Sunday Schools, with cheap publications of songs, recitations and dialogues for Sunday Schools produced throughout the nineteenth century. Here, however, I explore the disciplinary potency of the performance of hymns, which would have been an important aspect of the Sunday School entertainment in the workhouse. Reverend Millson, presenting at a meeting of the Manchester Unitarians in 1891, and speaking in a register that seems aimed directly at the child, insists on the *social* potency of hymn singing:

> [O]ur favourite hymns will be those which we have liked singing in the great wave of song which every voice helps to swell. That all may join in it, each one singing with and for the others, is what makes hymn-singing so good a part of worship. It makes us feel that we are worshipping together, and that in that worship everyone has a share. Take care to have *your* share. (Millson 1891: 19)

Considering Farrington's 1894 compilation of hymns for children used in Unitarian Sunday Schools during this period is useful here. Reading it as whole, a thematic arc that reflects Millson's commentary is noticeable and the 'emotional drama' this presents is far from the 'religious terrorism' of Sunday Schools noted by E. P. Thompson (1968: 415). It is, instead, remarkably life affirming. There are songs that celebrate the joy of coming together with others to sing, the otherworldliness of nature and the glory of God as a loving and nurturing being; songs in praise of cheerfulness, love, feeling, perseverance, truthfulness, faith, good habits, being kind to

animals, helping others, having courage. The hymn book includes strident
pieces about the positive role that young people can play in making the
world a better place – 'Come friends! The world wants mending! . . .
Though you can do but little, That little's something still.' The words of
hymns repeatedly stress the vital contribution of the small and obscure
things – little children, the poor, a whispered word of kindness, a brief look
of love, the 'lesser children' of God, including 'the helpless worm' and
'wind wafted seed' – to the well-being of the whole. Nothing is too small or
poor to be of value and, as the title of one of the hymns suggests, 'the least
may do something'. The hymns offer a joyful and embodied experience
that shapes the social world in ways that call into being self-belief, self-
respect, openness to others (including non-human life) and a profound
sense of well-being. They can be interpreted as an imposition of discipline
as well as a source of critical resilience, perhaps most evidently in their
illustration of an overarching, omnipotent force that is also a benevolent
and loving locus of order. This omnipotent force is founded on the
repression of certain feelings and experiences, but it also promises that
there is a time and place for all forms of life in an ordered universe,
a promise that can be translated into a disciplinary force to be utilised in
the face of dispossessing forms of authority. A chorus of voices come
together to materialise an affective landscape for an inclusive kind of
becoming, one that is quintessentially social and socially diverse.

Conclusion

In his reading of Plato's *chora*, Derrida shows how the word refers to a time
and place where children are 'sifted' into identity categories that remain
resilient over time (1995: 107). The forms of life that performances in the
workhouse opened up to, at least in part, are those that rest on the edges of
systems of political recognition and intelligibility – the economically
excluded – and this is most evident in the affective realm of each performance. As such, the *choric* nature of the performances resonate with arguments about the critical potency of the affective capacity of applied theatre
practice, arguments that have been articulated most clearly by James
Thompson (2009). Most importantly, the affective realm of each performance generated a radically open quality of reception and engagement –
open in the sense of projecting the possibility of a diversely constituted social
world, populated by multiple forms of life, and appearing as an
orderly mélange of equally valued beings. Each performance was also
embedded in an infrastructure of social support and critical pedagogical

practice that positioned those engaged in the theatrical transaction as knowing and capable world-making agents. It is important to embrace the contradictory nature of the performances and their contexts, as each also materialised a hierarchical and exclusive set of constructions that, at the same time as opening the social domain, made ongoing entry conditional on adherence to ideals of respectability, good character and work. The coexistence of coercive and emancipatory characteristics in each of the performances draws attention to their complex politics of reception. To return to Derrida, the *choric* theatricality of the performances evokes the 'fold of an immense difficulty', that is, the impossibility of fixing the relationship between what is being represented, and how it appears and is received. It is perhaps the undecideability of the relational transaction of theatre – the unfathomability of reception – that offers the most hopeful definition of applied theatre's politics, as it provides practitioners and researchers, and participants of theatre projects, embedded as they are in problematic economies of production and reception, with the possibility of escape into other kinds of relation, including relations figured by an acceptance of otherness.

The examples indicate the potential of further investigation of the hitherto untapped archives of the fledgling social theatres of the nineteenth century and particularly highlight the importance of missionary culture to the histories of applied theatre, in turn inviting attention to the colonial trajectories of these histories. There may also be fruitful connections between these histories and contemporary theatre initiatives taking place in aid, development and welfare contexts, which can be implicitly or explicitly framed by Christian discourses. The interwoven matrix of Protestant, utilitarian and Romantic discourse present in theatre as a practice of public service, ministry and amenity carries echoes across time and place and provides a fresh basis for arguments about social theatre's value, an understanding of value threatened by policies of austerity introduced by governments in response to economic crisis. The fledgling social theatres featuring here, for example, prefigured the later development of public subsidy for civic theatre in Britain, and insights gathered from their ongoing study might usefully map on to contemporary efforts to counter the neoliberalisation of creative social practices across a variety of contexts.

Acknowledgements

Lancashire and Cheshire Band of Hope Union records were accessed via the British Library, and archives relating to the Manchester District

Sunday School Association via the John Rylands University Library (University of Manchester). The research for this chapter was supported by the Arts and Humanities Research Council [Grant Ref: AH/L004054/1].

References

Arnold, M. 1869. *Culture and Anarchy.* Project Gutenberg e-book, available from www.gutenberg.org/ebooks/4212. Last accessed 20 April 2015.

Bailey, P. 1978. *Leisure and Class in Victorian England: Rational Recreation and the Contest for Control, 1830–1885.* London: Routledge & Kegan and Paul.

Barish, J. 1981. *The Antitheatrical Prejudice.* Berkeley, CA: University of California Press.

Barrett, W. 1886. *English Glees and Part-songs: An Inquiry into their Historical Development.* London: Longmans, Green & Co.

Bolton, G. 2007. 'A history of drama education: a search for substance' in Breser, L. (ed.) *International Handbook of Research in Arts Education.* Netherlands: Springer, pp. 45–62.

Butler, J. 1993. *Bodies that Matter: On the Discursive Limits of Sex.* New York & London: Routledge.

Carmen, B. 1904. *The World's Best Poetry Vol IX of Tragedy: Of Humor.* Philadelphia: John D. Morris and Company. Available from www.gutenberg.org/ebooks/43223. Last accessed 20 April 2015.

Cole, G.D.H. 1944. *A Century of Co-operation.* London: George Allen and Unwin.

Cole, J. 1994. *Conflict and Cooperation: Rochdale and the Pioneering Spirit, 1790–1844.* Littleborough: George Kelsall.

Department for Work and Pensions. 2008. 'No-one written off: reforming welfare to reward responsibility'. UK: The Stationery Office.

Derrida, J. 1995. (ed. T. Dutuit and trans. D. Wood) *On the Name.* California: Stanford University Press.

Ditchfield, G.M. 2007. 'English rational dissent and Sunday Schools' in Orchard, S. and Briggs, J.H.Y. (eds.) *The Sunday School Movement.* Milton Keynes, Colorado Springs, Hyderabad: Paternoster, pp. 17–41.

Engels, F. 1993. (ed. D. McLellan) *The Condition of the Working Class in England.* Oxford: Oxford University Press.

Farrington, C. 1894. *Hymns for Children, with Opening and Closing Services, and Songs and Hymns for Bands of Mercy and Hope.* London: Sunday School Association.

Foucault, M. 2008 *The Birth of Biopolitics: Lectures at the Collège de France, 1978–1979.* New York: Palgrave Macmillan.

Gowland, D.A. 1979. *Methodist Secessions: The Origins of Free Methodism in Three Lancashire Towns.* Manchester: Manchester University Press.

Gunn, S. 2000. *The Public Culture of the Victorian Middle Class: Ritual and Authority in the English Industrial City, 1840–1914*. Manchester and New York: Manchester University Press.

Gurney, P. 1996. *Co-operative Culture and the Politics of Consumption in England, 1870–1930*. Manchester: Manchester University Press.

Hallsworth, T.E. (ed.) 1885. *The Onward Reciter, Volume XIV*. London and Manchester: Partridge & Co, Onward & John Heywood. Available from archive.org. Last accessed 20 January 2016.

Harrison, B. 1994. *Drink and the Victorians*, 2nd edn. Keele: Keele University Press.

Holyoake, G.J. 1900. *Self-Help by the People: A History of the Rochdale Pioneers, 1844–1892*, 10th edn. Available from archive.org. Last accessed 20 April 2015.

Hopps, Rev. J. Page. 1885. 'Sermon: What is a Sunday School?' *The Unitarian Herald* 10 April 1885.

Jackson, Anthony. 2007. *Theatre, Education and the Making of Meanings: Art or Instrument?* Manchester: Manchester University Press.

Lancashire and Cheshire Band of Hope Union. 1888. *Twenty-Fifth Annual Report*. Manchester: Mount Street.

Laqueur, T.W. 1976. *Religion and Respectability: Sunday Schools and Working Class Culture, 1780–1850*. New Haven and London: Yale University Press.

Manchester District Sunday School Association. 1886. 'Report of the committee to the 41st Annual meeting'. Manchester: A. Ireland and Co., Pall Mall.

Manchester District Sunday School Association. 1879. 'Report of the committee to the 34th Annual meeting'. Manchester: H. Rawson & Co.

McAllister, Annemarie. 2011. '"The lives and souls of the children": the Band of Hope in the North West'. *Manchester Region Historical Review* 22: 1–18.

Millson, F. 1891. *Talks about the Sunday Services*. London: Sunday School Association.

Nicholson, H. 2010. *Theatre, Education and Performance: The Map and the Story*. Basingstoke: Palgrave Macmillan.

No author. 'Rochdale Board of Guardians' *Rochdale Observer*, 11 January 1888.

No author. 'Opening of Sudden coffee tavern' *Rochdale Observer*, 18 December 1880.

No author. 'Mr Cross's popular concerts' *Manchester Courier and Lancashire General Advertiser*, 12 November 1883.

No author. 'Christmas treat to the workhouse inmates' *Rochdale Observer*, 29 December 1877.

No author. 'A description of the new Dearnley workhouse, with an account of the proceedings at the opening ceremony' *Rochdale Observer*, 22 December 1877.

Olsen, S. 2014. *Juvenile Nation: Youth, Emotions and the Making of the Modern British Citizen, 1880–1914*. London and New York: Bloomsbury.

Plato. 2008. (trans. by B. Jowett) *Timaeus* Project Gutenberg e-book, available from www.gutenberg.org/ebooks/1572 Last accessed 20 April 2015.

Rancière, J. 2011. *Staging the People: The Proletarian and his Double*. London and New York: Verso.

Rancière, J. 2003 [1983]. *The Philosopher and his Poor*. Durham and London: Duke University Press.

Robertson, W. 1875. *Rochdale Past and Present: A History and a Guide*. Rochdale: Schofield and Hoblyn.

Rochdale Board of Guardians, Board of Guardians committee, 5 January 1888. Minute book PUR 1/24 (Rochdale Local Studies Unit).

Rochdale Board of Guardians, Board of Guardians committee, 6 January 1887. Minute book PUR 1/23 (Rochdale Local Studies Unit).

Rumens, C. 'Poem of the week: The Fine Old English Gentleman by Charles Dickens'. *Guardian* 14 May 2012.

Russell, D. 1996 [1986]). *Popular Music in England, 1840–1914: A Social History*, 2nd edn. Manchester: Manchester University Press.

Samuel, R., MacColl, E. and Cosgrove, S. 1985. *Theatres of the Left 1880–1935: Workers' Theatre Movements in Britain and America*. London: Routledge and Kegan and Paul.

Shiman, L. 1973. 'The Band of Hope Movement: Respectable recreation for working-class children'. *Victorian Studies* 17.1: 49–74.

Shiman, L. 1988. *Crusade against Drink in Victorian England*. London: The Macmillan Press.

Smiles, S. 1996 [1859]. *Self-Help*. Great Britain: IEA Health and Welfare Unit.

Snell, K.D.M. 1999. 'The Sunday School movement in England and Wales: Child labour, denominational control and working-class culture'. *Past and Present* 164: 122–168.

Thompson, E. P. 1968. *The Making of the English Working Class*. London: Penguin Books.

Thompson, J. 2009. *Performance Affects: Applied Theatre and the End of Effect*. Basingstoke: Palgrave Macmillan.

Turner, N. 1942. 'The drama in temperance work' in No author. *The Band of Hope Blue Book: A Manual of Instruction and Training*. London: United Kingdom Band of Hope Union.

Tyler, R. 1946. *The Hope of the Race*. United Kingdom Band of Hope Union: Hope Press.

Varty, A. 2008. *Children and Theatre in Victorian Britain*. Basingstoke: Palgrave Macmillan.

Vincent, D. 1976. *The Formation of the British Liberal Party 1857–1868*, 2nd edn. Sussex & New York: Harvester Press.

Weber, M. 2002. (ed. and intro P. Baehr and G.C. Wells) *The Protestant Ethic and the 'Spirit' of Capitalism and Other Writings*. London and New York: Penguin Books.

Wright, Rev. J.J. 1891. *Less Teaching and More Training*. London: Sunday School Association.

CHAPTER 4

Applied theatre and cultural memory in East and Southeast Asia

Wan-Jung Wang

A person standing in the downtown urban streets of Singapore, Hong Kong or Taiwan is surrounded by similar globally branded stores and coffee shops, and distinguishing locations can be difficult. A sense of placelessness overwhelms and bewilders both local inhabitants and travellers. Local inhabitants search for traces of sites that they have lost while growing up in their cities, whereas travellers seek the 'authentic' places of the city. Applied theatre practitioners in East and Southeast Asian global cities have responded sensitively to this sense of placelessness in their communities and have used it as a source when devising performances. They have attempted to rediscover invisible cultural memories by interviewing community elders, socially excluded individuals and marginalised indigenous people, compiling the stories and concerns attached to the places in which they lived into plays. In these performances, applied theatre practitioners have attempted to reconstruct communal memories of places, recovering a sense of connection between the specific sites of the city and those who inhabit them. Performances have questioned who has the right to 'authenticate' places and have sought to locate invisible cultural memories in the cities that people are yearning to grasp and re-experience. As part of these theatre projects, practitioners and communities have begun a journey through what Italo Calvino described poetically in *Invisible Cities* (1972) as cities made of memories, desires and imagination, often unseen and hidden by kaleidoscopic metaphors and the metamorphoses of signs and architecture. In the process of devising plays, applied theatre practitioners raise questions about the ownership of cities as well as of the relationship between cultural memories that are preserved and transmitted in processes of remembering and those that are discarded. They explore the remembering and forgetting mechanisms working in their societies and the power struggles behind those complex mechanisms.

The tremendous social and cultural changes brought about by globalisation in Singapore, Hong Kong and Taiwan since the 1990s, then, have stimulated a process of seeking local cultural and historical identities and reconstructing collective cultural memories. This process has been facilitated by numerous local cultural movements, and applied theatre is one such movement. David Harvey and Sharon Zukin have both demonstrated that global cities in Asia have been threatened by cultural commodification, gentrification, the imitation of supposedly fashionable and progressive Western cultures and erosion of local cultures by the entertainment industry and cultural tourism (see Harvey 2003, 2006; Zukin 2010: 9–15). How city populations can resist this shaping of sociocultural life is unclear. In this chapter, I draw on Foucault's notion of 'heterotopia' to argue that applied theatre's resistant potential might be usefully understood in relation to its practices of memory and space. Foucault describes 'heterotopia' as a kind of space that can be understood both as 'real' and as a mirror that reflects and comments on reality. He draws on the metaphor of the mirror to reveal how spaces contain hidden relationships to other, differently constituted spaces and a multiplicity of meanings, including remembered and historical meanings. As such, spaces, including the spaces of performance, are at one and the same time real and illusory, offering the inhabitant counter-sites from which she or he can reconstitute herself or himself in relation to cultural life (Foucault 1984: 4). This idea of heterotopia chimes with Edward Soja's concept of space as 'third space' – as both real and imagined. 'Third space' is a concept of space as a bringing together of practices of sociality and everyday life, historical experience, representational practice, subjectivity and abstraction, materiality and the imaginary. This concept opens up an understanding of space and spatial practice as a potential means for dwellers to rethink and recreate their lived space (1996: 79–82). Both notions – heterotopia and third space – rework and counterbalance Henri Lefebvre's conceptualisations of perceived and conceived space and present new possibilities for understanding how performance practices interact with lived spaces (1991: 38–44). I argue that the examples of applied theatre examined below work as heterotopia and third space, with representations of memories of places and their dwellers encouraging viewers and participants to reflect on their realities. From this, I argue that applied theatre praxes can facilitate the reconstruction of cultural memories and counter the manipulation of space by the forces of globalisation by establishing various types of heterotopias and third spaces in cities. The theatrical processes and performances that result can be considered a kind of cultural resistance.

This chapter investigates three examples of applied theatre, drawn from Singapore, Hong Kong and Taiwan, and explores how community theatre praxes can renegotiate contested and disappearing cultural memories and retrieve a lost sense of place by engaging diverse communities. I analyse the contents and forms of these examples, examining how they negotiate diverse cultural memories connecting to places by reflecting their contested sociality, historicity and geography, and resisting the orthodox memory practices of their respective contexts. In addition, I explore the distinctive aesthetic strategies that applied theatre companies have employed. This research is based on the analysis of data from interviews, scripts and rehearsal notes, and the approach to data collection here is characterised by an aim to engage with participants as reflective practitioners.

Community theatre praxes represent the invisible roots and routes of cultural memories in Singapore

Since the 1990s, Singapore has become an economically leading country in Asia and is regarded both as a garden city and city-state. Its communities have experienced various global and local conflicts related to issues of ethnicity and the commodification of local cultural identities. Geylang, a multicultural district near Singapore Harbour, can be considered a specific site where these conflicts are played out. Situated east of the Singapore River, Geylang has long been considered a place outside the city proper and is the site of microbusinesses for entrepreneurial immigrants, such as mechanical repair workshops, wood suppliers for boat and furniture manufacturers and iron and plastics merchants supplying the construction industry. The area is known for the preservation of shop buildings used by clan associations and was established as one of the earliest points of contact for newcomers, initiating them into local customs and ways of life. Positioned in the gap between East and West, Geylang features a natural deep harbour and therefore was of strategic convenience for European colonisers and their military personnel. Geylang, similar to other Asian seaports such as Shanghai and Calcutta, has played a role in trafficking women for prostitution for over a century. James Francis Warren has investigated how the red-light district moved eastwards from Chinatown to Beach Road and subsequently crossed the Kallang River to Geylang over the course of Singapore's transition to independence, with colonial and state controls segregating brothels from areas protected for the economic development of Singapore (Warren 2007: 228–229, 256–258). Due to the continuous trend of globalisation and an encouraging immigration policy in the face of demand for labour, immigration into Singapore has increased by almost 600,000 each decade since the 1980s, and Singapore's immigrant population has been estimated as one million and 300,000 people, more than 25% of the total population (Yeoh and Lin 2012). Geylang is now a destination for international working-class labourers seeking exquisite foods, warmth and emotional comfort, whereas 100 years ago, it served Chinese migrant coolies and rickshaw pullers.

Dramabox, a prominent applied theatre company in Singapore, has created three Geylang-related plays since 2007, all for local audiences. Founded in 1990, Dramabox's mission is to tackle current and provocative social issues by applying innovative theatrical forms and interactive strategies. Exploring the hidden histories of Geylang with site-specific performance resonates well with this core mission of Dramabox. The company has explored the invisible routes and roots of cultural memories associated with Geylang over time by interviewing stakeholders and inhabitants of this area and uncovering the everyday lives and problems of sex workers. Although sex workers are legal in Singapore, they do not operate publicly during the daytime because of generally accepted codes of moral behaviour and typically emerge in high numbers at night to conduct their business. Geylang has thus become a secretive tourist spot offering visual and sensual entertainment. Of significance for my argument here is that Foucault explored brothels as 'heterotopias', stating that 'the role that was played by those famous brothels was to create a space of illusion that exposes every real space, all the sites inside of which human life is partitioned, as still more illusory' (Foucault 1984: 8). Here, I argue that Dramabox's performances in Geylang make use of the heterotopic qualities of space to expose the ways in which economic development has created false partitions among the city, its population and its histories, based on exclusions of unwelcome realities. The theatre processes and performance reflected on Geylang as a heterotopia, mirroring but also criticising social realities of Singapore by unravelling alternative cultural memories.

One of the three Geylang community theatre plays, *IgnorLAND of its Desires – Geylang's Gods, Desires, Food, and History* (2009), addressed the origin of all the names of Geylang, described the history of the local 'Happy School' built by Geylang's Dancing Girls and included interviews with Geylang inhabitants regarding their perspectives and memories of living in Geylang. The play demonstrated that the name 'Geylang' sounds similar to 'mute' and 'deaf' in the local Fukien dialect, thus serving as a satirical symbol of the intentional negligence of the Singaporean government in addressing the problem of prostitution in the area since its establishment. Geylang's name can be traced back to Malay, in which it sounds like Kilang, a place in Malaysia where local coconut products were manufactured for British colonisers. In the Fukien dialect, 'Geylang' can also refer to an Indian sarong or the cages used for chickens and ducks. Because international sailors and soldiers sought sex workers near the harbour and the word for chicken in the Fukien vernacular is used to refer to prostitutes, Geylang came to be known as the 'chicken cage', with an obvious derogatory tone. The ironic tone of Geylang's associated names reflects the ambiguous social and political attitudes towards Geylang among Singaporeans. The criticism of the historic naming of Geylang in the play, therefore, can be read as a subversive act that critically engages with the ways in which dominant powers have perceived and manipulated the representation of the area and its populations over time. If Geylang is a heterotopia, marginalised and secluded from the city centre, replete with illusions to fulfil people's desires for food and sex, it also is a site that reflects the reality of the discontent, hypocrisy and ignored suffering of generations of sex workers. Everyone is partitioned in this heterotopia, and everything can be bought and sold as commodities. However, it is unclear who the real winners are. Everyone seems to lose because all are ultimately partitioned and treated as participants in the exchange of commodities. The blunt interviews dramatised by Dramabox featuring Geylang's street stories and histories reveal the invisible and very real origins of Geylang's illusions and their dehumanising effects.

The Happy School was founded on No. 24th Ave. 14th in Geylang in 1946 and was mainly funded by Ms Lina Ho, a well-known dancer working in the area. The show was performed in a derelict house where the school was originally built. The actress playing Lina Ho dressed in a traditional Chinese costume and elegantly presented her wish for the poor to receive free education in the area in front of projections of historical photographs of the school. Ms Ho and her board members were removed from the school board in 1950 because of her illicit profession and the school was converted into a commercial school before it was closed in 1979 due to dwindling student numbers. The story of Happy School was recovered by interviews with local inhabitants who were invited to share their memories. This practice of remembering itself works as a heterotopia and one that acts as a protest against the official demolition and negligence of local histories. The way the performance revealed Ms Ho's establishment of a local school and the scandal of excluding her from the school board because of her profession was an act of resistance against the hypocritical ideology of Singaporean authorities.

Although in the play Geylang's inhabitants complain about the noise and interference that the sex industry has caused, such as that caused by customers drinking and talking loudly late into the night, and the high numbers of immigrant Chinese girls moving into the communities, they also describe the innocence and beauty of these girls. The inhabitants express their inner conflict between whether to stay or move away because they have lived there for generations; many wish that the government would relocate these sex workers instead of having to move away themselves. The play features realistic scenes of Geylang and reveals how sex is traded on the streets and behind closed doors. It features sly pimps, helpless social workers, inexperienced but eager customers, passionate taxi drivers acting as local guides and a gloomy Chinese sex worker looking for her missing sister, as well as the desires and sufferings of these people. The dramatic language is mixed with irony, sympathy, street-smart humour and vitality. This play reflects on and criticises past and present Geylang, shifting between Brechtian alienation in mode of narration and empathy-evoking realism, with bilingual expressions in English and Chinese aiming to reach the broadest audience in Singapore. The production of the play involved engaging Geylang's local inhabitants and numerous stakeholders in the current sex industry through interviews and subsequently renegotiated their ever-evolving identities and their definitions and perspectives of Geylang. Furthermore, through the participation and involvement of locals in creating the play, the question of the direction of Geylang's development emerged. Representing the voice and concerns of Geylang residents in public was a type of local cultural resistance aimed at criticising the global political economy and the dubious governmental manipulation of Geylang's sex industry.

The other two plays created by Dramabox in Geylang are *Flowers* (2011) and *How Much?* (2011). All three plays offer intimate explorations of Geylang's sex industry, based on oral history interviews and fieldwork in the area, and have a bleak and realistic style. All present the social and economic structures that have violated the human rights, work rights and security of migrant sex workers. *IgnorLand* featured a Chinese sex worker accepting a job in order to look for her missing sister in the industry and revealed that both had been cheated, smuggled and subsequently forced into sex work. Because many sex workers are illegal immigrants, they do not receive fair payment and are legally unprotected, resulting in numerous abuses, disappearances and accidental deaths. The candle lit by the sister at the end of the play is symbolic: 'you lighted up the life of our family through your work, but not yourself' (Dramabox 2009: 21). *Flowers* explored the lives of local Singaporean sex workers. Sha Jie, fifty years old, raised her daughter as a sex worker and is despised and excluded from her daughter's family. She buys a cell phone as a gift for her granddaughter's birthday, which her daughter rejects. Sha Jie continues to work on the streets and hopes to reunite with her granddaughter one day. Helen is twenty seven years old and constantly faces the danger of being caught by the police, blackmailed by her pimp and exploited by her customers because of her illegal status. However, her desperate situation requires her to work in this dangerous environment. Jo Jo, a thirty-five year-old transvestite, must confront discrimination and exploitation from her customers on a daily basis. She is tough and tries to protect her female friend from physical abuse on the street. The play is shocking and illuminating and enables the audience to witness the difficulties of street life.

How Much? unravels the conflict between 'normal' family life and prostitution, and takes the form of a forum theatre in which the audience participates in the play through a debate. May is a young woman who once travelled to Geylang to find her father, who was seeing a sex worker; her mother ignores this and tells her to mind her own business. May has nowhere to vent her anger. She later returns to Geylang to photograph sex workers and their customers and expose them on websites. Numerous women join in her endeavour, reducing the number of customers and affecting the livelihood of the sex workers. A forum is conducted after the police arrest of a sex worker because of her exposure through a picture posted on the Internet, and the audience is asked to hold a mock trial and pass its own judgment on the case. This play uncovers previously invisible issues and experiences, relating to the rights of sex workers, customers' moral and family crises, and privacy and voyeurism in a media society. It involves the audience and invites people to offer their judgment, posing difficult social questions for the audience to reflect on and attempt to solve.

The three Dramabox plays represent the invisible cultural memories of Geylang's sex industry and its stakeholders. They expose the lives and problems of sex workers and customers and question the negligence of sex workers' rights to work and personal security. They also subvert the public's silence by revealing Geylang's sex industry, exploring the dilemma of covering and uncovering incidents that might endanger customers' reputations and sex workers' livelihoods. These plays thus create a heterotopia on a heterotopia, which reflects certain hidden aspects of Singapore's social reality. Their revelations transform the performance into a 'third space', drawing on Soja's notions of place and cultural resistance, by representing local histories and ongoing daily struggles for the audience, enabling people in Singapore to re-examine their perceptions of Geylang and its way of life and offering new perspectives on the lived spaces of Geylang. In addition, the plays preserve and communicate cultural memories of Geylang, enabling a large audience to encounter these memories, redefine its relationship with the place and reimagine what it could and should do with the place in the future.

Reminiscence theatre represents the heterotopia of cultural memories to counter forgetfulness in Hong Kong

Hong Kong is one of the most developed global cities in Asia and has undergone substantial political and social transformations since its reintegration with China in 1997. Its urban landscape, redevelopment and daily modes of living provide the intensely contested ground for the playing out of conflicts relating to the influences of the global political economy, the hegemonic nature of Chinese national identity and grassroots cultural and social movements. According to En-Tze Kuo's studies of the East Asian region, the commodification and gentrification of places is evident throughout Hong Kong and threatens the preservation of numerous historical sites, traditional buildings, industries and modes of life (Kuo 2011: 341). These changes are caused by urban rebuilding and have evoked protests from grassroots cultural activists fighting for their right to shape 'authentic' places. Zukin analysed how city cultures, as symbolic economies, are constantly changing and reshaping the urban landscape, and concludes her book, *The Naked City*, by citing Jane Jacobs' insights regarding the complex negotiations required to engage local inhabitants in authenticating places in cities (2010: 246). Zukin's argument about the 'authenticity of places' points to the importance of creating a sense of connection to place by working among diverse populations. She argues that the authenticity of places must be considered from a human perspective and that developing a sense of authenticity must be a bottom-up, democratic social process that engages local inhabitants, labourers and small business owners (2010: 246). All should have the right 'to inhabit a place, not just to consume it as an experience' (2010: 6). She also argues that it is a continuous process of living and working, a gradual build up of everyday experience, rather than patterns of consumption, which might produce a kind of forgetfulness. Applied theatre projects that explore and present local people's memories of daily inhabitation of a place have played a prominent part in Hong Kong's grassroots cultural movement for recovering the oral histories of various areas and reclaiming rights to the city. Here, diverse social groups strongly echo Zukin's resistance to the dominant power structures of estate developers and politicians, as well as their complicity in shaping and reshaping Hong Kong.

The reminiscence theatre, created and produced by the Chung Ying Theatre Group in 2008, is an ongoing project aimed at representing oral histories of older people arriving and settling in Hong Kong, countering the drastic changes and forgetfulness pervasive in Hong Kong's everyday urban culture. *Sustaining the Scent of Sham Shui Po* (2010), initiated and conducted by Jie-Ying Zhang, project manager of the Chung Ying Theatre Group's Outreach Department, was a one-year community theatre project designed to explore and represent the community histories interwoven with the personal and family histories of older local inhabitants living in a public housing estate in Sham Shui Po since the 1950s. Chung Ying Theatre Group was founded in 1979 and its main artistic objective is to create professional theatre performances that reflect both local and international concerns, specifically for Hong Kong audiences. Since the late 1990s, the community and school outreach programme has become a major part of its creative goal to reach local audiences and address their concerns through theatrical performances. The urgency in creating the project discussed here resulted from the plan to dismantle the housing estate as part of Hong Kong's urban regional redevelopment plan. Approximately fifty local elders gathered to train in theatrical expression techniques, sharing their life memories of the Sham Shui Po public housing estate, and approximately twenty of them performed their collaboratively devised play in a refurbished black-box theatre in a local nonfunctioning factory. The black-box theatre was located on the second floor of an industrial building within walking distance of the old area of Sham Shui Po's public housing estates and provided an architectural source of texture and feeling which was very resonant.

French philosopher Maurice Halbwachs argues that memories are collective, evoked by others and connected with people's surroundings and other memories. He further argues that collective memories can be reconstructed and retained through their related structures of meaning and passed down to subsequent generations (1992: 1–33). The performance of these older inhabitants' collective memories constitutes a heterotopia, representing what is absent as well as mirroring reality and at the same time offering a counter-site of memory to resist and criticise Hong Kong's urban development plan. The oral histories of how the elders of Sham Shui Po interacted with each other socially on the housing estate represent collective cultural memories of these people and the place in which they lived, important to the development of community identity. Halbwachs argued that forgetting would occur if structures of meaning dissolve and collective memories lose their connectedness. The representations of social and personal memories reinforce the structures of meaning of this community and strengthen the members' shared historicised identities, thereby helping them to resist the forgetting that is characteristic of Hong Kong's cultural life. Jan Assmann and John Czaplicka elaborated on Halbwachs' concept of collective memories, focusing specifically on how cultural memories are passed down through communicative practices such as signs, social interactions and narratives routinely performed during festivals, celebrations and rituals aimed at ensuring the continuation of shared cultural identities (1995: 125–133). *Sustaining the Scent of Sham Shui Po* retrieved the memories of numerous elders who had been relocated to a newly built public housing estate because of a massive fire in 1953 that destroyed the wooden temporary housing inhabited by the multitude of poor mainland Chinese immigrants fleeing the Chinese Civil War. The fire reportedly left 50,000 refugees homeless. The elders reported on the intimate social bond formed when they were relocated in the public housing estate together in small units, where they shared bathrooms and kitchens as well as limited food and daily goods, without considering that the recipients would return anything that was shared. The performance captured detailed personal histories of the people, including how they cooked, ate and washed clothes together, how children ran around and played, how elders told stories and chatted in the outside courtyard, how the moon festival was celebrated and how they held their candlelight lanterns together: precious memories of daily and yearly rituals practised by the entire community.

The elders also re-enacted their survival of one of the most turbulent riots – the right-wing nationalist Double Ten riot against British colonial rule in Hong Kong in 1956 – with vivid eye-witness accounts of bomb explosions in the streets. These personal memories were woven into and juxtaposed with social and historical events in the play, creating a holistic image of the area throughout the years. The social and family stories of the communities were relived, including the neglected memories of hard work in the textile factories which emerged amid Hong Kong's economic boom in the 1970s. The image of elders standing orderly in uniform, moving mechanically, operating the machines and performing various laborious tasks, provided a stunning evocation of the past in the present. Throughout the play, two men, friends since childhood, recall these memories during a conversation about the benefits and disadvantages of the redevelopment plan of Sham Shui Po, which involved destroying old housing estates and building modern skyscrapers in their place. One of the men runs for the position of a local political representative, and the other struggles to preserve Sham Shui Po's original spirit and history. The end of the play does not provide a conclusion but poses numerous questions to the audience. Arguably, this reminiscence theatre performance in Hong Kong mobilised cultural resistance and combatted the forgetting that is embedded in the redevelopment plans. The project transferred the spatial sites of cultural memories by re-inscribing these onto the bodies of the performers, transferring them in turn in performance to the audiences and enabling people to reconsider their perceptions regarding the shaping and reshaping of spaces in their city.

This argument is underpinned by my reading of Henri Lefebvre's theory of the production of space and Pierre Bourdieu's theory of cultural habitus. Lefebvre argued for the inter-influence of inhabited space and symbolic space, and Bourdieu argued for the possibility of cultural re-inscription to destabilise the fixed cultural habitus (Lefebvre 1991: 38–44; Bourdieu 1977: 116). Thus, the symbolic space of the performance and physical re-inscription of memories from the site of the estate onto the theatre representation can potentially reconstruct the cultural habitus and spatial conception of the elder inhabitants. Here, a reflective and critical performance materialises communal memories of a place. The main aims of the play were to act out the collective memories of Sham Shui Po through the oral accounts of the local elders, to resist forgetting significant personal and social experiences after the dismantlement of the public housing estate and to reassert the people's shared identities. By performing collective memories of a lost social bond in the old neighbourhood, memories of work in factories, as well as confused emotions and attitudes about living in the alien skyscrapers of the future, the performers created a reflective heterotopia of memories about Sham Shui Po's past, to mirror the present and provide a counter-site for audiences to reflect on what is now absent and to ponder on how to reconstitute themselves through shaping their own futures. The selection of specific spatialised cultural memories of Sham Shui Po reflects the elder inhabitants' questions and doubts regarding the redevelopment plans and their fears of forgetting and of the associated loss of shared values attached to their memories. Therefore, the elders' reminiscence theatre represents grassroots social resistance to the gentrification of places in Hong Kong.

The performance also represented a form of cultural resistance to the Chinese recolonisation policy, which connects to a long history of Chinese imposition on Hong Kong. It recovered stories of the development of Hong Kong from the original inhabitants who arrived in Hong Kong from diverse locations worldwide. David Harvey states that constructing a sense of place can be characterised as a movement from remembering to hope, a movement that facilitates a community's journey from past to future by revealing a vision and prospects for the future that arises from and is embedded in neglected or hidden histories. He argues that evoking grassroots traditions and local iconography, therefore, can provide the political base for countering the incessant flow of commodities associated with the monetary system, which overwhelm local practices of memory and place (1996: 306). According to the project manager Jie-Ying Zhang, *Sustaining the Scent of Sham Shui Po* resonated among the local inhabitants of Sham Shui Po and confirmed their shared cultural identity by reconstructing their cultural memories of the place in the creative and performance processes (2011). These complex cultural processes occurred, for example, during heated discussions in the rehearsal and after the performance among participants passionately exchanging their memories and among enthusiastic audience members who used to be neighbours. The continuous dialogue induced by the performance echoes Zukin's insights regarding the importance of engaging local inhabitants in renegotiating the 'authentic soul of a place to reimagine its future' (2010: 28–32). It does so by introducing a human perspective that helps to counter the overwhelming scale of the building plans proposed as part of the redevelopment programme.

Museum theatre creates multiple heterotopia to represent the neglected indigenous cultural memories in Taiwan

Anthony Jackson stated that 'the deployment of museum theatre varies across the world and its practice is almost as diverse as the sites in which it takes place' (2007: 236–237). Between 2008 and 2012, my colleagues and I at the Department of Drama Creation and Application at the National University of Tainan (Taiwan) collaborated with the National Taiwan History Museum to devise and perform four interactive museum theatre programmes to represent, renegotiate and debate Taiwan's contested histories in various historical periods. Here, I investigate how I worked with the museum researcher and indigenous descendants through fieldwork, interviews and meetings, as well as with my university students in rehearsals, to explore the neglected history and cultural memories of the Papora tribe through a play that I wrote and directed in 2012 – *The Legend of King*

Da Du. In addition, I present an analysis of the 'multiple heterotopia' this performance created, as well as the social, cultural and aesthetic meanings it generated.

The Papora tribe was one of the earliest recorded Ping Pu indigenous ethnic groups populating Taichung in Central Taiwan in the seventeenth century. Their history has been neglected in Taiwanese historical accounts and its people and cultures have been primarily acculturated and assimilated into mainstream Han culture in present-day Taiwan. In preparation for devising the performance, I visited the locations where their descendants lived, in Pu Li, a mountainous area in Central Taiwan. My guide was a museum researcher who had spent years researching the relevant historical period and the descendants of this ethnic group. Observing the original territory of the tribe, now featuring the current high-speed railway station in Taichung, I was astonished to discover how vast and rich their ancestral land was. However, there are few traces of the Papora people and culture left in these mountainous areas or in modern metropolitan Taichung. Indeed, before beginning the project I had not heard of the Papora or their legendary hero King Da Du, considered one of the greatest and most powerful leaders of seventeenth-century Taiwan. He was the leader of a tribal union of twenty self-governed villages and bravely resisted Dutch colonial powers in the seventeenth century. In Pu Li, the museum researcher and I interviewed Papora descendants regarding their memories of their tribes and cultures and found that many of them (presently construction workers) had also not heard of King Da Du and could not speak their tribal language. Only the leader of the Ping Pu Society, Ms Li-Pen Zhang, a retired journalist, knew of King Da Du and his stories through her own Papora research. The blank look on the faces of descendants motivated me to recreate the history of King Da Du, as an attempt to restore the tribe's cultural identity and dignity. Here, I sought to rebuild descendants' cultural memories by directly engaging their perspectives and feelings in the creation and performance of the play. Gong-Ming Hsu argued that aboriginal museums tend to exhibit and display aboriginal artefacts, perpetuating the representation of aboriginal cultures as ancient fossils and extracting aboriginal rituals and customs from their cultural and social contexts to present them as exotic exhibitions (2004: 271). The indigenous cultural researcher Sung Shan Wang analysed examples of contemporary Taiwanese aboriginal artwork and argued that a primary concern and feature of this contemporary art is to explore and produce the cultural 'subjectivities' of aboriginal people through artistic means (Wang 2014: 142–144). Wang argues for the importance of representing aboriginal

Figure 4.1. King Da Du asks audience members for advice – should he accept the
Dutch's offer to enter into a business relationship, or declare war?
Photo: Wan-Jung Wang.

cultural subjectivities – he proposes that the cultural identity of aboriginal
people particularly needs to be affirmed by accounts of historical agency,
and therefore explorations of cultural narratives of 'subjectivity' can be
especially important for aboriginal people.

The primary concern in the creation of the play related to the process of
negotiation between the cultural perspectives of the Papora, those of the
museum and my own. Here, it was important to avoid speaking for the
Papora and to respect the indigenous perspective. An interview with local
indigenous cultural and historical researchers, Shi Lang Jian and Shiang
Yang Deng, revealed numerous stories of the Papora and other indigenous
tribal migration histories around Pu Li. Shi Lang Jian sang a Papora ritual
song that he had previously heard, and the recording of his singing became
crucial in re-enacting Papora rituals in the play. The discussion with Ms
Zhang confirmed what the museum researcher and I had discovered in the
research documents regarding the dilemma that King Da Du had faced in
his own lifetime, relating to whether to expose his tribe to the outside
world or close it off and live autonomously. We developed the primary

perspective of the play through a series of discussions with researchers as well as descendants and chose to focus on producing Papora cultural subjectivity by presenting two generations of King Da Du's historical choices. This trans-historical perspective would highlight the struggles of the Papora people to survive through periods of war and peace and to preserve their unique and traditional modes of living and culture, as well as show how their population and culture has been eroded through time by the dominating Han culture.

Reconstructing Papora embodied memories by re-enacting their customs and rituals, such as Chian-Tian (a hand-in-hand ritual dance for worshipping ancestors during harvest) and Zou-Biao (a male field race among tribal teenagers to win favours from the opposite sex), was important. As anthropologist Paul Connerton argues, people remember by performing commemorative ceremonies, customs and rituals as well as sharing memories stored in their bodies in the form of habits, rather than preserved in textual forms of stories. His work demonstrates the crucial role of embodiment in the transmission of cultural memories (1989: 35–57). This is consistent with the argument of Laurajane Smith concerning the value of 'doing heritage' as a cultural process and performing intangible cultural heritage such as dancing, singing and practising other embodied social customs and rituals to both preserve heritage and experience cultures emotionally through performance (2006: 64–65 and 70–71). Therefore, during the rehearsal process, I invited an indigenous dance teacher to introduce the students to a dance developed in response to the rhythm of the recorded song, a process of development that was necessary because there is no living memory of how to perform a Papora ritual dance. Here, we performed a type of 'creative remembrance' to reinvent the Papora ritual dance for worshipping ancestors. This process represented a twist on Nietzsche's belief in the free spirit of the aristocratic intellectual, who engages in 'creative forgetting', an argument that has been critically contested by Andreas Huyssen (2003: 4–5). Huyssen contested Nietzsche's privileging of aristocratic and intellectual people's rights to practise creative forgetting and its concomitant forgetting of unprivileged social groups. Drawing inspiration from Huyssen, I tried to collaborate with the aboriginal dance teacher to re-imagine and recreate the ancient dance steps of Papora to practise 'creative remembering' of indigenous rituals.

Our creative remembering process also involved reimagining the Papora people's way of life by recreating their natural living habitat by building the stage settings in the form of traditional bamboo houses, adding a Ping Pu symbolic tree and reproducing artefacts such as clay urns, jars and wooden

Figure 4.2. King Da Du makes peace with the Dutch after the defeat of the Papora.
Photo: Wan-Jung Wang.

cups from historical accounts and drawings. The costume and makeup
designs originated from numerous historical drawings and were creatively
reinvented. The students recreated the manners, appearances, spirit and
physical demeanour of all characters in the play, including the Dutch and
the Japanese, again drawing on the historical illustrations that we had
gathered. The heterotopia created by this museum theatre performance is
a multiple heterotopia because it was a theatre representation (mirroring
and criticising the Papora people's marginalised political position) of
Papora history (mirroring their past in the present), taking place in
a museum (mirroring and contesting official historical accounts). This
multiple heterotopia reflected the contested identities of Papora people
and uncovered their hidden histories; it employed the aesthetic means of
stage, lighting, costume and makeup designs, as well as the re-enactment of
their dances, customs and rituals to reconstruct cultural memories.
Therefore, it both represented cultural resistance to the orthodox practices
of history as well as orthodox historical accounts of Taiwan, facilitating an
encounter with Papora historical struggles that are intentionally neglected
in contemporary Taiwanese society.

The play provided a political heterotopia to mirror and to reflect the
social reality of the Papora people and their present circumstances, and
therefore had a clear political and ethical impetus that argued that the
Taiwanese government might usefully reconsider its aboriginal policy.

The government has not granted the right to most Ping Pu ethnic groups to recover their tribal names in response to their campaign to reclaim tribal names, beginning in the early 1990s, including the Papora. The current government of Taiwan has proclaimed that multiculturalism plays a crucial role in facilitating social integration and cohesion. In a Taiwanese context, 'multiculturalism' means to respect different ethnic people's cultures and languages and give them equal rights and terms in citizenship. Nevertheless, for any ethnic group that has not been officially recognised, this agenda remains merely a propagandistic slogan. *Seeing Ping Pu* was the largest exhibition to date curated by the Taiwan History Museum. It displayed the historical artefacts and documents of all the Ping Pu ethnic groups in Taiwan in 2013. *The Legend of King Da Du*, the performance accompanying the exhibition, was staged four times during the exhibition period and was dedicated to reconstructing the cultural memories and historicised cultural identities of the Papora people. The main purpose of the exhibition, as a heterotopia, was to question the government policy towards the Ping Pu people and to challenge official historical accounts and perspectives towards them. From this perspective, the exhibition and performance clearly constituted cultural resistance within the official historical system of interpretation against the cultural hegemony of the dominant Han people. By addressing the negligence of various indigenous histories by the Han majority, the performance functioned as a form of public political activism supporting the movement for reclaiming the Ping Pu tribal name. Furthermore, during the performance of *The Legend of King Da Du*, the dramatic representation of the epic Papora story involved the participation of young audience members (primary and secondary school children in various performances), responding to the dilemma of King Da Du to either fight with the outsiders (first the Dutch colonisers, later the Han people) or make a peaceful pact with them during various historical periods. The heterotopic qualities of museum theatre, offering space for the interrogation of historical realities, can be identified in an interactive section that took place between the audience and characters, during which King Da Du approached the young audience members and asked for their advice to help him make a decision. Drama education methods such as 'conscience alley' and 'taking sides' were used to enable children to debate, question and make their own decisions regarding critical historical moments with their own multiple perspectives.

A total of 655 questionnaires were completed by members of an audience of approximately 1,800 people at thirteen public performances (four at the National University of Tainan, five at the Tainan Culture

Centre and four at the Taiwan History Museum). The educational purpose of this type of museum theatre is largely achieved by transmitting historical knowledge, transferring cultural memories of indigenous people, promoting minority cultures, arousing audience interest in exploring Taiwanese history and challenging official and orthodox historical accounts. The analysis of the questionnaire returns supported these claims by showing that more than 90% of the audience members stated that their historical knowledge about the Papora people and culture had improved and 85% expressed their growing awareness of the importance of preserving minority cultures after seeing the performance. Over 77% were interested in viewing additional historical exhibitions and performances about Taiwanese ethnicities and over 80% stated that they enjoyed interactive participation in the performance (Wang 2013: 68–103). The questionnaire returns contained numerous empathetic remarks regarding King Da Du's story and audience members also indicated their willingness to facilitate the preservation of minority cultures in Taiwan. This suggests that the interpretation of history concerns not exclusively the past but also the present and the future, resonating with the perspectives of Owain Jones and Joanne Garde-Hansen, who have pointed out that experiences of identity and place in the remembering process are constantly in flux and in a process of becoming. The remembering process engages empathy towards and reflection on collective memories as an active way of stimulating possible imagination and social action for changing the present and shaping the future (Jones and Garde-Hansen 2012: 1–3).

Conclusion

Cultural memories presented in applied theatre approaches such as community theatre, reminiscence theatre and museum theatre in East and Southeast Asia assume diverse forms and serve different purposes in various contexts. They often engage directly with contested categories of politics, ethics and aesthetics. In this chapter, I have critically analysed and examined three case studies in Singapore, Hong Kong and Taiwan to investigate how applied theatre in East and Southeast Asia has represented cultural memories and generated different kinds of heterotopia as a mirror and counter-site to reflect and criticise various realities. These heterotopias can be understood as examples of active cultural resistance in each specific site. They include hidden cultural memories of marginalised social groups such as sex workers in Geylang Singapore, buried cultural memories of Sham

Shui Po's demolished public housing estates in Hong Kong and neglected cultural memories of seventeenth-century Papora people in Taiwan. These applied theatre projects employed different aesthetic strategies in devising and rehearsing their performances, such as Chung Ying Theatre Group's interviewing and retrieving the inhabitants' oral histories, Dramabox Theatre Company's engaging of site-specific performance and interviews with stakeholders of sex work industry in Geylang, as well as my own employment of creative remembering processes and interactive strategies to engage stakeholders and audiences. These aesthetic strategies offer effective examples for other practitioners to follow and develop in similar projects. They also provide vivid examples of how artists and communities in East Asia and Southeast Asia are striving to recover their disappearing cultural memories through theatre devising and performance processes, countering a sense of placelessness created by the globalisation and commodification of their cultures and places. The heterotopias represented by applied theatre thus offer a means to examine social realities – to combat the inequalities experienced by sex workers, the forgetfulness of urban redevelopment plans and also affirming minority people's histories, helping them to reclaim their agency in the struggles of identity politics. The heterotopias of applied theatre are ongoing battlegrounds of cultural resistance, continuing to induce interrogation and action for change.

References

Assmann, J. and J. Czaplicka. 1995. 'Collective memory and cultural identity'. *Journal of New German Critique-Cultural History/Cultural Studies* 65: 125–133.

Bourdieu, P. 1977. (trans. R. Nice) *Outline of a Theory of Practice*. Cambridge: Cambridge University Press.

Calvino, I. 1972. (trans. W. William) *Invisible Cities*. London and New York: A Harvest Book.

Connerton, P. 1989. *How Society Remembers*. Cambridge: Cambridge University Press.

Chung Ying Theatre Company. 2010. *The Program of Sustaining the Scent of Sham Shui Po*. Hong Kong: Chung Ying Theater Company.

Ding Tsun, J. Z and H. Y. Shi Ze. 2012. (trans. Y.B. Su) *The Sociology of Cities*. Taipei: Chun Shue (In Chinese).

Dramabox Theatre Company. 2010. The Unpublished Script of *Flowers*. Singapore.

Dramabox Theatre Company. 2011. The Unpublished Script of *How Much?* Singapore.

Dramabox Theatre Company. 2009. The Unpublished Script of *IgorLand of Its Desires-Geylang*. Singapore.

Fong, Y.L. 2012. (ed.) *The Reader of Cultural Memories Theories*. Beijing: Beijing University Press (In Chinese).

Foucault, M. 1984. 'Texts/contexts of other spaces'. *Diacritics* 16: 22–37.

Hallbwachs, M. 1992. *On Collective Memories*. Chicago: Chicago University Press.

Harvey, D. 2003. *The New Imperialism*. Oxford: Oxford University Press.

Harvey, D. 2006. *Spaces of Global Capitalism: Towards a Theory of Uneven Geographical Development*. London and New York: Verso.

Hsu, G.M. 2004. *Indigenous Art and Museum Exhibitions*. Taipei: Nang Tian (In Chinese).

Huang, K.H. 2012. The Unpublished Script of *Sustaining the Scent of Sham Shui Po*. Hong Kong (In Chinese).

Huyssen, A. 2003. *Present Pasts: Urban Palimpsests and the Politics of Memory*. California: Stanford University Press.

Jackson, A. 2007. *Theatre, Education and the Making of Meanings*. Manchester: Manchester University Press.

Jacobs, J. 1992. *The Death and Life of Great American Cities*. London: Vintage Books.

Jones, O. and Garde-Hansen, J. (eds.) 2012. *Geography and Memory: Explorations in Identity, Place and Becoming*. New York: Palgrave Macmillan.

Kuo, E.T. 2011. *The Spatial Production in Eastern Asian Cities*. Taipei: Garden City Cultures (In Chinese).

Lefebvre, H. 1991. (trans. D. Nicholson Smith) *The Production of Space*. Oxford: Blackwell.

Lefebvre, H. 1996. (trans. E. Kofman and E. Lebas) *Writings on Cities*. Oxford: Blackwell.

Smith, L. 2006. *Uses of Heritage*. London and New York: Routledge.

Soja, E. 1996. *Thirdspace: Journeys to Los Angeles and Other Real-And-Imagined Places*. Oxford: Blackwell.

Wang, S.S. 2014. *The Original State of Art: Taiwanese Indigenous People's Creative Anthropology*. Taipei: Hiking Cultures (In Chinese).

Wang, W.J. 2013. The Unpublished Report on the Museum Theatre Project from 2012 to 2013. Tainan: Taiwan History Museum (In Chinese).

Wang, W.J. 2009. *The Legend of King Du*. Tainan: Taiwan History Museum (In Chinese).

Warren, J.F. 2007. *Pirates, Prostitutes and Pullers: Exploration in the Ethnohistory and Social History of Southeast Asia*. Crawley: University of Western Australia Press.

Yeoh, B and W. Lin. 2012. Rapid Growth in Singapore's Immigrant Population Brings Policy Challenges. Migration Information Source. Singapore: Migration Policy. Available from www.migrationpolicy.org. Last accessed 3 April 2015.

Zhang, J. Y. 2011. 'On the multiple forms of community drama and theater' in Hong Kong Drama Association (ed.) *Hong Kong Yearly Book of Drama 2011*.

(Hong Kong: International Association of Theatre Critics, pp. 30–38 (In Chinese)).

Zukin, S. 1995. *The Cultures of Cities*. Oxford: Blackwell.

Zukin, S. 1988. *Loft Living: Culture and Capital in Urban Change*. London: Radius.

Zukin, S. 2010. *Naked City: The Death and Life of Authentic Urban Places*. Oxford University Press.

CHAPTER 5

Dear Nise

Method, madness and artistic occupation at a psychiatric hospital in Rio de Janeiro

Paul Heritage and Silvia Ramos

In 1995, the Brazilian psychiatrist Nise da Silveira wrote seven letters to Baruch Spinoza. Already in the ninetieth year of a pioneering life dedicated to psychiatric reform, the heroine of the anti-asylum movement and former colleague of Carl Jung used her correspondence with a seventeenth century Dutch philosopher to reflect on the interconnections between ethical, artistic and scientific questions that had fascinated her since she first graduated in Medicine in the 1920s. There could be no answer to her letters or to the questions that she raised, beyond the need to keep asking them even as she faced the end of her own life.

In 2014, we (Paul Heritage and Silvia Ramos) wrote three unsolicited letters to Nise da Silveira because the questions that she asked with such rigour and passion – and for which in the final years of her life was awarded Brazil's highest cultural and human rights prizes[1] – remain as necessary today as they were for Nise as she sought to breach the divisions between arts, medicine and life. One of us, Silvia Ramos, is a Brazilian sociologist, with a background in public health policy. She has been a government special advisor on issues of security, citizenship and human rights and has developed a series of research projects on young people and violence. The other, Paul Heritage, is a theatre practitioner and academic from London, who has been working between Britain and Brazil for the last twenty-three years.

---

[1] *Nise de Silveira added footnotes to her letters so the authors have adopted the same mode of referencing in their own letter essay here.* She was awarded the Order of Rio Branco in 1987 and the Chico Mendes Medal in 1993.

Paul Heritage

London

25 September 2014

My dear Nise,

   You are unique. Your death in Rio de Janeiro at the age of 94 in the final year of the twentieth century has not diminished the reverberations of your deeply philosophical and unashamedly poetic revolution. A psychiatrist who invited us not to seek to cure ourselves beyond what is necessary, you knew that we all have a little madness within us and would be more boring if completely cured. We continue to need doctors like you, who temper certainty with the artistry of the unknown and unknowable. In your quest for a better understanding of madness and of art you became a correspondent with Carl Jung in the 1940s, exploring with the founder of analytical psychology what you discovered as a medical doctor about the use of the arts as a means of understanding chronic psychosis. But it is the resonance of the questions you raise in your letters written to the seventeenth-century Dutch philosopher Baruch Spinoza in the 1990s that have encouraged Silvia Ramos and me to write to you now fifteen years after your death. We also want to take the opportunity of our letters to introduce you to Dr Vitor Pordeus who now works in the same psychiatric hospital in Rio de Janeiro where you practised. He is an immunologist and an artist who has been utterly infected with the spirit of Nise da Silveira.

   I wonder how you would feel to know that the institution where you worked for almost five decades in Rio's northern suburb of Engenho de Dentro is now called the Municipal Institute Nise da Silveira? When you joined the staff as a psychiatric doctor in 1944 it was home to over 1500 patients and bore the name of Pedro II, the second and last Emperor of Brazil. Now it is named after you – the woman who fought so hard to deconstruct and dismantle all such institutions. I am glad that we can write and tell you that the Museum of Images of the Unconscious that you set up within the hospital complex in 1952 is still open. Works produced by psychiatric patients under your care are still displayed there, paintings and sculptures by Fernando Diniz, Adelina Gomes, Emygdio de Barros and Carlos Pertius. Many of these artists continue to occupy a significant place in the pantheon of Brazilian modernist art, consecrated by their exhibition at the 1st São Paulo Biennale in 1951 and subsequent tours to European art galleries. But we want to tell you about a new generation of artist-activist-healers who are re-thinking the boundaries between medicine and performance alongside your Museum at a site they call the *Hotel and Spa of Madness.*

In 2014, Erika Pontes e Silva is the director of the Municipal Institute Nise da Silveira. Around her office are dark oil paintings of previous directors who have occupied the heavy wooden chair in which she now sits. She described your work to me as a landmark in the history of Brazilian psychiatry:

> When we think about psychiatric reform and how we treat people with mental illness today, it has so much to do with Nise's work. She divides the waters so that we must talk about before and after Nise da Silveira. She was a pioneer. She blazed a trail. None of the medical authorities at the time dared to follow the route she took. She was against traditional psychiatry and had the courage not just to say no, but also to show that there are other ways of treating madness.[2]

Despite all the reforms in psychiatric care and treatment in the second half of the twentieth century, the Institute still has a hospital structure. Erika describes the unresolved conflicts involved in deconstructing a mental health institution whilst at the same time responding to legal and medical regulations. The wards for patients who have been sectioned require a certain number of qualified staff to control medication and determine their release or continued incarceration. In addition to approximately 400 patients who have been sectioned, the hospital has 50 temporary beds for those experiencing short-term crises as well as approximately 200 people who live in different levels of monitored hostels within the hospital complex because there is no alternative accommodation in the community. The challenge for Erika and her team is to try to change this context into a different sort of everyday reality so that patients are not totally overwhelmed by the hospital environment. Over the last three years, the transformation of the hospital environment has meant that immunologist, cultural psychiatrist, medical doctor and theatre-maker Vitor Pordeus has been able to establish the *Hotel and Spa of Madness* in two abandoned wards of a building that still houses patients with chronic psychosis. The *Hotel* is described by Vitor as a centre for culture, health and transcultural psychiatry and hosts a wide range of artistic and cultural activities with the direct participation of acute and chronic psychiatric patients, as well as professional actors, painters, dancers, directors, poets, educators and graffiti artists.

[2] Erika Pontes e Silva – Interview with Paul Heritage, 24 July 2014.

A portrait of you in your nineties, Nise, hangs above the *Hotel* 'reception', frail but luminous alongside Jung, Einstein, Shakespeare, Paulo Freire and Spinoza. A neologism is painted across the wall, encouraging us to find your name in the Greek god Dionysius whose own theatre adorned the hillside of ancient Athens. *Dio-Nise*! Your name is re-conjugated as an imperative verb of command, but is surely best thought of as a performative inspiration to the artists and arts collectives that occupy the 35 beds of the *Hotel and Spa of Madness* on the 4th and 5th floor of the Nise da Silveira Institute, alongside the crisis ward and the ward for the chronically ill. During our visits, Silvia and I experienced the deliberate confusion the *Hotel* seeks to establish in which patient, doctor, nurse and artist become unidentifiable from each other as they combine to participate in the performance rituals. Two young artists residing there during our first visit can better describe for you what they are doing:

> Gabriela: We host an open soiree here every Friday night called *Tropicaos* – tropical chaos.[3] There's an intense exchange between the patients and those that come from outside. Artists and audiences are often afraid initially because the space is so free and uninhibited, but gradually they enter to perform and participate. It's an amazing experience of exchange and freedom. The place offers a unique environment and energy. *Tropicaos* starts in the grounds of the hospital and then moves inside. From about 6pm onwards, the nurses gather the patients, bringing them down from the wards. As they begin to participate it is always powerful. You see 'wellbeing', as people sing, recite, express themselves. Pelezinho, one of the patients, is singing, and you can see what good it does for him. He's a natural artist. To be there amongst those people is a cure for him. And for us.
>
> Carlos: The only commitment that is required for any artist or group who comes to visit the Hotel is to never forget that the moment they enter from outside, they are affected by those who are inside. I am curing them, and they are curing me. We feel in direct contact with the ideas of Nise da Silveira in a site that has been a magnetic pole of creativity in Rio for over 70 years.[4]

I cannot know if you would recognise or accept your legacy in the free creative spirits that paint, dance, sing, perform and process down the

---

[3] The name is borrowed from *Tropicaos*, a book by Brazilian designer Rogério Duarte who collaborated with some of the most important Brazilian musicians of the last sixty years including João Gilberto, Caetano Veloso, Gilberto Gil, Jorge Ben Jor and Gal Gosta. In 1964, he designed what would become an iconic poster for the seminal film of Brazilian New Cinema *Deus e o diabo na terra do sol* (1964), directed by Glauber Rocha.

[4] Interview with Paul Heritage and Silvia Ramos, May 2013.

corridors and wards you once walked. Where you fought to establish Occupational Therapy as a creditable alternative to electroconvulsive and psychopharmaceutical treatments, these young artists have staged an Occupation. You brought the arts to the centre of a mental health institution, establishing workshops that led to the creation of an internationally renowned collection of paintings and sculptures by artists only previously recognised as schizophrenics. They bring the activist irreverence of guerrilla art, the exuberant aesthetic of street theatre and the participatory collective celebrations of Brazilian Popular Culture. Perhaps I might not be so convinced that this seemingly anarchic experiment was attached to the lifeline you threw, were it not for Dr Vitor Pordeus. He is co-actor and co-director both with the artists he has invited from outside and those he has found living and working in the hospital compound. Binding his intellectual training from disparate disciplines into an application of theatre-based methodologies, Vitor has sought to remain true to your principle that research must be rooted in what is around and in ourselves: the imperative to seek knowledge in every being.

In 1665, Spinoza wrote to Henry Oldenburg, attempting to clarify the grounds for his belief that 'each part of nature agrees with its whole, and is associated with the remaining parts'.[5] Spinoza asked his friend's permission to imagine a worm living in the bloodstream and I ask the same permission now as I invite you to reflect on the artists who make theatre at the *Hotel and Spa of Madness* in 2014. These artists are something like that little worm, which Spinoza tells us is able to distinguish the particles of blood and to understand the manner in which 'each particle, on meeting with another particle, is either repulsed, or communicates a portion of its own motion'.[6] The worm can see and consider each particle but not understand the nature of blood in its entirety. Spinoza asks Oldenburg to think about the way we as humans live in the universe as akin to that worm, constantly seeking to attend to and understand the relationship between the part and the whole.

Dr Pordeus has opened a *Hotel* in which patients, family members, health workers, visiting artists and the general public are encouraged to participate in theatrical rituals as a form of research that sets bodies in motion in order to value and reveal the knowledge that is within all of us. In Spinoza's words, 'each body, in so far as it exists as modified in a particular manner, must be considered as a part of the whole universe, as agreeing with the whole, and associated with the remaining parts'.[7] Vitor

---

[5] Spinoza 1883: 291.   [6] Spinoza 1883: 293.   [7] Spinoza 1883: 293.

follows the line that connects you so closely to Spinoza, who you identify as the first person to investigate the nature of the sentiments. Theatre is not introduced at the *Hotel and Spa of Madness* as therapy, entertainment or as a form of cultural or social rights but rather as a means of overcoming a limited understanding of the world – *an antidote to* an approach that considers only some of us as able to contribute to its meaning and value. Spinoza's words become your own and are echoed in what Vitor is proposing, which is to create performance rituals which allow us to identify and study human actions and desires as if they were the lines, planes and bodies of geometry. Understanding the impulsive forces of severe psychosis is necessary to the contemplation of who we are in this world and how we might change or modify what we have learned to be our nature.

You directed us to seek a cure for madness through a greater understanding of what it is that makes us human, which requires the revelation and contemplation of the shapes, forms and sentiments of psychosis. Spinoza's reminder that we are finite within an infinite world and must always recognise the consequent limitations on our understanding meant that you Nise could stand in front of what you did not know – the impenetrable world of psychosis and madness – and create a new itinerary of knowledge that depended on recognising that what we can know is always contingent and dependent on how we connect with and are contaminated by the other.

Obrigado, doutora!
Thank you,
Paul

Silvia Ramos

Rio de Janeiro
2 October 2014

Dear Nise

You cannot imagine the madness that has taken over Engenho de Dentro. Young people have occupied two floors of the old Psychiatric Institute with their theatre groups, graffiti crews, video makers, dance companies, and cultural collectives.

Arts collectives are the most contemporary and surprising way in which young people from Brazilian peripheries have been organising themselves over the last ten years. These multiple and diverse initiatives are a second generation of cultural movements by young people from *favelas* and the impoverished suburban neighbourhoods that have emerged in our cities.

You will remember, Nise, that to be young in our city of Rio de Janeiro in the 1970s was synonymous with being middle class and to be a rebel was synonymous with belonging to the student movement or to the left-wing armed resistance (also middle class). At that time no one talked about young people from the *favelas* or young people from the peripheral suburbs. It was as if they didn't exist. The youth scene in Brazil has changed so much over the past two decades that today when we speak about 'youth questions', we are referring to the problems faced by the young poor people who live in suburban metropolitan areas and the agenda that they are setting for their city and the country.

I remember in 1974, when I attended your famous C.G. Jung Study Group, that the majority of us were students, filling the library of your flat on Rua Marquês de Abrantes in the affluent neighbourhood of Flamengo. Every Wednesday night you opened that house to anyone who wanted to study. The atmosphere was magical and you were a mythical figure. The door was always open. One of your many cats would walk down the long table, lording it over the room and, if they sat on the book that was being read, then the reading had to stop. You had an enigmatic aura, offering a generous welcome with the firm voice, direct eye and unmistakable air of one who seemed to be organising the world. At important moments, you would scratch your head, rub both hands on your mouth and fall silent, just watching us. There were long periods of silence before you spoke. Or didn't speak. Sometimes you just left the room in silence. Few stood up to you.

In the 1970s, the psychology faculties were bursting with middle-class students ready to fight the military dictatorship with their readings of Michel Foucault and eager to empty the asylums, fired up by their readings in anti-psychiatry. We were armed with frenetic readings of your friend Ronald Laing, and also with anything we could get hold of by David Cooper, Franco Basaglia, Félix Guattari, Erving Goffman, Robert Castel, Ivan Illich, then later on by Brazilian authors such as Joel Birman, Jurandir Freire Costa and Roberto Machado. But it was your voice above all that showed us the importance of listening to those that society has forgotten or wants to remove. A major milestone on this journey was the publication of your book *Imagens do Inconsciente* (Images of the Unconscious) in 1981, an astonishing, pitiless slaughter of traditional psychiatry, drawn from four decades of studying artist-patients. This book's excavations of the archaeology of the psyche through the world of images, rituals and mandalas introduced the works that are still on permanent display at the Museum of Images of the Unconscious, and brought your artists to stand alongside the novelists, painters and poets who have taken us into the world of the excluded.

During those encounters in your apartment in the 1970s you insisted that as young students from the rich Southern Zone of Rio de Janeiro, we should cross the city and go to Engenho de Dentro. We were encouraged to travel to the Northern Zone – home to Rio's poorest suburbs – and pay attention to the inmates at the Psychiatric Centre Pedro II. Only many years later would I understand that the youth movements that arose in Brazilian *favelas* in the 1990s, with their demand to be heard and to be seen, echoed what you had asked of us in the 1970s. When I began to visit the *favelas* in the 1990s and spend time with young people engaged in art and culture, the most impor-tant lesson for me as a researcher of urban movements was to realise that groups such as AfroReggae, Cufa, Nós do Morro and others no longer needed 'translators'. Just as you had insisted on recognising the agency of psychiatric patients in their acts of interpreting, communicating, translating their hidden worlds through art, so the *favela*-based arts groups demanded attention when for the first time they spoke in the first person plural as 'we the young people from the *favelas*'. Throughout the 1970s and 80s, 'we' – the researchers and sociologists – had talked about and for 'them'. Young people from *favelas* in the 1990s stepped up to the microphone and announced, 'now we are speaking for ourselves'. For example, Racionais MC, hip hop artists from peripheral communities in São Paulo, sang in *Negro Drama*[8] that they themselves are 'the Black Drama', and that they do not need 'sociolo-gists' to speak for them. In my research I call these emerging artists the 'new mediators'. They were the ones that were translating and creating a bridge between an unknown Brazil – the world of the *favela,* the territory domi-nated by armed drug gangs – and the other side of society: the politicians, media, business and NGOs.

I believe, Nise, that the rise of young groups in the *favelas* became the most important social development of the 1990s. This phenomenon reminds me so much of feminist, black, and gay identity-based movements that characterised the 60s and 70s. Not only have these groups of young people from the *favelas* discovered a new agency through art and culture: they have changed our way of thinking about the identities they reveal and also revelled in a new entrepreneurship that challenges the traditional no-profit constitutions of regular NGOs. They have created hybrid organisa-tions and shown as much creativity and persuasion in their handling of the

---

[8] Composed by Mano Brown and Edi Rock for the album *Nada como um Dia após o Outro Dia* (Cosa Nostra Fonográfica: São Paulo, 2002).

media as they do in their mastery of the rhymes of rap and rhythms of percussion. They have produced a fervent territorial affirmation, valorising their own *favela* (Vigário Geral, Cidade de Deus, Capão Redondo, for example) without becoming provincial, and in consequence insist that they are part of a global dialogue. They have denounced the violence of the hidden lives of the *favelas* in a way that no other sector of the country – especially not the intellectual Left – has ever managed and in so doing have changed the political consciousness so that the problems of young people from the peripheries became the problems of Brazil.

I know that you dedicated your whole life to understanding and working with psychiatric patients, but you were also never indifferent to wider social issues. In 1993, already almost 90 years old, an entire edition of the journal produced by your Jung Study Group was entitled *The Death of the Immortal Child: the Extermination of Street Children.*[9] That was the same year that Rio de Janeiro was traumatised by the murders of eight street children at Candelária and twenty-two residents in the *favela* of Vigário Geral. You couldn't have known it, Nise, but Grupo Cultural AfroReggae was founded in that massacre by the police in Vigário Geral, and young people began to create an art movement that went on to achieve national and international renown over the following two decades.

Just as you always focused on the stories and narratives of people's lives, the cultural activism of the art organisations of the *favelas* makes a radical investment in subjectivity. This is a significant shift from the traditions of previous social movements such as trade unions, political parties and community parties that sought to suppress the first person singular: 'I'. When we fought against the Dictatorship, the action was conjugated in the first person plural: 'we'. The politics was authorised by individual experiences subsumed into and represented by a collective agenda (based on class or other categories of identity). Subjectivity and a personal, individual worldview were seen as the enemies of collective struggle. Recent years have seen the rise of community-based organisations on the periphery of Brazilian cities that are strongly anchored in individual trajectories and life stories, changing everything we know about collective action. These new groups have structured themselves more as arts organisations than as NGOs or other socio-political movements. You too preferred to be part of the world of culture and art instead of that of psychiatry and the politics of mental health. You concentrated on the paintings and works of the artists at Engenho de Dentro and forged links for them with critics, writers, poets, actors and cinema directors.

[9] Walter Melo 2007.

That's why when Nise da Silveira is remembered today it is alongside some of the towering figures of twentieth-century Brazilian art: Manuel Bandeira, Ferreira Gullar, Carlos Drummond de Andrade, Leon Hirchman, Rubens Corrêa, Di Cavalcanti, Mario Pedrosa and Abraham Palatnik.

But there has been another shift in recent years with the emergence of independent and inter-dependent artists from peripheral communities who are no longer rooted within large-scale *favela*-based organisations. These individuals perform in one company, make graffiti in another, write blogs, set up cultural projects that are deliberately transient as well as holding down some sort of employment that pays the bills. They intervene in debates about the politics of culture and associate themselves momentarily with other individuals or groups to make a funding application or undertake specific tasks. Such initiatives, which are often only localised in one or two people, strengthen their impact through participation in networks, promoting a more spontaneous activism that is less dependent on big structures. This is a new generation of young people from the peripheries that is constantly re-inventing their ways of articulating themselves. And to our surprise, it is those young people that have taken up residence in Engenho de Dentro.

I am sure you would see beauty in the chaotic mix of artists who have been invited by Vitor Pordeus to be resident at the *Hotel and Spa of Madness* alongside the psychiatric patients and medical staff. In conversation with Paul Heritage and myself, Vitor drew attention not only to the significance of the age of the artists who have taken up his invitation to be resident at the *Hotel,* but also to their territorial origins:

> The *Hotel and Spa of Madness* is mobilising young people, something that the anti-asylum movements never managed. With these artists we have been able to re-open a ward without public investment and thus intervene in this space through making symbolic modifications .... Just like those young artists, I'm from the northern suburbs of Rio. I only became an artist after I had trained as a doctor, but I can see that I had the same hunger as these young people. And all of us are from the periphery of the city: Tijuca, Maré, Realengo, Camp Grande and Bangu.[10]

Vitor is just as aware of the history and significance of the peripheral suburbs as you were, Nise, when you brought the artists from Engenho de Dentro to prominence. You and Vitor are bound together by the necessity to re-calibrate the value and make audible the voices of a vital force of the city, especially those that have been excluded, unheard and invisible. Vitor

---

[10] Vitor Pordeus – Interview with the authors, September 2014.

understands that young people from the periphery and those that society deems 'mad' have strong points of connection and that's why they must be brought together to care for and heal each other. This can be seen in a report about an extraordinary event that took place in your name at the *Hotel* in September 2014. Over 400 people came together for a week of activities called *Occupy Nise* and a young blogger called Tatit wrote about it with a title that I like to imagine you and Spinoza would have loved, 'Affect yourself, affect your body, because to be human you need the other':

> *Occupy Nise* is an act of courage and faith. More than that. It is a privilege for whoever allows themselves to go to the bottom of the sea of self to reach the other. The other is also us. It is a profound desire to see collective dreams being constructed in the direction of a more loving and less excluding society. I heard someone say one day that health is dialogue and sickness is monologue. Illness is not cured individually; the cure is in the collective. 'To care for someone else is to care for myself' – the words of a song that constantly echoed through the corridors in this week of light and love. *Avante! Occupy Nise!*

Dear friend, while it is inspiring to see the hospital complex in Engenho de Dentro occupied by young people and animated by arts projects, the state of the buildings provokes a deep sensation that everything and everyone has been abandoned. It's shocking to see the precarious conditions in which the remaining patients live. This is the paradox of the fight to close the asylums: as the wards empty, state investment diminishes and leaves just the rubble of the asylum. The ruins of society's own insanity, such institutions are part of the archaeology of a collective failure to imagine a world that safely integrates the full range of how we are human.

I hope that your revolutionary spirit, *Doutura*, inspires the health authorities to revitalise the whole Institute. It deserves to be occupied in ways that acknowledge the unique history of Engenho de Dentro, by doctors that share your courage and artists that continue to be inspired by the extraordinary creativity of the *Hotel and Spa of Madness*.[11]

Yours affectionately,
Silvia Ramos

---

[11] Translated from the Portuguese by Paul Heritage.

Figure 5.1. Senhor Geraldo as Claudius in *Hamlet*. Photo: Ratão Diniz.

Figure 5.2. Grafitti image of Nise da Silveira on the walls of the Hotel and Spa of Madness. Photo: Ratão Diniz.

Figure 5.3. Dr Vitor Pordeus. Photo: Ratão Diniz.

Figure 5.4. Performance in open air arena in the grounds of the hospital. Photo: Ratão Diniz.

Figure 5.5. Processional performance by patients, families, health staff and artists through the grounds of the hospital. Photo: Ratão Diniz.

P.S.

When Vitor heard that we were sending these letters, he asked us to deliver a short note to you from Hamlet, Prince of Denmark:

Dear Nise,

The spirit of madness unites us across the centuries. Our destiny is to unmask the torments that threaten to lead any one of us to unspeakable acts.

I am at your Hospital in Engenho de Dentro, being embodied by those that seek to hold the mirror of theatre up to nature. Just as when your fellow alchemist William Shakespeare invoked me in London, the political, ethical and aesthetic crises in Brazil today are profound. At all such uncertain moments, values unravel, violence takes centre stage and mediocrity takes the place of virtue. Rogues disguise themselves as good men, infecting the real culture of the age with the putrid gangrene of guilt and lies.

Nise! You know better than anyone that the madness of our rulers must be carefully watched, that the fever of those that govern us ripples like a convulsion through the population. Ghosts of vile murderers stir up people today, just as in Elsinore in the thirteenth century, in Shoreditch in London in the seventeenth century and today in Rio de Janeiro in the twenty-first century. We need constantly to return to certain memories and traditions to reveal the addictions and the shadows of our eternal slavery. We are all arrant knaves. If only human beings, forever perplexed by their own stupidity, could listen to the whole truth before new errors lead us to the same misfortune.

You were Hamlet, Nise. You refused to accept the destiny of modern psychiatry. You wouldn't violate the spirit of those who have become beside themselves through the slings and arrows of outrageous fortune. You travelled to the undiscovered country, through the paintings, images and delirium of your patients, imprisoned and tortured unjustly in Elsinore-like dungeons called psychiatric hospitals.

I know that the performance of crime can catch the conscience of the one that committed it, just as you the psychiatrist knew that the performance of disease can bring transformation for those that are diseased. We are needed in this world, because we seek to suit the action to the word, the word to the action. I, Hamlet, place myself beside you, Dr Nise da Silveira, so that once again I can tell the world that madness has a method.

Nise, you achieved equilibrium between reason and passion, revealing injustice, curing the wounds of our human spirit that in dark times explodes into madness. To be or not to be? I will always be Nise.

Adeus

Hamlet[12]

---

[12] Translated from the Portuguese by Paul Heritage.

Paul Heritage

Rio de Janeiro
10 October 2014

My dear Nise,

It intrigues me to know that at the age of 30 you spent eighteen months as a political prisoner in Brazil's oldest prison in the Penitentiary Complex of Frei Caneca. It was the first prison I visited when I arrived in Rio de Janeiro in 1991, and one I got to know well over fifteen years of directing theatre projects in the Brazilian prison system. In 1936 you were taken to the women's prison within Frei Caneca still wearing your doctor's white coat, arrested because a nurse found 'communist books' in your bedroom at the psychiatric hospital where you worked. The last time I visited Frei Caneca, before the Penitentiary Complex was blown up in 2010, I was running workshops with Lois Weaver and Peggy Shaw from the American post-modern performance troupe Split Britches. In that same prison where you were held over sixty years before, Lois and Peggy spent two weeks playing with lesbian, queer, dyke, butch and femme identities with twenty women prisoners. Perhaps we were in Cell N⁰ 4 in which, thin and pale, you waited each day for the hour when they came to remove the women who were to be tortured, some of them into madness. It was from Cell N⁰ 4 that you heard their screams and it was there that you treated the burns on their breasts when they returned. You shared Cell N⁰ 4 with some of the most extraordinary women of your time, including the young militant communist leader Olga Benário Prestes, later to be taken from that same cell to be deported to certain death in Nazi Germany. It is no surprise that when you wrote to Spinoza sixty years later you told him that deep in the eye of some men you have seen the spark of real evil.[13]

You understood the damage done by imprisonment, both to those who are locked up and to those who hold the keys. The psychiatric hospital where you were finally able to resume your work in the 1940s presented the same symptoms, tendencies, impulses and urges as the prison where you had held ten years before. It was a sickness that you spent a lifetime trying to 'cure' in the knowledge that no healing of an individual is possible if the institution is infected by the imperative of incarceration. I wish I could have talked to you as I was beginning my own journey as an artist through the Brazilian prison system twenty years ago. I had to let go of everything I had previously been doing in Britain, where I had created offence-focused drama programmes that placed the responsibility for change on the individual prisoner. It all

---

[13] da Silveira 1995: 74.

seemed irrelevant and inadequate when I arrived in Brazil. I had to learn how to make theatre that focused on effecting change to the institution through building new affective relations between those who work there as guards and those that are held there as prisoners. Madness for you is an imprisonment where the subject is chained to a passion or an idea, an entanglement in space and time where self has become forgotten. Making theatre with guards and prisoners became for me a search to untangle the relationships that produce the real and imagined horrors, to discover the possibility of un-forgetting the self in the creative imperative. I want to ask of you, as you asked of Spinoza, if it is ever possible that the language of the imagination once released can be translated into what you articulated as a rational world or will it always remain heterogeneous to rational discourse? Can art offer a cure for the madness of the prison or the hospital?

At the same time as you were entering your second year in Frei Caneca, a French poet, playwright and philosopher just a few years older than you was being locked up in the psychiatric hospital of Sotteville-lès-Rouen at Le Havre. When France itself became an incarcerated society during the Nazi Occupation, Artaud's friends managed to get him transferred to Rodez to avoid *l'extermination douce* of the 40,000 inmates of psychiatric hospitals who died of starvation in occupied France.[14] When you came across his writings from Rodez in an art bookshop many years later, it is no surprise that an artist who himself had been subject to the extreme barbarities of a psychiatric system spoke to you with such an authoritative voice. Derailed from logical thinking, Artaud was able to express the chaos, conflicts and agonies of psychosis just like your painters and sculptors at the Museum of the Images of the Unconscious. Subjective lives were made visible. But Artaud gave you much more than just an insight into the troubled mind of the psychotic patient. He blew open the doors of theatres, art galleries, opera houses, concert halls and demanded that art cease to be trivial and return to its essential role in our lives. You knew his writings so well that I wonder if you sensed a thrill when you read the artist-patient from Rodez insist on what he called 'applied culture'. He created a terminology for what you were doing: applying arts to new uses while returning culture to its original roots. You shared Artaud's need for art that 'gets to the heart of the matter ... which stops being a pointless game unrelated to events, especially unrelated to what is deep and dramatic in our present-day preoccupations'.[15] Like Artaud, you expected art to offer a means by which we may incorporate chaos into our understanding of life.

[14] Wilson 2009.   [15] Artaud 1970: 4.

While for Artaud the arts were a vital magic, your approach was always rigorously methodological. In the spirit of the advances in psychiatry being pursued in Brazil in the 1940s, you developed a clinical practice in occupational therapy based in artistic practices. Where others turned to electroshocks and lobotomies, you sought out and applied the arts as if they were another technology. You were defiant in your resistance to what was the overwhelming tendency in psychiatric treatment at the time. It was rare enough for a woman to be pursuing the career you took, and more extraordinary still that you refused to participate in what were seen as the modern, forward-thinking practices offered by the latest technological and pharmaceutical interventions. Were you strengthened in your opposition by the hours spent in Cell N° 4 at Frei Caneca Prison, hearing the blooded cries of fellow inmates and watching the tortured, almost life less bodies of Olga, Elisa, Carmen, Maria, Rosa and others being returned to your care? Or was it the memory of Nestor, the prisoner who had served your daily coffee in the Cell and reprimanded you with a steely look when you squashed the ants who escaped from his sugar jar. From the torture of your fellow inmates, from Nestor the thief, from your disgust at the senseless experiments on live animals during your teenage years at medical school, from reading your beloved Spinoza, you gathered a life-long commitment to investigating how physical life should be thought of as a constant process of interaction with the things, animals and people surrounding us as human beings. You wanted to reveal the vision and hear the voice of the schizophrenic, not open up his brain to surgery or submit her body to electric shocks. You established arts practices that would enable an entry into their worlds and a deeper understanding of their pain.

The arts became your research field, as you carefully collected and published the studies of arts and crafts workshops, including bookbinding, cabinet making, dress making, music, dance, theatre and the visual arts. You will be heartened that the creative outcomes of those workshops are still housed at the Museum of Images of the Unconscious, making possible new research that builds on what you observed and published in your lifetime. Opening up the creative and learning capacities of patients deposited in the institution, you sought to prove the efficacy of the arts in comparison with what you understood to be the impact of traditional psychiatric treatments. Each of my visits to the Museum reveals something more about what you created and what you have passed on to us. The depth, complexity, mystery and abundance of the visions of those artists is displayed today in a permanent exhibition taken from the

Museum's collection of over 350,000 works created by the patients at the Institute over the last five decades. Walking through the galleries, the vital and compelling artistry of each canvas and sculpture shows not only the wealth and value of the lives of those who crafted them but also the inadequacies of society's attitudes towards those who are mentally ill. I begin to see how you took that art and those artists into the world beyond doctors and hospitals as part of your own fight to transform psychiatric institutions and treatments. Art was something you discovered to be contagious: a biomedical happening. You observed and documented the affectivity of art for people living unknown states of being outside socially normative parameters of space and time. You showed how the affect of art could penetrate the hermetic world of the schizophrenic, but also that the art works produced by your patients could become antibodies to neutralise the viruses that infect a society characterised by such monstrous institutions. The artists were not just your patients; they joined you as the healer.

Vitor Pordeus has constituted the *Hotel and Spa of Madness* with the same precision that you named the Museum of Images of the Unconscious. A hotel is not the name of a medical institution and a spa does not suggest a secure environment. Hotels and spas are desirable, leisurely and transitory places, evoking unknown memories of luxury cures in beautiful locations across Europe in the nineteenth century. The *Hotel and Spa of Madness* opens itself up to artists to check in for a residency alongside the psychiatric patients and encourages the general public to come for just a few hours to take the artistic cures on offer at the Spa. Following your example, Vitor has ensured that art flows outwards from the psychiatric hospital in Rio de Janeiro's northern suburbs. He regularly leads a troupe of actors from Engenho de Dentro to cross the physical and cultural divides of the city of Rio de Janeiro and perform Shakespeare against the iconic backdrop of Ipanema. Where the beautiful people swing down the beachfront made famous in your time by the Bossa Nova artists, every Wednesday for the last three years a motley troupe has spilled out of municipal mini-buses to perform Act III, Scene 2 of *Hamlet*. As the sunset is applauded from the rocks that curve out at the beginning of Ipanema Beach, the actors come hither from the *Hotel and Spa of Madness* to perform the scene in which Hamlet gives his advice to the players and creates his own act of applied theatre in which he hopes to 'catch the conscience of the King'.

Like the Danish prince, Vitor offers enigmatic evidence that there is method to the madness of his theatre. In a consulting room at the end of a corridor collectively painted in a multicoloured tropical delirium, Vitor explains the ways in which he formulates and aligns his theatre at the *Hotel*. Our conversation is constantly interrupted by the screams of patients: the doctor is ever alert for the sounds of a psychotic attack that might indicate something more urgent than the high-voltage human soundtrack that constantly pervades the whole environment. He insists always on drawing attention to the artistic skills of the patients as actors, to their capacity to give themselves to poetry, music, dance and theatre and their freedom from the need to please an audience. They express and, in doing so, they reveal. Even in the extremely chronic patients with whom Dr Pordeus works, there is something for Vitor the director to channel.

Vitor Pordeus is a biologist who writes research papers on immunology, has qualified as a medical doctor with a specialisation in psychiatry, and trained as an actor in street theatre. In his own words, he medicates symbolically and biologically. He announces himself a doctor-actor whom indigenous tribes would recognise as a *pagé* or shaman. He welcomes descriptions of himself as a healer and invites those around him – doctors, nurses, administrators, cleaners, patients, visiting actors and audience – to assume this function within the *Hotel*. The method he proposes is based on the creation of collective experiences in a public space, of building inter-relationships through the valorisation of each meeting between the artists and their subsequent encounter with an audience. Their theatre is ancestral, drawing on Afro-Brazilian stories, popular cultural *festas*, indigenous chants, and the *repentistas* from the north-east of Brazil who convert the quotidian into rhythm and rhyme. The aesthetic of the *Hotel* is drawn from Iberian religious processions and Latino carnival as well as from Shakespeare, Brecht, Lope de Vega, Molière and all those who made theatre in open spaces as a collective, political act. Pordeus re-imagines theatre as dialogue, and like Augusto Boal he looks to Paulo Freire as the inspiration for an art that must always be incomplete. But it is in you, Nise, that Vitor finds the most consistent affirmation of his method by which patient and non-patient become inter-dependent co-therapists as they join each other in an artistic collaboration. By opening up deserted corridors to radical cultural collectives from across the city of Rio de Janeiro, he has invited young artists to collaborate with him in a process by which expressivity, emotional responses and cultural manifestations are therapeutic keys to improving mental health. The invitation is for them to cure not to compete, to incorporate and create with others in the recognition that as an individual artist none of them is ever complete.

Has the resistance of the institution you knew so well been dispersed, diluted or disappeared entirely? No. It is a miracle that the *Hotel* exists and a credit to the current director and her staff that it thrives within the medical contexts in which it must operate. But for each of the patients who is able to participate, there is another whose doctor or nurse has prevented them from leaving the ward where they have been sectioned and are now becoming resident. Like so many other such institutions around the world, there are rules and regulations more reminiscent of a prison than a healing or curative environment. Outside the *Hotel* the institution still feels like the end of the party, not the beginning. The essential vitality of the *Hotel* dares to suggest that the medicine and theatre that exist beyond its world are moribund, or rather are both part of a unified dead tradition.

Nise, you found beauty in scientific thinking so that clinical observation and documentation remained intrinsic to your methodology. In the partnerships and collaborations you created with artists you always preserved your own distinct position as a psychiatrist. In opening up psychiatric treatment within your institution to become a site of interdisciplinary practices, you recognised that others could reveal through artistic languages what the medical specialist alone would never find. Thus you set the stage for what has been created at the *Hotel and Spa of Madness*. You didn't bring the clinic and the *atelier* together in order that people could be distracted from their illnesses by learning to paint or playing an instrument. You created a 'clinical happening'. In anticipating artists from the Sixties who created signification from playing with the relationships between objects, bodies, spaces and time, your process not only produced art works that went on to be seen in galleries across Europe, it was itself a performance that produced its own meanings: an installation that re-structured realities, a happening that staged a resistance. Your work continues to be a challenge and an invitation to all artists working in fields such as Applied Theatre. How can we reveal the richness and complexity of the lives of people who are degraded by their environment or circumstance or by disease?

Last night I thought about you in silent contemplation of Baruch Spinoza in your library in the apartment above where you lived. You sit peaceful, eyes open but looking beyond written words towards the unknown. Above you there is a straw sieve and two handmade fans hanging over the door to the bedroom that you made into your study. A reminder of your aunt who made the most delicious dessert by sieving oranges seven times while she flicked the fans to keep the fire burning below the pot. Your own research was just as meticulous, crafted by hands as well as by the mind. Vitor Pordeus is still fanning the flames you lit all those years ago. He knows that you have to sieve the same oranges over and over again. Every Wednesday: *Hamlet* Act III, Scene 2. From you he has acquired a methodology that requires him to combine the curiosity of intellectual discovery with the ingrained instinct of the cook and the human heart of the woodcarver.

As I have been writing this letter to you, Vitor has sent me two emails. One contains a scientific article he has just published in the *Journal of Psychology and Psychotherapy Research*.[16] In the other he has sent me a poem that begins:

> *Hamlet is the strong medicine*
> *That we use in cases of serious madness*
> *Where you see the Ghost*
> *And let the Prince of Denmark*
> *Teach you Theatre, Politics, Psychiatry*

Nise, Vitor practises what you taught through his own academic and clinical practice and the liberation that he seeks through art. In his words, I hear the echo of the lines from the Persian poet Kabir that you sent to Spinoza in your final letter to him:

> Seek knowledge and understanding while you live . . .
> If you cannot break out of your prison while you are
>   alive, what is the hope of freedom when you die? . . .
> Dive into the truth[17]

Nise, in your search for truth you broke out of every prison.

Now and always,
Paul

Acknowledgement

Paul Heritage's research for this chapter was made possible by a Major Research Fellowship from the Leverhulme Trust.

References

Artaud, A. 1981 [1970]. (trans. V. Corti) *The Theatre and its Double*. London: Calder and Boyars.

[16] Pordeus 2014.   [17] de Silveira 1995: 108.

Duarte, R. 2003. *Tropicaos*. Rio de Janeiro: Azouge.

Melo, W. 2007. 'Será o Benedito? Livros à espera de improváveis leitores'. *Mnemosine* 3.1: 41–65.

Pordeus, V. 2014. 'Restoring the art of healing: A transcultural psychiatry case report'. *Journal of Psychology and Psychotherapy Research* 1.2: 1–3.

da Silveira, N. 1995. *Cartas a Spinoza*. Livraria Francisco Alves Editora.

Spinoza, B. 1883. (trans. R.H.M. Elwes) *Correspondence*. www.sacred-texts.com/phi/spinoza/corr/corr12.htm. Last accessed 13 October 2014.

Wilson, S. 2009. Artaud, homo sacer. www.courtauld.ac.uk/people/wilson-sarah/ARTAUDtext.pdf. Last accessed 13 October 2014.

PART II

Place, community and environment

CHAPTER 6

Performing location
Place and applied theatre

Sally Mackey

This chapter privileges and holds up for scrutiny the intimate relationship between applied theatre and place. Applied theatre researchers and practitioners engage with people in their contexts and locations, and people's relationship to their *locus* is immanent in our work. Our practices can trouble the meanings of place, destabilising suppositions of locality, dwelling, inhabitation, territory, indigeneity, community, residence, belonging, connection and ownership. Here, I present an argument about how applied work identifies, makes explicit, interrogates and shifts or alters relationships with place. Such practice can manifest itself in many different ways: places from the past, or that have been left behind, can be glimpsed through performance-related projects as part of a palimpsest of personal narrative; quotidian, dull and embedded places might be defamiliarised and re-envisioned; places of fear can be made familiar and more comfortable; performance practices can invoke or construct allegiance to 'special' places, perhaps even replacing long-lived rootedness with attachment to temporary places. These different outcomes from 'performing place' suggest that a simple rendering of place and its inhabitation is not possible. Place can be reconceived conceptually and practically to reference alienation *and* attachment, roots *and* routes, stasis *and* mobility and practices can reveal, expose, heal, enhance and alter people's response to their inhabitation and dwelling.

The relationship between place (and space) and applied theatre has been interpreted simply, perhaps too simply, in applied theatre scholarship. As has been noted, work happens in non-traditional venues, in *places* that are not associated with formal performance (Prentki and Preston 2009: 9). Some applied work might be performed in theatres, of course, and non-theatre sites themselves can be interpreted as performative (Thompson and Schechner 2004: 13), but there is broad agreement that most applied work takes place in community locations, educational settings or alternative sites. It is 'ambulant and peripatetic' as Nicola Shaughnessy suggests (2012: 98), making use of sites and places that are often local for the participants if not for the practitioners. An additional and also reasonably straightforward understanding of the relationship between applied theatre, place and space is the familiar concept of the 'safe space' to work in. Juliana Saxton and Monica Prendergast regard such a space as physically and emotionally safe (2011: 33–34) and Mary Ann Hunter considers space as facilitating risk-taking as well as providing protection (2008: 5). This is a relatively uncontested and embedded mantra of the field. I take these starting points as axiomatic and build an argument from an alternative standpoint that recognises a complexity of place, drawing on cultural theories of space and place, and moving on to present a detailed analysis of a place-focused initiative with a group of migrants, refugees and asylum seekers in Oldham, UK. The initiative with this group exemplified the potential for breaking down familiar binaries in place discourses, such as the binary of fixity and mobility. It also suggested that the value of performance practices with – in this instance – dislocated people, living in places unrelated to their personal history, may reside in the way performance works to 'fill out' or 'thicken' place for such participants.

Place-threads

Challenging the academic largesse awarded to space and time as key tropes for contemporary thought and existence in the last third of the twentieth century, and concomitant neoliberal, capitalist agendas, some scholars regretted what was perceived as a relegation of 'place' in the ways we think about our lives. Phenomenologist philosopher Edward Casey made a rigorous and passionate case for humans to 'get back into place' (1993), and anthropologist Arturo Escobar drew attention to this as part of his sustained critique of 'development' agendas and their impact on the deracination of local economies, suggesting that the 'globalization craze' negated place (2001: 141). Certainly, such relegation is unhelpful for understanding applied theatre's potential relationship with place and I make use of certain place theories below (Casey, Massey, Amin) that help challenge this position. In this opening section, three overlapping conceptual place-threads are explored that are relevant for practice and research in applied theatre: that place is animated space; that place might be temporary but can still be affective; that place *matters*. These three points help refigure the 'practising' of place in applied theatre as a major focus for work with people alienated and disenfranchised from – or even, in contrast, too much inured to – their physical location

First, place is space (or site) animated through operations and actions and made personal. That is to say, place is geographically located, inhabited briefly or over a long period, constructed through a range of operations, actions and behaviours which, in turn, help people develop a personal and subjective relationship with place. This latter may not necessarily be a positive relationship although frequently place *is* associated with 'attachment', as discussed below. Place is animated by the inhabitant. It is this locatedness through animation that has significance for applied theatre when, for example, we work with people to facilitate the location of self in place with more ease, confidence and sense of belonging.

Such an emphasis on place as operations-in-space or on sites, such that the area becomes one of affinity, has its roots in the ideas of Michel de Certeau (1984), Henri Lefebvre (1991 [1974]) and others who were rethinking matters of place and space in the 1960s and 1970s. Lefebvre was seminal in establishing spatial *practices* at the forefront of debates on how space is produced. His implication of space as relational and contingent has had a significant influence on later theories of space and place, even if a distinction between space and place can seem blurred when reading his work now ('place' might well be considered a more nuanced alternative to aspects of Lefebvre's 'space', for example).

To separate place and space is not helpful and an insistence on the blurred boundaries between these two ideas is foundational to my discussion. Space is immanent to place. Place *is* spatial; it cannot exist without dimensions; it is geophysical. Doreen Massey's arguments are interesting here; she does not accept certain distinctions between space and place such as those that align 'place' with localised experience and oppose this with a notion of 'space' as an abstract and globalised mapping of experience (2005: 5). Making the point that 'local/global' and 'place/space' do not map onto 'concrete/abstract', she suggests that 'global' is no less concrete than 'local', for example, and that space is as grounded and lived as place (2005: 185). She argues that the 'local' cannot be simply understood as territorial because where would you draw a line around it? Where would the local end? Massey's conjunction of place with space offers a useful repositioning although she does not attend extensively to the personal and subjective experience of place. When I suggest that theatre animates space into place, crucially I am referring to place as located space (the space of a geophysical site) where a personal affinity or familiarity is perceived and experienced by the inhabitant. This affective identification will be shaped by a broader context, the extensive sum of all our connections so far, as Massey suggests, but it becomes a specific location with its own related practices that embodies, also, a primal sense of place. Place is an aura of a location together with the location itself and one with which a person builds a relationship and interaction, even if not necessarily a positive relationship and even if temporary.

In suggesting the conceit 'animation of space into located place' as particularly useful for applied theatre projects, I anticipate a shift from untenanted or 'indifferent' space that is associated with unfamiliar, new or, indeed, *too* familiar sites through a process of change by performative accretions of behaviours, activities and operations such that space or site becomes newly- or re-interpreted place. 'Places' are locations that are significant, inhabited and meaningful because of these activities. They are indeed spatial: they have dimensions and they embrace Massey's notion of global simultaneous collections of stories-so-far (2005: 130). It is the currency of new practices, however, that can de-historicise place and offer a re-imagined present and future.

Second, animated by theatrical intervention, place provides a way to reconcile perceived tensions between mobility and stasis that feature in examinations of contemporary experience of, for example, globalisation and displacement. Part of my thesis on the critical importance of place within applied theatre work is that *performing* place enhances, effects and provokes a constructive conjunction of pause and movement. Place has often been positioned in contrast to mobility or 'liquidity' (as well as to space and site). I am suggesting that if we rethink place as temporary, then we are able to reconsider mobility and stasis without the implicit binary.

Place has been perceived as static, hermetic and defended, destructive and invoking prejudice. 'Mobility' became an alternative in contemporary thought, a term used to describe the changes in population, fast communications and conceptions of modern life in the new millennium. An outcome of discourses around globalisation, diasporas and postmodernism, 'mobility' became a much-used metaphor, described by Tim Cresswell as 'the ironic foundation for anti-essentialism, antifoundationalism and antirepresentationism' (2006: 46). In such academic discourses, static and sedentary place might indeed appear relegated and, simply, oppositional to a global, fluid and exciting mobility. I have suggested elsewhere that we may usefully reconcile certain aspects of place with mobility rather than maintain the binary, however, by rethinking place as always already 'temporary' (2007). Here, the local is sensitively understood as constituted by *periods* of dwelling. Ash Amin suggests that '[place] is a subtle folding together of the distant and the proximate, the virtual and the material, presence and absence, flow and stasis, into a single ontological plane upon which location – a place on the map – has come to be relationally and topologically defined' (2007: 103). Place may well be located but is also relational in such an interpretation and can be provisional and transitional. It need not be somewhere devoid of feeling, however. That place becomes a pause, part of being 'up, across and along' (Ingold 2006: 21), need not *necessarily* reduce or relinquish feelings of familiarity, an experience of being located, care for the environment or security in actions. We can make places quickly. Temporary locations need not lack attachment. In this iteration, 'place' challenges the well-established binary of rootedness or fluidity. Together with the first place-thread, this theory has implications for practical theatre projects. Attachment to temporary (or recently arrived in) places can be increased or thickened and dull places re-envisioned through performance practices in physical locations. One's affinity to place might be reimagined. The second section of this chapter will offer an example of such activities in a specific context.

The third place thread I want to suggest is implied in the first two: that place matters. Rethinking site or space as place or reconciling mobility and stasis into a place that is not bounded or territorial are invoked here because place matters. Casey's work privileged place above space and time (1993: 11) and positioned place as critically central in understanding our culture and identity. His work is a form of proactive yet philosophical exhortation and perhaps does not have as central an influence on discourses of place today as it might warrant. As geographer Terence Young said, '[g]lobalization's critics, as well as place preservationists ... will discover in Casey a noneconomic justification for their resistance to international capital's feckless treatment of the world as little more than spaces waiting to be filled and unfilled in order to maximize production and consumption' (2001: 682). Casey's work still offers a clear and timely provocation: *heed place more*. It is this that provokes my arguments for applied theatre and place. Casey despairs at the loss of places (1997: 197). In applied theatre, we are often working with people who are disenfranchised from place for multiple reasons. They are not in a position, perhaps, to dwell in the manner that Casey implies. My practice and research reifies much of Casey's extensive philosophical exhortations to engage with place or to heed place and results in a belief that we have the ability to invoke 'placedness' in people through performance practices – even if dwelling is brief.

If not directly in response to theories and philosophy of place, a revival of interest in how places matter has increased. Of particular note in the United Kingdom, attention has been given to lived experiences of place in recent years by social policy research. 'Place attachment' and 'place-making' are phrases that have become popular as incitements to action change in policy reports, for example. Place attachment has been described as 'emotional or affective bonds which an individual feels to an area or place . . . Attachment is generally seen as having positive impacts for both individuals and for neighbourhoods' (Livingston et al. 2011: 1, 5). Echoing the findings of a further commissioned report with low-income neighbourhoods (Batty et al. 2011), Livingstone and colleagues suggest some preference for perceived homogenous communities in facilitating place attachment as well as longevity of place inhabitation. They also suggest that higher affluence and age contributed significantly to place attachment although Batty et al. contradict this: 'neighbourhood mattered most to people where both the economic legacy and future prospects for their community were least favourable' (2011: 4). A high turnover of residents can also decrease people's attachment to place (Livingstone et al. 2011), although there are perceived benefits as community spaces and primary schools can be revitalised through in-migration of cultural groups – however, this does not *always* lead to a sense of shared spaces (Batty et al. 2011). There are two points here that are useful in this consideration of place in applied theatre. First, that perceived mobility decreases attachment to place yet such attachment is deemed as important for people to feel positive about their locality and community. This suggests a role for performance activities that accelerate the attachment to places, such that place matters. Second, place attachment is promoted as an affirmative affective relationship; 'attachment' is assumed as emotionally 'good'. Bounded, hermetic, defended place is also noted as a negative ramification of place attachment, however, suggesting caution in encouraging wholesale place-making or place attachment. Place attachment needs qualifying. Whilst this last is not at the forefront of the project analysed in the second section of this chapter, it is something to generally consider in the practices of applied theatre.

By way of a coda to this first section, then, I offer one example of how we might attend to 'qualifying' place attachment. How might we consider place attachment when it may be undesired and unwished for? When writing of activist and community theatre work in Palestine, Maurya Wickstrom asks for a new performance and a new politics – or what she describes as a 'conceivable rupture' (2012: 14) – in current performance practice built in places of destruction and shattered lives. She argues for performance that returns us to an 'Idea' (*pace* Badiou) growing out of resistant, deracinated spaces (Wickstrom 2012: 188). Wickstrom's attention to deracinated spaces, part of an argument for how theatre practice might challenge neoliberalism, is synchronous with Jenny Hughes' articulation of performance in a time of terror, where she debates the possibilities of performance to 'evoke dreams of habitable environments and affirm life as *possible*' (2011: 197) in a time of uncertainty, crisis, terror and transience – where places have become uninhabitable. Both authors consider 'camps' in their texts as symptomatic of difficult-to-inhabit conflict zones. We might now interpret camps as representing a *particular form of contemporary place*, one that is a distorted mockery of 'traditional' place, a material symbol of not-so-temporary rootedness in the wake of mass deterritorialism. Camps might be iconic of a particular contemporary global politics of place – albeit perhaps a site of resistant and hopeful performance as Wickstrom and Hughes suggest.

My point in this coda is that in considering performance practices of place as an intended positive reconciling of mobility and stasis and arguing that place matters, it is moot to consider loaded assumptions of normative dwelling. Is such place attachment desirable, for example, in such forced loci? Any interpretation of place, place attachment and applied theatre performance practices of place must be contextual. The following section exemplifies work with those who have been displaced in Oldham. Both examples (the camps and the Oldham migrants) concern the deracination of people's relationship to place and some level of transient occupations of space; yet, each situation is very different. We cannot assume a generic approach to enhancing place – and people's attachment to it. Such practice needs to attend to place differently and contextually.

Challenging place in Oldham

My Arts and Humanities Research Council (AHRC) funded research project 'Challenging concepts of "liquid" place through performance practices in community contexts' (2011–2014) (Challenging Place) investigated ways in which specific communities experience and relate to the concept of 'place' using performance practices. I have argued elsewhere that the performance of place is a participant activity with participants as *actants* rather than as recipients of work prepared *for* them (2007). This is an accepted applied theatre model. The participant activity of the research experimented with the ideas expressed so far in this chapter: the animation of place, mobility (and 'liquidity') and that place matters.

Three community groups were invited to take part in Challenging Place, each with different relationships to locality and migration, although sharing an element of social vulnerability. The research asked to what extent contemporary theories of dislocation and transience are evidenced in particular 'real world' contexts, how performance practices can be used to consider relationships to place and whether dislocation – if and where it exists – might be eased through such practices. One clear provocation for this research project was to further scrutinise assumptions about 'traditional' place and 'contemporary' mobility. What was the reality of these claims? How do those who might be perceived as vulnerable or even at risk *actually* perceive their places? If dislocated from place, how was this manifest in their daily lives? What other forms of dislocation might exist? As the project progressed, of course, questions became blurred and muddied as the situated gaze, knowledge and imaginations of people's lives moved us further away from what had appeared clear theoretical arguments in planning the work.[1] In this chapter, I explore one of three projects that took place, this one in Oldham, UK.

The northern town of Oldham (population 103,544 in the 2011 census) is best known for two, not unrelated histories. First, it was once the most 'successful' textile mill town in the United Kingdom with 337 cotton mills at its peak in the early part of the twentieth century (Stacey 2013: 20), after well over 100 years of a developing mill trade. The last mill closed in 1998. This history is still present in the town's architecture although most mills have been pulled down. Its heritage remains a source of pride for many. With the twentieth-century waning of that industry, Oldham became a town of some poverty, its overreliance on the dying cotton trade perceived to be the root of this falling economy. In the 1960s, a number of British Commonwealth migrants settled in Oldham, recruited to take hard-to-fill work places in the town such as night-shift work in the remaining mills and leaving areas of India and Pakistan believing promises of wealth. As Ed Stacey notes, some Asians had been expelled from Uganda in 1972 and had been businessmen there (2013: 122). Tensions grew between white right wing and predominantly second-generation young Asian males in the last years of the twentieth century, however. This erupted into the Oldham 'riots' in 2001, three days of fighting, echoed in nearby towns of Bradford and Burnley, and the second reason for Oldham's fame. The subsequent – and contested – *Oldham Independent Review* ('The Ritchie Report', 2001) cited deep segregation between cultural communities and two-way racism as key factors leading to the riots. It is worth noting that the term 'riot' was perceived by some as a misrepresentation of the events in Oldham.

Stacey notes that the Asian community 'came through [the riots] with enhanced reputations and confidence' (2013: 124) and Oldham Metropolitan Borough Council (MBC) was praised for the significant advances made in community cohesion after the riots. In 2006, Ted Cantle's review team were impressed by the effort, thought and resources invested by Oldham MBC, the Oldham Partnership and other stake-holders, finding that 'few cities, towns or districts in other parts of the country have done as much as Oldham in seeking to build community cohesion' (Cantle 2006: 4). Recommendations from the earlier 2001 Ritchie Report were being enacted such as merging schools to facilitate bringing those from different cultural backgrounds together at a young age. Oasis Academy and Waterhead Academy (both opening in 2010) are each mergers of two schools, one predominantly Asian and one white, for example. Built over a number of years, a new Cultural Quarter opened with a magnificent arts and museum space, Gallery Oldham (2002), and this has been followed by the Oldham Library and Lifelong Learning Centre extension (2006). 'One Oldham' and more recently 'Oldham United' have been terms used as signatures to the ambitions of rallying community cohesion in the town.

Writing from his perspective as a political geographer, Ash Amin offers a different recommendation to the Reports on the 2001 riots in Oldham, Burnley and Bradford:

> The [post-riots] emphasis has come to fall on community cohesions and consensus. The dynamics highlighted in this paper, however, point in a different direction, towards a politics of presence that is capable of supporting plural and conflicting rights claims and that is ready to negotiate diversity through a vigorous but democratic clash among equals. What is at stake is the culture of the public domain – whether it is capable of sustaining plural demands without prejudice, rather than whether difference and disagreement can be sublimated to the imperative of community cohesion. (Amin 2003: 463)

Amin advocates a response that favours equal plurality rather than community consensus. It is not yet clear if that distinction has been realised although it could be argued that this is evidenced in the council's updated Corporate Plan, subtitled 'Delivering a Co-operative Oldham' (2014). Certainly, the different positions of Ritchie/Cantle and Amin prompt considerations for applied theatre with its deep commitment to 'community'. Our work on place in Oldham was not explicitly aimed at the community cohesion urgently stressed in the Ritchie and Cantle Reports of 2001 and 2006, however. 'Community' and 'place' are frequently conjoined, and perhaps too easily. We were more interested in facilitating and interrogating new inhabitants' relationship with place. The town has continued to be a site for settling migrants in some number, whether refugees, asylum seekers or otherwise, and our small-scale practical research project aimed to explore the performance of place with relatively new migrants in an area where ideals of 'place' might be challenging for newcomers. We were to use extended performance practices of place, experimenting with the aim of easing location for these migrants. This is more aligned with Amin's demands for plurality in the public and cultural domain, I suggest, rather than the overused notion of 'community cohesion'.

Oldham's recent history of ethnic tensions was part of the reason for inviting Oldham Theatre Workshop to be in the Challenging Place research project. Oldham Theatre Workshop is a community theatre organisation, part of the local government body, Oldham Council. Predominantly a youth theatre, over 400 young people attend weekly. Situated in a town famous for its migrant populations, Oldham Theatre Workshop was keen to expand its community, participatory work and a project group of 'drop-in' migrant adults was newly established for the research project. Following three preliminary workshops within a council-led English-speaking class, *Place* at Oldham Theatre Workshop comprised eighteen two-hour weekly sessions together with a final four-day summer intensive, 2012/2013. Sometimes twenty, and sometimes two in number, the group was drawn from members of the English class together with 'off the radar' migrants who visited a charitable venue where medical, food and other care was provided on a weekly basis. The group who run this weekly charity event decline publicity and so are not named here. Run by James Atherton, Craig Harris with additional support from older teenage members of Oldham Theatre Workshop and occasional other facilitators, apart from the four-day intensive, sessions were individual and rarely continuous because the group varied most weeks. A wide range of performance-based workshop activities were undertaken that prompted engagement with new and reconsiderations of known places.

Casey described places as 'thick' and 'thin'. Thinned-out places do not '*hold*, lacking the rigor and substance of thickly lived places' (2001: 684). The practical research in Oldham explored how performance practices might accelerate the thickening of thin places, particularly by layering

Figure 6.1. A *Place* workshop, Oldham, 2013. Photo: Dayna Brannick.

alternative and unexpected memories of undertaking practical performance-related activities in sites (e.g. the studio, the park, the indoor
market). There are two particular points I wish to make about this project
that offer something to the theorising of performing place. Each point is
framed by existing research in refugee, asylum seeker and migrant contexts
and, also, builds from a specific example of practice.

Re-experiencing place

As identified in the first section of this chapter, familiar ideas of place
suggest that it is formed through turning the strange into the familiar, the
new into old and the vacant into full. A place is experienced, practised,
'performed', embodied. It is relational; it might reference elsewhere, yet is
physically located. From Edward Relph (1976) onwards, familiarity and
ease have characterised descriptions of 'a sense of place' in the theorisation
of place. Relph used the term 'existential insideness' to describe an

experience of being most at ease through a deep, subconscious familiarity with the environment (1976: 51). The strange is made familiar and the vacant 'lot' is filled with personal history; this was certainly an intention of the Challenging Place project. Less expected in the animation process, and therefore more interesting, was when the phrase became inverted: that is, when the *familiar* was made *strange* – not an unknown conceit in performance history. The theme 're-experiencing place' arises from this. Re-experiencing and subverting place is part of a theory I had developed before in relation to ideas of performing place and was something I wished to 'test' in 'real world' contexts. Two moments from the Oldham Theatre Workshop Place project exemplify this.

In the very first session, the last activity undertaken invited each participant to draw onto small pieces of coloured lighting gel something that represented pleasure (15, that week). Scenes were drawn, a flower and a birthday cake for a child, for example. On the main wall at the front of the Oldham Theatre Workshop building, a transparent, clear pane of glass existed. This window lay on a key thoroughfare for migrant communities leading to the lifelong learning centre and library. Not only are classes held in the library but there was access to computers for communication with home. The 'picture-gels' were taken to the inside of the blank windowpane and formed into a collage, a medley of flowers, seaside, a birthday cake and other pleasurable moments, and the group were gathered outside and shown 'their picture' with the collage clearly visible to passers-by (see endnote). One participant said that he would smile every time he passed it to go to church. In an interview nearly a year later, Sofia talked of this moment with some pleasure, explaining that it had a Chinese picture on it and she liked to think a Chinese person passing by would recognise it. She felt she had become 'part of the culture' because her gel was there and that she and the place 'seems to have melted in together'. At the time of writing, the gels remain in the Oldham Theatre Workshop window.

One of the underpinning ideas of the Place project work was to engage new residents with their environment by subverting and reframing locations of the everyday through performance practices, building a palimpsest of memories that would, in the future, prompt positive, wry and even fond memories of performance-in-sites each time the site was encountered. The performance practice would animate that space (or site) differently. The exercise with the gels both filled a vacant lot – literally – and also added a layer of the unexpected, an unusual memory of that site; it shifted the quotidian. It was no longer simply a thoroughfare to the library; the site was re-experienced or re-encountered because of the arts practice. Another example extends this idea. During the final intensive week of the project, the group visited an everyday place, Oldham Indoor Market. From this, a movement piece was built up using actions or gestures seen in the market (led by co-investigator Margaret Ames) together with a soundscape and rhythm (led by James Atherton). A return visit to the market was undertaken and the piece was 'performed' in an empty shop with a glass frontage in the market place. In addition, each member of the group was given headphones and MP3 players with the downloaded rhythmic soundscape on them. Each 'walked' round the market performing the movement motif. This project was striking for the group, who were not artists or performers. Six months later, in interview, two of the participants described how they now smiled when in the market remembering the time they 'danced' through it. One of the two admitted to still gently and almost imperceptibly doing some of the movements as she walked round, finishing with: 'I feel good, happy because I'm taking part in this project and never forget, forever'. The market had become a personal performance site; a subaltern strategy of localisation (to draw on Escobar 2001) had taken place and an indifferent site transformed into a place of layered memories.

Theorists on place have paid attention to the differences *between* places and how they might materially change. Rose states, for example, what is now axiomatic: '[places] differ from one another in that each is a specific set of interrelationships between environmental, economic, social, political and cultural processes' (1993: 41). Escobar suggests that our sense of place alters as the 'environment' changes. He refers to the deterioration of landscapes through activities such as mining and the negative impact this has upon the inhabitants (2001: 149). In *performing* place by, for example, setting lighting gels into a blank window or dancing in a market, I suggest that what takes place is an additional layer of unexpected experience in the *same* environment. The environment itself barely changes but our perception of it does because of the less-than-usual activities enacted there. Place is re-experienced for the participants through performing it pleasurably, enhancing and shifting its quotidian properties into a place that is heightened, beyond the ordinary, augmented and differently embodied. Such re-experiencing can be infinite and, indeed, some of the sites in and around the building of Oldham Theatre Workshop were performed several times during the course of the project. A collected group of memories formed, changing the understanding of that site for those relatively new to the town. The already familiar – if not cared for – sites (the walk to the library, the indoor market, Oldham's Alexandra Park) were made just slightly strange and, in the process, endeared themselves to the participants. Location was thickened, I suggest. In addition, these places in the public domain seemed capable of sustaining Amin's suggested plural demands, as a result of representatives of different cultures emplacing parts of themselves within sites and reinterpreting others through their own practices.

Dwelling in the present

The *Place* project at Oldham Theatre Workshop was *not* many things. It was not a project to specifically address community cohesion, perhaps irreverently in the town of Ritchie and Cantle Reports. It was not a cultural performance at a refugee arts festival, which would typically involve 'groups of performers from countries that are represented by refugees in the host community performing mostly music and dance that is "traditional" to their home location' (Jeffers 2012: 113–114). Neither was it refugee participatory theatre where projects might involve 'a group of refugees, often with little or no experience of theatre or performing arts in general, working with artists to create and perform a piece based on their own stories and experiences' (2012: 137). It was absolutely not performance that set out to specifically engage with, for example, Loomba's postcolonial hybridities as Adam Perry aspired to in his Boalian theatre of the oppressed work with migrant workers in Canada (2012, citing Loomba 2005). In fact, we were never entirely sure who was an asylum seeker, who had refugee status and who was a European migrant. We did not seek specific identity information from the group. This was a drop-in, mainly adult, group, with participants encouraged to attend from other venues (an English class at the local library; a charity support group) or who attended having heard of it by word of mouth. All in the group were within a year or so of being new to the United Kingdom and the group probably included at least one refugee, asylum seeker and European migrant, as became clear from casual conversations. They were a group of people that most closely resembled Appadurai's *ethnoscape*, perhaps, a 'landscape of persons who constitute the shifting world in which we live [including] ... immigrants, refugees, exiles, guest workers, and other moving groups and individuals' (2006 [1990]: 589).

For much of the project, this was a concern to me. As a researcher armed with carefully planned 'permissions forms', and intent on publishing outcomes, I felt I needed to know the specifics of the status of the participants. But the project – in engaging migrants with new places – had deliberately not set out to address the past by acting as, for example, a post-conflict therapeutic encounter. It was surprising how sustained this focus on the present became, in fact, and intriguing enough to consider in theorising the performance of place. Very occasionally someone would offer a moment of memory but this was rare. It transpired that Oldham Theatre Workshop staff (including myself as researcher) felt awkward and ill-equipped to ask the drop-in participants about their pasts. Rather than this being a problem, however, a part-time facilitator, himself a Rwandan refugee, told me that in his view a significant and highly successful factor of the project was that it did *not* dwell on the past or seek to address memories of previous lives. This was a project for the present. In an interview after the project, Stella Barnes, perhaps London's most well-known and experienced facilitator of drama with refugee youth, supported this 'presencing', saying of her own work at Oval House: 'they don't carry a label here … we don't say: you're a refugee, you're an asylum seeker or you're a migrant. So they don't have to wear that label' (2014). She feels strongly that this is important in the work they produce with young people and understood why such a strategy – however unplanned – had been effective for the Oldham Theatre Workshop project.

It might be assumed that the performance of place with migrants is implicitly concerned with past histories, a deliberate and constructed meshing of places for hybrid peoples. What emerged from the Oldham workshops is that one iteration of a performance of place, and particularly relevant for recent migrants, may usefully focus on a performance of the immediate, the 'now', a de-historicisation. This practical research, it transpired, was not so much about alleviating dis-ease by reconciling old and new but about offering new ways of considering, and dwelling in, the present. One of our interviewees described new dwelling and ownership of places, talking of a path by a reservoir, the site of some performance work, saying 'you might as well call it Yolinda's path now'. A participant, Yolinda, had created a story in that site, about a clay figure she had placed there. Sofia's pleasure at her part in the gel collage was about feeling culturally emplaced. Both examples suggest *new* stories of place and illustrate the excitement of the participants arising from this.

As part of her detailed and lengthy engagement with place and space, Massey suggests: '[i]f space is rather a simultaneity of stories-so-far, then places are collections of those stories, articulations within the wider power-geometries of space' (2005: 130). What intrigued me about the work with Oldham Theatre Workshop's *Place* group was the clear indication that the *writing of the new* was important, not the articulation of stories-so-far. In that it is impossible to part anyone from their 'stories', their historical narrative, then of course those histories are embodied; this is not about suggesting *tabula rasa* people. This project suggested a different nuance, however: the importance of de-historicising for our participants and building new narratives of place through performing multiple presents.

End and on

As exemplified through the place-focused research project with Oldham migrants, the specifics of animating space into place and reconciling mobility with temporarily locating through performance practices suggests a particular use of performing place. The enquiry presented in this chapter was characterised by the subversion of everyday lived environments and the re-experiencing of places (sometimes many times) through such subversions, alongside a particular focus on the present. Such 'findings' help develop a participatory, grounded, performance-based approach to encountering, re-viewing and easing our relationship with place. This is one manifestation of place performance as applied theatre activity, where place and location is foregrounded and *the* focus for participatory, socially engaged practices. We worked towards animating spaces into place, reconciling mobility and stasis and encouraging place attachment such that these locations in Oldham *mattered*. Whilst not guiding the research, in retrospect it is tempting to suggest that such practices have relevance for Amin's 'politics of presence' and the plural demands of the 'public domain' (2003: 463). Perhaps the thickening of place for individuals also undercuts an overwrought and flat emphasis on community cohesion.

Whilst researching this chapter, I considered developments that might extend discourses and practices of performing place in applied theatre in the future. This final section is not so much about an ending, therefore. Two emerging fields interest me. First is 'virtual place'. Matters of place, their representation and inhabitation utilising digital technology is not new, of course, although 'place' conjoined with 'the digital' is yet to be considered in any detail in applied theatre research. Digital technology plays a part in many applied theatre projects, but its connection with place-making is as yet under-explored. Whilst there is increasing broad-based interest in the relationship between digital technologies and place (Wilken and Goggin 2012), and there are examples of the use of GPS mapping technologies as part of innovative performance practices (in the work of Blast Theory for example), it will be interesting to see how the relationship between *applied* theatre, the digital and place (or virtual places) interweave in the future. In some ways, there is little to contest about the advantages of digital technology used creatively as part of arts projects as a means to enhance places and their import. Indeed, during one session in Oldham, participants were invited to use ipads to take photographs of small details of local places (e.g. the edge of a desk in the nearby library), and these photographs were then displayed by the participants back in the studio. The close encounters with the quotidian that this exercise generated was an important part of enhancing a sense of connection to place. A larger-scale example of experiment with digital technology and place-making comes from James Thompson and colleagues, who have created an online 'global place' for performances and art made by artists in sites of conflict. Since its launch, the *In Place of War* site has become an inclusive testament and supportive location for hundreds of artists and organisations – 'an online meeting place for artists to share their response to war', allowing artists to 'connect with others across the world'.[2] It acts as an instantly accessible digital dropbox for arts that might not survive tempestuous and fragile warzones. Such examples raise the question – can *virtual* places assume the mantle of *inhabited* place, for example? Making reference to the lived experience of community that is in danger because of increasing use of the digital, Sherry Turkle presents a counterargument in a way that has immediate resonance with the shibboleths of applied theatre, with its privileging of live community-based practice. She pays particular attention to the impact of the digital on young people, urging care and caution as communities become increasingly alone together: '[w]e have invented inspiring and enhancing technologies, and yet we have allowed them to diminish us' (2011: 295).

Second, it is clear that the important issues of climate change and environmental concerns have become part of the consideration of place within our field. Conjunctions of applied theatre and environmentalism are generating new conditions for practice, as Deirdre Heddon and I discovered when editing an edition on environmentalism for *RiDE: The Journal of Applied Theatre and Performance* (2012). Theatre in education and participatory programmes addressing climate change have been limited in the United Kingdom, however, although this is changing elsewhere. Recent shifts in Australian school curricula point to a greater awareness of environmental concerns, for example. One of the most successful UK pieces I have seen, Theatre Venture's *The Carbon Footprint Detective Agency*, toured to London primary schools (ages 5–11) from 2008 to 2010. It invited youngsters to participate in decisions to save energy in their own school and home places. Each school nominated its own carbon footprint detectives to monitor and advocate energy savings. The intention was that this would be replicated at home, although director and performer Ray Downing suggested this was, of course, difficult to track (Downing 2010). Return visits to the schools with 'assemblies' about the results of energy savings were offered as part of this tour. This was Theatre in Education as light eco-activism and was straightforward in its agenda. Because of funding cuts, and after a thirty-year history, Theatre Venture closed down in 2011. Even this rare UK example of environmental theatre for young people was lost, therefore.

Issues of climate change will become increasingly relevant and complicated as we move from climate change mitigation towards adaptation strategies. It is noticeable that the Intergovernmental Panel on Climate Change (IPCC) report of 2007 references adaptation *and* mitigation, yet the 2014 report focuses on impacts, adaptation and vulnerability[3] suggesting it is too late for mitigation activities – too late to prevent climate change – and there is instead a need to focus on *adapting* to the consequences of climate change. This is likely to be reflected in profound changes in the environment which will in turn shift how artists and communities approach and explore 'place'. The fragility and mutability of place has become an increasingly global issue, arising from climate change rather than (or as well as) warzones or related forms of human-directed deterritorialisation. There will surely be an increasingly important role for participatory, applied performances of place, responding to, initiating or critiquing environmental change and its impact on our understandings and animations of place.

References

Amin, A. 2003. 'Unruly strangers? The 2001 urban riots in Britain'. *International Journal of Urban and Regional Research* 27.2: 460–463.

Amin, A. 2007. 'Re-thinking the urban social'. *City* 11.1: 100–114.

Appadurai, A. 2006 [1990]. 'Disjuncture and difference in the global cultural economy' in Meenakshi G.D. and Kellner, D.M. (eds.) *Media and Cultural Studies Keyworks*, Rev edn. Malden, MA and Oxford: Routledge, pp. 584–603.

Barnes, S. 2014. Interview with the author.

Batty, E., Cole, I. and Green, S. 2011. *Low-income neighbourhoods in Britain: The gap between policy ideas and residents' realities* www.jrf.org.uk/sites/files/jrf/poverty-neighbourhood-resident-experience-full.pdf. Last accessed 4 July 2011.

Cantle, T. and the Institute of Community Cohesion, 2006. *Review of Community Cohesion in Oldham: Challenging local communities to change Oldham*, http://news.bbc.co.uk/1/shared/bsp/hi/pdfs/25_05_06_oldham_re port.pdf. Last accessed 2 June 2012.

Casey, E. 1993. *Getting Back into Place: Toward a Renewed Understanding of the Place-World*. Bloomington: Indiana University Press.

Casey, E. 1997. *The Fate of Place: A Philosophical History*. London: University of California Press.

Casey, E. 2001. 'Between geography and philosophy: What does it mean to be in the place-world?' *Annals of the Association of American Geographers* 91.4: 683–693.

Cresswell, T. 2006. *On the Move: Mobility in the Modern Western World*. New York and London: Routledge.

De Certeau, M. 1984. (trans. S. Rendall) *The Practice of Everyday Life*. London: University of California Press.

Downing, R. 2010. Interview with the author.

Escobar, A. 2001. 'Culture sits in places: Reflections on globalism and subaltern strategies of localization'. *Political Geography* 20: 139–174.

Heddon, D. and Mackey, S. 2012. 'Environmentalism, performance and applications: uncertainties and emancipations'. *RiDE: The Journal of Applied Theatre and Performance: Environmentalism* 17.2: 163–192.

Hughes, J. 2011. *Performance in a Time of Terror: Critical Mimesis and the Age of Uncertainty*. Manchester: Manchester University Press.

Hunter, M.A. 2008. 'Cultivating the art of safe space'. *RiDE: The Journal of Applied Theatre and Performance* 13.1: 5–21.

Ingold, T. 2006. 'Up, across and along'. *Place and Location: Studies in Environmental Aesthetics and Semiotics* 5: 21–36.

Jeffers, A. 2012. *Refugees, Theatre and Crisis: Performing Global Identities*. Basingstoke: Palgrave Macmillan.

Lefebvre, H. 1991 [1974]. (trans. D. Nicholson-Smith) *The Production of Space*. Oxford: Blackwell.

Livingston, M., Bailey, N. and Kearns, A. 2011. *People's Attachment to Place: The Influence of Neighbourhood Deprivation*. York: Joseph Rowntree Foundation.

Loomba, A. 2005. *Colonialism/Postcolonialism*. London: Routledge.

Mackey, S. 2007. 'Transient Roots: Performance, place and exterritorials'. *Performance Research: On the Road* 12.2: 75–78.

Massey, D. 2005. *For Space*. London: Sage.

Perry, J.A., 2012. 'A silent revolution: "Image Theatre" as a system of decolonisation'. *Research in Drama Education: The Journal of Applied Theatre and Performance* 17.1: 103–119.

Prentki, T. and Preston, S. (eds.) 2009. *The Applied Theatre Reader*. Abingdon: Routledge.

Relph, E. 1976. *Place and Placelessness*. London: Pion.

Ritchie, D. 2001. *Oldham Independent Review: One Oldham, One Future.* www.te dcantle.co.uk/publications/002%20One%20Oldham,%20One%20Future%20Ritchie%202001.pdf. Last accessed 3 August 2003.

Rose, G. 1993. *Feminism and Geography: The Limits of Geographical Knowledge.* Cambridge: Polity Press.

Saxton, J. and Prendergast, M. (eds.) 2013. *Applied Drama: A Facilitator's Handbook for Working in Community.* Bristol: Intellect.

Shaughnessy, N. 2012. *Applying Performance: Live Art, Socially Engaged Theatre and Affective Practice.* Basingstoke: Palgrave Macmillan.

Stacey, E. 2013. *Cotton, Curry and Commerce: The history of Asian businesses in Oldham.* Oldham Council.

Thompson, J. and Schechner, R. 2004. 'Why social theatre?' *TDR: The Journal of Performance Studies* 48.3: 11–16.

Turkle, S. 2011. *Alone Together: Why We Expect More from Technology and Less from Each Other.* New York: Basic Books.

Wickstrom, M. 2012. *Performance in the Blockades of Neoliberalism: Thinking the Political Anew.* Basingstoke and New York: Palgrave Macmillan.

Wilken, R. and Goggin, G. (eds.) 2012. *Mobile Technology and Place.* New York and Abingdon: Routledge.

Young, T. 2001. 'Place matters'. *Annals of the Association of American Geographers* 91.4: 681–682.

CHAPTER 7

Peacebuilding performances in the aftermath of war
Lessons from Bougainville

Paul Dwyer

London, 2006. I'm part of a 'community performance' working group, meeting at the Performance Studies international conference (PSi #12) on the theme of 'Performing Rights'. An opportune moment to reflect on the challenges and potential benefits of applied theatre interventions in places marked by violent conflict. By this time, I had completed some preliminary fieldwork in the Autonomous Region of Bougainville in Papua New Guinea (PNG), the first steps in an ongoing inquiry into how ceremonies of ritual reconciliation are being used to progress the peace process there in the wake of a decade-long civil war. I had received kind support from local non-government organisations (NGOs) and invitations to observe the practice of village-based mediators.[1] The question I wanted to discuss with fellow conference delegates was what, if anything, I might be able to offer by way of cultural exchange with my Bougainvillean contacts. One possibility, for which my training and the bulk of my professional experience in applied theatre was particularly relevant, would have been to run workshops on the methods of Augusto Boal's 'Theatre of the Oppressed'. Indeed, one of the NGOs with which I had consulted was already using educational materials – in their campaigns to promote literacy, health, environmental awareness, good governance and respect for human rights – that were clearly inspired, as Boal had been, by the strategies of Paulo Freire's 'Pedagogy of the Oppressed'. Apart from the inevitable logistical difficulties and funding issues, why was I hesitating? 'Why', as one conference delegate bluntly put it, 'would you want to withhold these empowering tools from the people who need them?'

History provides part of the answer. Flashback to Bougainville, 1988–1997. When, as an Australian theatre practitioner and researcher, you know that the war started as an attempt by Bougainvilleans to secede from PNG, when you know that one of the triggers for this unrest was to do with grievances over the environmental damage from a giant copper mine imposed on Bougainville by Australia in the run up to PNG's independence, when you know that Australia committed to supporting the commercial interests of the PNG national government, as well as Australian companies and foreign shareholders, by supplying the PNG Defence Force with patrol boats, mortars and high-powered automatic rifles, when you know that Australian military advisors later recommended the strategic withdrawal of PNG troops and the imposition of a blockade, cutting Bougainville off from the rest of the world, cutting off all access to government services, medical supplies, trade and the scrutiny of media and human rights observers, when you know that the consequent breakdown of civil society in Bougainville – the lawlessness and insecurity it generated – became the pretext for the PNG Defence Force to return, to start corralling people into 'care centres', to start arming local home guards and using them as frontline troops in what was now a dirty civil war between the Bougainville 'Resistance' and loyalists of the Bougainville Revolutionary Army (BRA), when you know that Bougainvilleans have seen the PNG Defence Force using Australian helicopters, flown by Australian mercenaries, to strafe villages and dump the bodies of victims at sea, then it is probably not a bad thing to pause before offering to jump in and lead a peacebuilding arts project.[2] History, however, does not explain all of my reticence, nor was my Australian citizenship necessarily an impediment for my gracious Bougainvillean hosts (as one of them put it: 'Don't worry, Paul – we'll let you know if you're being too colonial!').

By now, there is a substantial body of scholarship on applied theatre and other forms of aesthetic, cultural or social performance, together with extensive documentation of practice, that considers the ways in which performance functions in place(s) of war, potentially legitimating a war culture but also potentially interrogating it and promoting peace in the aftermath of conflict (see, most notably, Cohen et al. 2011; Thompson et al. 2009). In a parallel development, scholars working across the disciplines of peace and conflict studies, international relations and transitional justice, as well as policy-analysts and aid-workers, have also begun to consider the potential of theatre and other arts-based initiatives as tools in grassroots peacebuilding (Lederach 2005; Lederach and Lederach 2010; Rush and Simic 2014; Schirch 2005). While this interdisciplinary research has provided inspiration for the practice-led research that I have gone on to develop in relation to Bougainville and its peace process, it also confirms the need for cautious, critical reflexivity when it comes to developing applied theatre projects in the context of peacebuilding.

This chapter looks at two major concerns that have been aired in recent scholarship. First, I address the argument that the value of an applied theatre intervention is not reducible to any simple measure of its social efficacy. Second, I consider the claims that are advanced by applied theatre practitioners with respect to the kinds of 'safe space' they hope to create for participants and the special role that is often allocated to first-person testimonial narratives within this space. I will then offer an account of the lessons learned from what might best be described as a form of cultural barter between myself and a small group of Bougainvillean associates, an exchange that moved from their support of a performance ethnography project instigated by me to my support of a ritual reconciliation process instigated by them. The conclusions to be drawn from this Bougainvillean case study challenge certain principles of applied theatre, evident in genres such as Forum Theatre or Playback, and highlight the scope for expanding the repertoire of applied theatre practice beyond such canonical forms.

The lure of efficacy: between ritual and applied theatre

Many scholars have reported on the wide gap that can exist between, on the one hand, the ways in which artists and audiences might make sense of their experience of an arts-based peacebuilding project and, on the other hand, the limited monitoring and evaluation frameworks within which aid agencies and donors tend to assess projects (Haseman and Winston 2010). While the focus of funding bodies on a narrow range of measurable outcomes is understandable, given the competition for resources across various development agendas, the current situation is unsatisfactory: at best, it results in artists and aid-workers adopting a tick-a-box approach to evaluation (gathering demographic data regarding workshop attendees, running surveys to suggest attitudinal changes, and so on) rather than attending closely to the forms of aesthetic, embodied, affective engagement that characterise participation in an arts-based process; at worst, it leads to recycling, in bad faith, ambit claims about the empowering effects of participatory art. This problem is not specific to *arts-based* peacebuilding work – as Diana Francis points out, the bureaucratisation of peacebuilding activities in general imposes 'pressure to do what is measurable, rather than what matters' (2010: 42) – but it is a problem which even the most sympathetic advocates of the arts have sometimes exacerbated.

For instance, conflict resolution scholars Michael Shank and Lisa Schirch (2008) outline the function of 'strategic arts-based peacebuilding' within a conceptual framework that moves between stages of conflict escalation, conflict management, conflict transformation and conflict prevention. Their diagrammatic representation of this framework – a neatly drawn bell curve with the above-mentioned stages of conflict as its x-axis and levels of conflict intensity as its y-axis – purports to chart the optimal periods during which different arts-based approaches might best be deployed. Their suggestions range from the use of hip-hop or documentary filmmaking in situations where participants are 'waging conflict non-violently' through to drama therapy in contexts where the goal is 'reducing direct violence' and 'transforming relationships', and on to Forum Theatre as a tool for 'capacity building' (2008: 231). This modelling suggests a crudely instrumentalist approach, as if arts-based practices are simply a novel delivery mechanism for a well-established set of peacebuilding concepts and the only substantive methodological issue to be addressed is the timing of the intervention. That said, Shank and Schirch do at least point towards the capacity of participatory art practices to represent conflict situations bluntly or obliquely depending on the needs of the moment, to incorporate non-verbal forms of communication and, by placing issues within an artistic frame, to move people from seeing conflict as intractable to seeing it as malleable (2008: 231–237).

Similar notions are emphasised by Cynthia Cohen (2005) whose strong theoretical account of the ways in which arts-based peacebuilding can foster processes of reconciliation attends closely to the nature of aesthetic experience. In particular, she addresses art's appeal to both sensory and cognitive capacities, its bounded nature which allows for intense engagement from a safe distance, and its capacity to mediate between innovative and conventional responses:

> [W]hen a work of art works, *as art*, it is because the sensibilities of the viewer or listener are anticipated in the expression itself. It is this calibration of the form of expression with the sensibilities of the viewer that gives rise to the perception of beauty; and it is through beauty that a work of art issues its invitation. It is by virtue of this reciprocity that aesthetic transactions are inherently other-regarding. They involve an awareness of the other, a sensitivity akin to respect. This quality of aesthetic experience alone makes cultural work and the arts especially valuable in situations of enmity when groups act with utter disregard for the well-being of each other. When individuals have been tortured, when homes and centers of community life have been destroyed by war, when the dignity of an ethnic group has been assaulted through longstanding oppression, the arts can remind people of what it is like to be acknowledged and respected, and, in time, to acknowledge and respect. (Cohen 2005: 73)

Cohen's insistence upon the aesthetic dimension of arts-based peacebuilding is an increasingly important theme in applied theatre scholarship and her efforts to develop a framework for documentation and evaluation of practice that honours this dimension are valuable (Cohen and Walker 2011). Furthermore, this valorisation of aesthetics can be seen as part of a larger 'affective turn' in applied theatre, most forcefully articulated by James Thompson: 'applied theatre has tended to miss aspects of practice that could strengthen its claims ... [I]t is limited if it concentrates solely on effects – identifiable social outcomes, messages or impacts – and forgets the radical potential of the freedom to enjoy *beautiful radiant things*' (2009: 6; original italics).

While sympathetic to such views, I would argue that the problem was never the notion of efficacy *per se*, but rather the looseness with which this notion was popularised by Richard Schechner as a key trope within the discipline of performance studies. Schechner, as is well known, based his understanding of efficacy on the ritual theory of anthropologist Victor Turner. Turner saw ritual processes as a form of redressive action through which a collective aims to repair the crisis inaugurated by a breach in social order. In this 'social drama' model, ritual performs a function analogous to, and can operate alongside of, political and legal-judicial forms of redressive action: elections, wars, court cases and so forth. At the heart of ritual practice, participants negotiate a *liminal* ('threshold') phase in which they are 'betwixt and between' their former and future social selves – an 'instant of pure potentiality when everything, as it were, trembles in the balance' – providing a powerful, therapeutic experience of *communitas* and a glimpse of alternative social arrangements before the normative constraints of everyday life settle more or less back into place (Turner 1982: 44).

For Schechner, the key enabling move in Turner's work was the latter's view that, in technologically complex societies, theatre and other performing arts take on a similar role to that played by the rituals of small-scale agrarian or hunter-gatherer societies. Emboldened by Turner's suggestion that all aesthetic performances have some ritual-like qualities and may be similarly geared towards redressive social action, Schechner (1976) made not only formal but also functional analogies between, on the one hand, avant-garde or community-based performances that he had produced or witnessed in New York from the 1960s onwards and, on the other hand, ritual practices that he observed or read about in Melanesian, Aboriginal Australian and other contexts. The potential for 'socio-political efficacy', as Baz Kershaw (1992) puts it, quickly become a staple justification for many performance practices that we would now characterise as forms of applied theatre.

Three difficulties are apparent in the way the notion of efficacy has been promoted as a cornerstone of applied theatre (and performance theory more generally). First, interest in the redressive potential of performance *qua* ritual has too often been pursued in isolation from any consideration of its contextual links to the other forms of redressive action that Turner considers in his original social drama model. In this regard, the recent studies by Ananda Breed (2014) and Catherine Cole (2009) – tracing relationships between aesthetic performance practices and, respectively, the Rwandan *gacaca* courts and the South African Truth and Reconciliation Commission – are particularly welcome. Second, Schechner and other scholars have tended to downplay, or simply ignore, the differences that Turner noted between the experience of fully liminal ritual practices and the more diffuse forms of participation involved in ritual-like *liminoid* genres. As Jon McKenzie (2001) puts it, performances came to be valorised only to the extent that they approached the 'liminal norm' of performance theory. Third, however, it is now clear that the grounds on which Turner argued for a distinction between liminal and liminoid genres are themselves unstable. As Lowell Lewis has recently argued, Turner posited that 'the position of play' is crucial in distinguishing the liminoid from the liminal but '[w]hat he didn't clearly realize is that this avowed centrality of play casts doubt on his contention that ritual is the primordial source of all kinds of human special events' (2013: 23).

Rather than assuming that applied theatre practices must 'take after' ritual in some fundamental way, I want to argue here the case for stepping back and letting different genres of performance do the work for which they are designed. This is not to deny the possibility of complex, complementary relationships between ritual and theatrical practices but it is calling into question the notion that a singular version of efficacy is always and everywhere at stake. It is also a call for applied theatre practitioners to think twice before taking on labels such as 'joker', 'healer' or other terms analogous to those used for ritual specialists, to scale back the pretensions of what we sometimes claim as the empowering quality of our arts practice and to accept that we can't always know in advance what the shape, let alone the vocation, of a piece of theatre might turn out to be.

Place and the uses of storytelling

One of the promises that applied theatre practitioners make (implicitly or explicitly) is that the drama workshop provides a 'safe space' in which to

Figure 7.1. Communal room in a hamlet near Hari, south-west Bougainville.
Photo: Richard Manner.

explore our understandings of difficult themes and social issues. However, as Mary Ann Hunter (2008) has observed, this discourse of safety is often only fleetingly engaged with the corresponding notion of risk. Furthermore, ideas of safe space are rarely developed with specific reference to the actual places within which the workshops are held. This issue is particularly pertinent to applied theatre practice in the context of peacebuilding and never more so than when the location is a developing nation where the majority of the population continues to live in small rural villages. To speak of Bougainville specifically, there is something incredibly exciting but also deeply unsettling to realise the porousness of the settings in which a performance or workshop might take place: underneath a galip nut tree in a clearing beside a church; under the thatched roof of a roadside market; in a classroom or communal room the walls of which are never fully enclosed (see Figure 7.1). The physical openness of these spaces is matched by a constant, unpredictable flow of people in and out of the workshop practice: you often have no idea who will turn up and how long they will stay, so you have little control over what people will hear and what they might do with this knowledge.

Such spatial relations and fluid modes of participation raise particular challenges. For example, one of the consequences of the war in

Bougainville is that it legitimated a culture of widespread sexual violence by men against women and this would be an obvious theme to tackle in an applied theatre project in Bougainville. Many stories could be told that would lend themselves readily to dramatisation and could potentially stimulate a problem-posing dialogue in the manner of Forum Theatre. But is a drama workshop, conducted in such open spaces, the right context in which to stage a scenario based, for instance, on the situation of a young woman who, having been raped in a school dormitory, was now pregnant and suicidal while the family of the rapist were shielding him from prosecution? The details of this story could, of course, be altered from the way they were told to me and, as here, anonymised but when you are working at the grassroots level, in a village culture where gossip sometimes goes hand in hand with beliefs in sorcery and payback violence, confidentiality is a harder promise to keep and a dangerous game to play.

Narrative storytelling modes are not a feature of all arts-based peace-building strategies but they are central to many and, as Thompson (2009) argues, applied theatre often draws uncritically on understandings of the therapeutic value of storytelling that have their origins in a culturally and historically specific discourse regarding post-traumatic stress.[3] While the clinical diagnosis of post-traumatic stress disorder (PTSD) has had a long and complex history, reminding us that it is a social construct as well as an undeniably painful psychological state (Balfour et al. 2015; Edkins 2003), there are several sound reasons for resisting the notion that trauma relief must always proceed by way of speaking out, as if bringing narrative order to bear on chaotic memories is the only way of mastering, or at least managing, the traumatic experience. In the first place, many individuals, despite exposure to calamitous accidents or horrific incidents of violence, do not develop PTSD symptoms. Furthermore, whatever the uses of storytelling as part of an individual therapeutic intervention, a linear narrative approach is not necessarily advisable in a larger-scale project. As Jenny Edkins puts it, with reference to collective experiences of trauma and state-sponsored practices of memorialisation, 'the process of [re-inscribing trauma] into linear narratives ... is a process that generally depoliticizes ... there is an alternative, that of *encircling the trauma* ... "to *mark* it in its very impossibility"' (Edkins 2003: 15, citing Zizek; original italics). Finally, in many non-Western settings, silence or non-verbal forms of expression, including dance and ritual, are more highly valued and culturally appropriate coping strategies (Väyrynen 2011).

Given that applied theatre practices in the aftermath of widespread violent conflict – if we follow the implications of Turner's social drama model described above – may have a relationship to larger-scale political or legal-judicial processes, it is also worth noting that some scholars in the discipline of transitional justice have begun to express similar reservations regarding the use of testimonial narratives as a default strategy for peace-building. Rosalind Shaw and Lars Waldorf, for instance, critique the indiscriminate application of mechanisms such as truth and reconciliation commissions:

> Ideas concerning the empowering, redemptive, and apotropaic powers of speaking and remembering [...] were forged over the *longue durée* of western religious and psychological thought and entered the transitional justice paradigm during the postauthoritarian period at the end of the Cold War, when truth telling and public remembering became critical weapons against the repressive violence of strong states. But subsequently, during its current globalised phase, transitional justice is more usually applied after (and, increasingly, during) low-intensity intrastate conflicts in weak or collapsed states characterised by violence 'among neighbours'. Those who have to live with their neighbours in contexts of chronic insecurity do not necessarily share the priorities, memory projects and speech practices of transitional justice mechanisms that developed to address the aftermath of political repression in other places. (Shaw and Waldorf 2010: 11)

In developing this critique, Shaw and Waldorf call into question 'the ethics of inciting people to talk about things that we cannot repair' (2010: 13). Their argument for 'localising transitional justice' highlights the need for ethnographic case studies to shed light on what 'justice, redress and social reconstruction look like from place-based standpoints' (2010: 6). The fact that the peace process in Bougainville – which is widely claimed to be one of the most successful of recent decades (Braithwaite et al. 2010) – has, to date, eschewed the options of war crimes prosecutions and truth commissions, relying instead on indigenous rituals of reconciliation, suggests again that storytelling genres, such as Playback and Forum Theatre, may not be the obvious choice for an applied theatre project focused on peacebuilding.

Before turning to my account of a Bougainvillean reconciliation ritual, there is one final point worth making about the tensions that would likely arise between a Boal-based applied theatre intervention and the Bougainvillean cultural context. Boal's techniques are based on a dramaturgy of opposition: the audience witnesses an oppressed protagonist struggling against their oppressor/antagonist; audience members are then asked to take sides with this protagonist and rehearse as many tactics as they can envisage by which s/he might win this struggle. This dramaturgical model has been critiqued many times, of course, and there are ways of using Boal's techniques that soften the binary opposition between oppressor and oppressed (Diamond 2007; Dwyer 2007). The question remains: is it the right place to start, culturally speaking?

For one thing, Bougainvillean people are already highly attuned to ethnic and other differences that are strongly marked in numerous local customs and in language. These may not be obvious to the numerous international aid workers who operate exclusively in English (relying on the fact that most Bougainvilleans count English among the several languages they speak fluently). Yet in *Tok Pisin*, the lingua franca enabling easy communication between people from different regions, when you want to say something about 'we' or 'us', you need to make explicit whether you are talking inclusively about 'we' as in 'all of us' (*yumi*) or whether you are talking exclusively about 'we' as in 'not you, but me and my group' (*mipela*).[4] The corollary of such ingrained sensitivity towards cultural differences is a deft, light touch when it comes to talking about divisive social issues. It is not for nothing that Bougainvilleans generally avoid speaking in binary terms of 'perpetrators and victims' and refer obliquely to their civil war as simply *taim bilong crisis* ('the time of crisis'). The healing of social divisions involves processes of 'shuttle mediation', driven by respected cultural leaders who will often, as a result of inter-marriage, have strong tribal ties to both parties involved in a dispute. It is a process that may take years before culminating in a ceremony that may require significant (economic and cultural) capital.

From performance ethnography to ritual performance

My first visit to Bougainville, in 2004, was animated by the following research questions: What resources for peacebuilding are available in this culture? How is the 'dramaturgy' of ceremonial actions performed within reconciliation rituals already modelling some of their hoped-for effects? To what ways of being-in-the-world are people reconciling themselves through these actions? Alongside these scholarly questions, as I have explained in detail elsewhere (Dwyer 2008), there was also a significant sentimental reason for seeking out fieldwork contacts in Bougainville. My initial reading about the history of the mine and the conflict had had the salutary effect of bringing back to mind some long-forgotten stories of my father, an orthopaedic surgeon who worked *pro bono* in Bougainville during visits to the region in 1962 (the year before I was born), 1966 and 1969. My father died when I was eleven years old and, in the three decades between that event and the piquing of my own interest in Bougainville, I had almost completely forgotten that he travelled there. Some fossicking in the attic of my mother's home yielded a box of old Kodachrome slides – images of people and places in Bougainville – some of which I digitised, printed and made up into a booklet, just before my first visit, thinking that it might make for a useful conversation starter.

Not only did my father's old photos achieve this modest end, allowing people to place me in relation to events long before the war; I also had the unexpected and humbling experience of meeting Bougainvilleans who, as nurses or as patients, had actually encountered my father in the small hospital clinics where, forty years earlier, he had performed his operations (principally to relieve the crippling effects of polio on dozens of young people). Soon, the pages of my hastily compiled booklet were covered with annotations as my companions provided names of some of the people in the images, showed me the places where my father must have stood to take his photos, and recounted stories of what had happened in these places during the years of the crisis (see Figure 7.2).

I also started to realise that the names of villages scribbled by my father across the bottom of his Kodachrome slides were often the same as the place-names I was seeing mentioned in a dossier of human rights abuses (Havini 1995). A particularly strong point of connection existed in the district of Siwai, in south-west Bougainville, where my father had spent much of his time and where I, too, even before realising this, had already begun to develop a relationship with some key cultural advisors. In 2004, John Tompot, Ces Kahuru and Willmo had spoken with me about the fighting in Siwai as a 'crisis within the crisis', an analysis that is widely supported in the literature on Bougainville's peace process. Writing in 2010, Braithwaite et al. refer to this conflict as the 'most dramatic local power struggle, whose effects are still not healed . . . most of the leaders who were at one another's throats in the Siwai crisis were still not reconciled in 2008' (Braithwaite et al. 2010: 30). While, ultimately, I became directly involved in attempts to redress this crisis, this was not what I initially envisaged.

Shortly after my first Bougainville trip, recognising that much more fieldwork would be required to make serious progress on the research questions mentioned above, and uncertain about how to proceed, I began gathering a range of documentary materials to complement my father's photographs and the rich vein of oral history that had been opened up in conversations about them. Some old manila folders buried in another box in my mother's attic yielded correspondence between my father, the

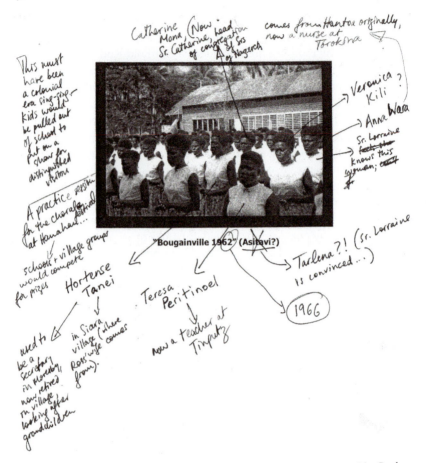

Figure 7.2. Photo by Dr A. F. Dwyer of Tarlena Girls Choir, annotated by Paul Dwyer.

missionaries on Bougainville and even some of the patients he had treated. I pored over medical textbooks, x-rays, surgical slides, transcripts of parliamentary debates, press coverage and academic writing about the crisis, archival film footage and so on. Slowly, thinking to fill in the time before study leave would allow another fieldwork trip, I began to generate a solo performance piece out of these materials. Thematically, and in its narrative structure, *The Bougainville Photoplay Project* (Dwyer 2010) interweaves accounts of the events leading up to, and during, the war; the recollections of Bougainvilleans and Australians (including some of my siblings who had accompanied my father on his travels) of life during the colonial era, before the mine and the crisis; and a running commentary on my fieldwork in progress. The show opens as a more-or-less formal lecture but soon slides into other territory (a Berlitz-style crash course in *Tok Pisin*; performative renditions of fieldnotes; the recreation of surgical procedures, and so on), inviting an audience to ask what kind of relationship might be possible now between Bougainvillean and Australian people.

While storytelling is certainly an important feature of this work, there is no linear narrative and no attempt to tie up loose ends. The performance rarely operates in the mode of first-person testimonial narrative: my voice within it remains that of the somewhat baffled traveller and ethnographer, aiming to 'speak nearby' the stories of others (Trinh Minh-ha, cited in Grimshaw 2001: 6). Another premise for the work is that it is Australians who have a memory problem in relation to the Bougainville crisis, not Bougainvilleans themselves. Most Australians have never heard of Bougainville and have no idea about our involvement in the mine and the war. Many do not even recall that Australia was once the colonial authority in control of PNG. Hence, from the outset, I understood Australians to be my main target audience, although I was, of course, concerned to have feedback from Bougainvillean people about the ways in which I was narrating parts of their history. By the time of my second trip to the region, in 2007, I was able to show a work-in-progress version of the *Photoplay Project* in a series of performances attended by some of my father's former patients, by nurses, doctors, teachers and local politicians, by ordinary Bougainvilleans on market days or after church, and by all of the cultural advisors I had met three years earlier.

In the aftermath of one particularly memorable open-air showing of the *Photoplay*, to several hundred villagers at Monoitu, in Siwai, I sat down again with John, Ces and Willmo who gravely explained: 'When we first met you a few years ago, we weren't really sure why you were here. Now we should find a way to work together.' Since 2004, they had also been busy, having formed a Peace Committee and set their sights on bringing about a reconciliation between former combatants from Siwai district (members of the PNG-backed Resistance militia) and from Buin district (members of the BRA H-Company). The epicentre of this conflict was a place called Hari whose chiefs were among the first to re-align themselves with the PNG Defence Force against the BRA. This inter-district reconciliation project was a major undertaking. John Tompot and his colleagues had successfully carried out shuttle mediation and a truce between the warring parties had been negotiated in 2005. However, further rounds of meetings were required in order for the families of those who had suffered injury, destruction of property, or the death of a loved one, to impress upon the former combatants the consequences of the war. The families, the former combatants and their leaders also still needed to agree on appropriate amounts of shell-money and other traditional gifts to be exchanged at a reconciliation feast.[5] And money – some 12,000 PNG Kina (6,000 Australian dollars) – would need to be found to pay for food and transport.

A bargain was struck. John would keep me informed of any further progress in the mediation between the Hari Resistance and BRA H-Company, and the Peace Committee would allow me to document any resulting reconciliation ceremony as part of my research. I would continue to develop the *Photoplay Project*, folding some of their stories into it, I would perform it back in Australia wherever possible and, should I make any money from it, I would repay their contributions to the performance by helping to fund the reconciliation. I pointed out that the market for a work that has been variously billed as 'performance ethnography' or 'slide-show with fireside chat' was likely to be small, yet, back in Australia, the show was actually well received critically, playing to fringe and 'alternative mainstream' theatre audiences, as well as some smaller festivals.[6] Thus, in 2012, my colleague, Richard Manner, and I found ourselves shadowing members of the Peace Committee, crisscrossing Siwai in Willmo's truck, as they negotiated deals on the cost of pigs, chickens, fruit and vegetables, met with local performance troupes who were rehearsing their songs and dances, organised flat-bed trucks to transport former combatants, liaised with those who took on the huge task of cooking food and with those building a stage on the football field where the final act of reconciliation took place.

A brief word about methodology is in order at this point. Ethnographers are often reluctant to talk about the money, used to facilitate the staging of events like the Hari reconciliation, that changes hands during fieldwork, as if such exchanges constitute a distortion of the ideal balance between 'empathic involvement' and 'disciplined detachment' in participant-observation (Margaret Mead, cited in McAuley 1998: 77). This reluctance is closely paralleled, I would suggest, by the reticence among 'first world' applied theatre workers when it comes to detailing funding arrangements, production budgets, and the ways in which their work in developing nations or 'at risk' communities may be part of a career-building strategy. I say this not to denigrate the good intentions and commitment of many colleagues (there are, after all, easier ways to make a living!) but simply to foreground the fact that an applied theatre intervention, like any ethnographic fieldwork encounter, generally involves an exchange between parties that are unequal. As Kirsten Hastrup (1992) explains, ethnographic research requires the fieldworker to maintain a certain pressure on 'informants', through constant questioning. Notwithstanding the shift in anthropology towards greater reflexivity and 'polyvocality' (Clifford 1986), it is ultimately the researcher who controls the discourse when fieldwork, as here, becomes academic text.

In talking with my friend, John Tompot, about the subsidy I was able to provide for the food and transport costs of the reconciliation, I have often made reference to the idea of it being a 'cultural barter'.[7] The *Photoplay Project* would never have come to fruition had it not been for the practical support and storytelling sessions that I experienced in Bougainville and it seemed only fair to plough some of the proceeds back into the ceremony that John and his colleagues had been actively working towards. Of course, in years gone by, reconciliation ceremonies may well have required less external financial support. The local economy is still struggling to recover from the crisis; the mine is closed; many of the copra plantations and other cash-crops are still devastated; there is little surplus food from gardens, and so on. Moreover, the traditional source of authority on Bougainville – *kastom* ('custom') knowledge administered by the chiefs – has also been a casualty of the war. This knowledge is fragile, creating a situation whereby reconciliation rituals demand a knowledge of, and respect for, *kastom* that the rituals themselves must help to foster. The motto of the Peace Committee in Siwai is *Kisim Bek Kalsa* ('Recovering Our Culture') and supporting their project, in exchange for being able to further my research, seems not unreasonable.

Tradition and innovation in Bougainvillean reconciliation ceremonies

When speaking of 'traditional' rituals in Bougainville, it is important to remember that these practices are still experienced as a contemporary phenomenon by those involved. The suppleness with which Bougainvilleans are able to adapt their reconciliation ceremonies to present circumstances is remarkable. The design of the reconciliation stage at Hari, for instance, involved an almost profligate layering of multiple symbols, one on top of one another, referencing different meaning-making frameworks and allowing participants as many ways as possible of coming inside the ceremony.

Figure 7.3 shows the flag of PNG, on display for those who still identify with the national government, alongside the Bougainville regional flag, long associated with the movement for independence. Both the national anthem and the regional anthem were sung as local police raised these flags.

Figure 7.3. The stage for the reconciliation at Hari. Video Still: Richard Manner.

Then prayers were led, and hymns were sung, during the start of the ceremony, by pastors and choirs of various Christian denominations. Meanwhile, in front of the stage, members of the Peace Committee placed a carved wooden post featuring totemic emblems that are important in some of the surviving animist beliefs of people from this area. However, by far the most compelling device for framing the event as a significant ceremonial occasion were the pigs that were trussed up on strong, light-weight tree trunks, specially selected for this purpose, and carried onto the field by former combatants. The fact that the appearance of these pigs – a traditional form of ceremonial exchange – coincided with many of the attending villagers surging forward towards the stage (foregoing any hope of shade on a blisteringly hot day) points to the residual strength of *kastom* vis-à-vis the other frameworks just mentioned.

The adaptability of traditional practices also extends to finding work-around solutions when parts of the ritual are not going to plan. The day before the final BRA–Resistance reconciliation ceremony, members of one of the families torn apart by the fighting at Hari felt that they needed a personal reconciliation before they could come out of mourning and accept the gifts and celebratory dances that were planned for the main event. One of the men who had been killed was the brother-in-law of a local man aligned with the BRA. The brothers of the deceased man held their sister's husband responsible for helping to organise the BRA attack on Hari. We met under the house of the brother-in-law for a *troim aut* session

Figure 7.4. Embodying the liminal moment in reconciliation. Video Still: Richard Manner.

(where you 'throw out' or 'vomit up' your feelings). The bereaved brothers spoke of their grief; the accused brother-in-law explained the context of his actions while fully acknowledging his responsibility and offering an apology that was accepted amid quiet tears and an exchange of shell-money. Without the time to stage this smaller reconciliation in full *kastom* regalia, the participants created the most simple, literal embodiment of what Turner describes as the liminal threshold in redressive rituals. Two mediators stretched out their arms and held a sustained handshake across which the eldest brother and his brother-in-law reached out to one another and shook hands in turn (see Figure 7.4). They each took a bite from the same piece of betel nut, chewed it briefly (exhibiting none of the relish that normally accompanies chewing this mild narcotic) and spat into a small hole that had been dug. The senior chief in attendance then planted a stone on top of the hole and pressed it into the ground with his foot before inviting everyone else in attendance to shake hands. Then we all shared a meal.

Notwithstanding the sober, low-key tone of this intra-family reconciliation, skilfully mediated by John Tompot, there was a strong ritual efficacy to the process, being the first time that these brothers and brother-in-law had communicated in sixteen years. Moreover, in the practised economy of their reconciliatory gestures, there are signs of a particular 'matrix of sensibility' at work (Geertz 1983) – a performance of what Diana Taylor (2003) refers to as the 'repertoire' of a culture's embodied memories – as well as a rich affective exchange between individuals. The act of spitting, if we follow the affect theory of psychologist Silvan Tompkins, is bound up with a visceral disgust, a need to expel not only food that doesn't quite taste right but also concepts or actions that strike us as morally unpalatable (see Sedgwick and Frank 1995). The planting of a stone atop the place where saliva from the eldest brother and his brother-in-law has commingled adds several layers of significance to this act. Emotional experience for Bougainvillean people is centred not in the mind or in the heart but in the gut, such that the deep sorrow of those present at the reconciliation would be described as *bel hevi* ('heaviness in the gut'): in this sense, the hardness and the weight of the stone function iconically to represent these feelings. The stone is also an indexical sign to mark the occasion of this reconciliation ceremony: notably, it is placed in the middle of a well-trodden path beside the brother-in-law's house so that it becomes a 'stumble stone', a mnemonic protrusion of the past into the present.[8] Finally, symbolically, the ceremony references a *kastom* belief that, once a reconciliation has been completed, one should remain silent as stone: the actions that caused the *hevi* will not be forgotten but they have been forgiven.

On the following day, with much more lavish ceremony, commanders of the Resistance and BRA factions met in front of about six hundred people on the football field at Hari. Again, a particular sensibility towards reconciliation was on display, along with the flexibility of *kastom* knowledge, despite (or, perhaps to some extent, enabled by) further signs of its fragility. For instance, in one part of the ceremony, the Resistance and BRA commanders were expected to charge back and forth at each other, brandishing spears in mock combat, before agreeing to break the spears and bury them. Both men were visibly uncertain about how to perform this sequence and what transpired was somewhat more akin to watching a pair of rugby footballers tentatively stepping onto the dance floor at a Blue Light disco. Wry smiles from some of the elders and members of the Peace Committee, along with warm applause from the rest of the crowd, suggested that any breach in protocol was a minor concern. However, the act of chewing betel nut, spitting into a hole in the ground and planting a stone – again a focal point of the ceremony – was harder to interpret on this occasion. Compared to the intra-family reconciliation of the day before, the Resistance and BRA commanders chewed their betel nut for longer, mixing it with mustard seed and lime to bring on its more pleasant effects. A slightly awkward pause followed before they shook hands under the instruction of Chief Joseph Hampeku.

Such details could be taken to imply that the BRA and Resistance commanders were not as sincere as the parties involved in the private reconciliation the day before but this would be to misread the situation. These leaders were acting politically, having been called upon to take up a role as representatives for all the ex-combatants who once served under them, in a public ceremony to mark the end of conflict. Both men made speeches that were well received even though they passed very lightly over the details of the fighting in Hari all those years ago and offered little that resembled the ideal-typical form of an apology that one often finds in the scholarly literature on restorative justice and reconciliation (Nathanson 1992; Tavuchis 1991). Rather, their words – and their demeanour – suggested calmness, civility and a common resolve to support the fledgling Autonomous Bougainville Government as it prepares for a referendum on independence from PNG. In this regard, the ceremony had much in common with observations made by Rosalind Shaw in her study of reconciliation rituals that have been used in the wake of Sierra Leone's civil war of the 1990s: 'the performance of truth as the recounting of specific actions was less significant than their embodied performance of the "truth" of moral subjectivities, the display of a change in the speakers' hearts ... [indicating a] changed basis for social relationships' (2010: 129–130).

Towards a 'slower' applied theatre practice

Having highlighted the powerfully efficacious, and complex affective, qualities inherent in Bougainvillean reconciliation rituals, I should stress that I am not suggesting the only, or indeed the best, option for building peace through performative means would be to pump large amounts of money into the staging of ceremonies like the event at Hari. Arguably, there has already been too much of this, placing great pressure on the Autonomous Bougainville Government to match the lavish budgets for some of the early post-war reconciliation ceremonies that were largely bankrolled by international agencies such as the United Nations Development Program. While the Hari ceremony was very cheap by comparison, the challenge of continuing this practice in a sustainable, grassroots manner is considerable. There are also hard questions to consider with respect to whether the rituals can unerringly achieve 'peace with justice' (Lederach 1997).

There was undoubtedly a strong reconciliatory rhetoric coming from both parties to the conflict at Hari but former combatants on the BRA side did seem more extroverted and one suspects that this reflects the relative ease with which they can attach themselves to a narrative of heroic struggle against the PNG Defence Force. As James Thompson (2004) has argued in relation to Sri Lanka, such narratives, and counter-narratives, can themselves be the cause for future conflicts. The practice of reconciliation rituals in Bougainville also raises the question of what to do about the cases of gross violation to human rights that occurred during the crisis. Victims of human rights abuses (particularly women) may feel pressured to give up on claims to legal redress, although several mediators I have spoken to stress that this is not a given: ritual reconciliation does not have to substitute for a perpetrator being sentenced by a court but can occur, for instance between a victim and the family of the perpetrator, as an adjunct to, or long after the outcome of, any criminal proceedings.

Many Bougainvilleans are asking themselves questions such as those raised above and, importantly, taking the time to search for a communal response. Volker Boege (2006) describes the situation in Bougainville as the peacebuilding equivalent to the 'slow food' movement and slowness is undoubtedly one of the key lessons here. Over time, the reservations I expressed at the outset of this chapter, regarding the prospects for developing a Boal-based applied theatre project in Bougainville, have shifted to a cautious embrace of the openness of applied theatre as a category. Of course, *The Bougainville Photoplay Project* was not originally conceived in these terms and was performed mostly in 'art house' theatre settings in Australia. Yet, it did grow organically out of a sustained dialogue with a number of key Bougainvillean associates and, as a fundraising tool, ultimately supported their objectives as much as it helped me to take account of my own interests, and the legacy of Australia's historical interests, in Bougainville. At the very least, the unanticipated outcomes of the *Photoplay Project* suggest that the category of applied theatre cannot be adequately explained with reference to any particular set of aesthetic forms or genre conventions.

What seems to have been forgotten, in the haste with which applied theatre practitioners have sought to press genres such as Forum Theatre into the service of peacebuilding, is the need simply to dwell in a context long enough to become aware of possible contradictions between indigenous and non-indigenous practices. On the one hand, this is surprising since careful participant-observation fieldwork was once a critical component in planning and delivery of the literacy programmes developed by Paulo Freire, Boal's mentor. On the other hand, it no doubt reflects something of the impatient bureaucratic culture of contemporary peacebuilding.

So the argument for a slower applied theatre practice is as much about deepening the dialogue between artists and sponsoring organisations or funding bodies with respect to evaluating outcomes as it is about creating the circumstances in which communities are able to drive much of the creative process. Above all, when I think about the skills of mediators like John Tompot and his colleagues from the Peace Committee in Siwai, I am reminded that best practice rarely results from 'fly-in, fly-out' interventions and that the most creative acts of peacebuilding can occur 'off-stage', as it were, around the edges of whatever activities might be planned as the main performance event.

References

Balfour, M., Bundy, P., Burton, B., Dunn, J. and Woodrow, N. 2015. *Applied Theatre: Resettlement. Drama, Refugees and Resilience*. London: Methuen.

Boege, V. 2006. 'Bougainville and the discovery of slowness: An unhurried approach to state-building in the Pacific'. *Australian Centre for Peace and Conflict Studies Occasional Paper Series*, 3. Brisbane: ACPACS.

Boege, V. and Garasu, S.L. 2011. 'Bougainville: A source of inspiration for conflict resolution' in Brigg, M. and Bleiker, R. (eds.) *Mediating Across Difference: Oceanic and Asian Approaches to Conflict Resolution*. Honolulu: University of Hawai'i Press, pp. 163–182.

Braithwaite, J., Charlesworth, H., Reddy, P. and Dunn, L. 2010. *Reconciliation and Architectures of Commitment: Sequencing Peace in Bougainville*. Canberra: Australian National University Press.

Breed, A. 2014. *Performing the Nation: Genocide, Justice, Reconciliation*. Calcutta: Seagull Books.

Clifford, J. 1986. 'Introduction: Partial truths' in Clifford, J. and Marcus, G. (eds.) *Writing Culture: The Poetics and Politics of Ethnography*. Berkeley: University of California Press, pp. 1–26.

Cohen, C. 2005. 'Creative approaches to reconciliation' in Fitzduff, M. and Stout, C. (eds.) *The Psychology of Resolving Global Conflicts: From War to Peace*, Vol. 3. Westport, CT: Praeger, pp. 69–102.

Cohen, C., Gutiérrez Varea, R. and Walker, P. (eds.) 2011. *Acting Together on the World Stage: Performance and the Creative Transformation of Conflict*, Vol. 1 and 2. Oakland: New Village Press.

Cohen, C. and Walker, P. 2011. 'Designing and documenting peacebuilding performance initiatives', in Cohen, Gutiérrez Varea and Walker, Vol. 2, 219–28.

Cole, C. 2009. *Performing South Africa's Truth Commission: Stages of Transition*. Bloomington: Indiana University Press.

Diamond, D. 2007. *Theatre for Living: The Art and Science of Community-Based Dialogue*. Bloomington: Trafford Publishing.

Dorney, S. 1998. *The Sandline Affair: Politics and Mercenaries and the Bougainville Crisis*. Sydney: ABC Books.

Dwyer, P. 2007. 'Though this be madness? The Boal method of theatre and therapy'. *Applied Theatre Researcher* 8: 1–12.

Dwyer, P. 2008. 'Theatre as post-operative follow-up: *The Bougainville Photoplay Project*'. *About Performance* 8: 141–160.

Dwyer, P. 2010. *The Bougainville Photoplay Project*. Sydney: Currency Press.

Edkins, J. 2003. *Trauma and the Memory of Politics*. Cambridge: Cambridge University Press.

Francis, D. 2010. *From Pacification to Peacebuilding: A Call to Global Transformation*. London: Pluto Press.

Geertz, C. 1983. 'Art as a cultural system' in *Local Knowledge: Further Essays in Interpretive Anthropology*. London: Fontana, pp. 94–120.

Grimshaw, A. 2001. *The Ethnographer's Eye: Ways of Seeing in Modern Anthropology*. Cambridge: Cambridge University Press.

Haseman, B. and Winston, J. 2010. '"Why be Interested?" Aesthetics, Applied Theatre and Drama Education'. *RIDE: The Journal of Applied Theatre and Performance* 15.4: 465–475.

Hastrup, K. 1992. 'Writing ethnography: State of the art' in Okley, J. and Callaway, H. (eds.) *Anthropology and Autobiography*. London: Routledge, pp. 116–133.

Havini, M.T. (ed.) 1995. *A Compilation of Human Rights Abuses Against the People of Bougainville, 1989–1995*. Sydney: Bougainville Freedom Movement.

Howley, P. 2002. *Breaking Spears and Mending Hearts: Peacemakers and Restorative Justice in Bougainville*. Sydney: Federation Press.

Hunter, M.A. 2008. 'Cultivating the art of safe space'. *RIDE: The Journal of Applied Theatre and Performance* 13.1: 5–21.

Kershaw, B. 1992. *The Politics of Performance: Radical Theatre as Cultural Intervention*. London: Routledge.

Lederach, J.P. 1997. *Building Peace: Sustainable Reconciliation in Divided Societies*. Washington: United States Institute of Peace.

Lederach, J.P. 2005. *The Moral Imagination: The Art and Soul of Building Peace*. Oxford: Oxford University Press.

Lederach, J.P. and Lederach, A. 2010. *When Blood and Bones Cry Out: Journeys through the Soundscape of Healing and Reconciliation*. St Lucia: University of Queensland Press.

Lewis, J.L. 2013. *The Anthropology of Cultural Performance*. Basingstoke: Palgrave Macmillan.

McAuley, G. 1998. 'Towards an ethnography of rehearsal'. *New Theatre Quarterly* 14.1: 75–85.

McKenzie, J. 2001. *Perform or Else: From Discipline to Performance*. London: Routledge.

Nathanson, D. 1992. *Shame and Pride: Affect, Sex and the Birth of the Self*. New York: Norton and Company.

Rush, P. and Simic, O. 2014. *The Arts of Transitional Justice: Culture, Activism and Memory after Atrocity*. New York: Springer

Schechner, R. 1976. 'From ritual to theatre and back' in Schechner, R. and Schutzman, M. (eds.) *Ritual, Play and Performance*. New York: Seabury Press, pp. 196–222.

Schirch, L. 2005. *Ritual and Symbol in Peacebuilding*. Bloomfield, CT: Kumarian Press.

Sedgwick, E.K. and Frank, A. (eds.) 1995. *Shame and its Sisters: A Silvan Tomkins Reader*. Durham: Duke University Press.

Shank, M. and Schirch, L. 2008. 'Strategic arts-based peacebuilding'. *Peace and Change* 33.2: 217–242.

Shaw, R. 2010. 'Linking justice with reintegration? Ex-combatants and the Sierra Leone experiment' in Shaw, R., Waldorf, L. and Hazan, P. (eds.) *Localizing Transitional Justice: Interventions and Priorities after Mass Violence*. Stanford: Stanford University Press, pp. 111–132.

Shaw, R. and Waldorf, L. 2010. 'Introduction: Localizing transitional justice' in Shaw, R., Waldorf, L. and Hazan, P. (eds.) *Localizing Transitional Justice: Interventions and Priorities after Mass Violence*. Stanford: Stanford University Press, pp. 3–26.

Sirivi, J.T. and Havini, M.T. (eds.) 2004. *As Mothers of the Land: The Birth of the Bougainville Women for Peace and Freedom*. Canberra: Pandanus Books.

Tanis, J. 2002. 'Reconciliation: My side of the Island' in Carl, A. and Garasu Sr. L. (eds.) 'Weaving consensus: The Papua New Guinea–Bougainville peace process'. *Accord* 12: 28–31.

Tavuchis, N. 1991. *Mea Culpa: A Sociology of Apology and Reconciliation*. Stanford: Stanford University Press.

Taylor, D. 2003. *The Archive and the Repertoire: Performing Cultural Memory in the Americas*. Durham: Duke University Press.

Thompson, L. (dir.) 2001. *Breaking Bows and Arrows*. Documentary Film. Waverly, NSW: Firelight Productions.

Thompson, J. 2004. 'Digging up stories: An archaeology of theatre in war'. *TDR: The Journal of Performance Studies* 48.3: 150–164.

Thompson, J. 2009. *Performance Affects: Applied Theatre and the End of Effect*. Basingstoke: Palgrave Macmillan.

Thompson, J., Hughes, J. and Balfour, M. 2009. *Performance in Place of War*. Calcutta: Seagull Books.

Turner, V. 1982. *From Ritual to Theatre: The Human Seriousness of Play*. New York: PAJ Publications.

Väyrynen, T. 2011. 'Silence in Western models of conflict resolution' in Brigg, M. and Bleiker, R. (eds.) *Mediating Across Difference: Oceanic and Asian Approaches to Conflict Resolution*. Honolulu: University of Hawaiʻi Press, pp. 38–56.

CHAPTER 8

Applied theatre and climate change in Bangladesh
Indigenous theatrics for neoliberal theatricks

Syed Jamil Ahmed

In the mid-1990s, a non-governmental organization (NGO) based in Khulna in south-western Bangladesh named Rupantar deployed Pot Gan, an indigenous form of performance, to devise a theatre process. Rupantar literally means 'transformation', and in Pot Gan (also known as Potuya Gan), narratives are visually illustrated with scroll paintings. This chapter examines how Rupantar successfully recreated, restored and adapted the 'indigenous theatrics' of Pot Gan to meet the challenge of climate change in Bangladesh, and at the same time will also chart how the process inevitably slips under neoliberalism. In consequence, 'indigenous theatrics', that is, 'the art of theatre produced in Bangladesh', emerges with a silent 'k' noxiously accommodated within 'the art', such that the notion of 'theatrics' now manifests itself as 'theatricks' to signify 'theatre tricks'.

The chapter is informed by the explication of neoliberalism as a project concerned with institutional changes ushered by 'the core tenets of Chicago School economics – privatization, deregulation and cuts to government services' (Klein 2007: 561). Underpinned by the ideology that is generated from the quotidian experience of buying and selling commodities to become an image of the society, neoliberalism is a political project 'that tries to render the social domain economic and to link a reduction in (welfare) state services and security systems to the increasing call for "personal responsibility" and "self-care"' (Lemke 2001: 203). Informed by the findings from two field-level investigations conducted in 2013 and 2014 in south-western Bangladesh, the chapter proceeds in four sections: the first locates Rupantar and its recreated indigenous theatrics in the context of climate change threats in Bangladesh; the second examines how Rupantar's Pot Gan is devised and performed to serve as an interventionist tool to challenge climate change; and the third uncovers the slippage of Rupantar's practice under neoliberalism, and the consequent emergence of applied theatricks. Summing up the findings of the previous three, the concluding section enlarges the scope of the examination from the local to the global to present a metadiscourse on intervention, neoliberalism and performance. But it is necessary to insert a disclaimer at the outset: this is no finger-pointing exercise; if there is an 'other' that this examination addresses, it is necessarily the 'self'.

Rupantar, indigenous theatrics, and the context of climate change in Bangladesh

Bangladesh is situated on an extensive alluvial floodplain at the confluence of three immense rivers (the Ganges-Padma, Brahmaputra-Jamuna, and Meghna) and is intersected by over 200 rivers. It also experiences a humid and sub-tropical climate and receives over 80% of its annual precipitation (1,600 mm to 2,300 mm) during the monsoon period between June and September. These hydro-meteorological features are so unique and influential to the life of the people that Bangladesh has been called 'a hydraulic civilization' (Yu et al. 2010: 5). At the same time, these features make the country susceptible to a range of climate risks, including severe floods tornados, tidal bores and droughts. 'The high exposure of the country to extreme hydro meteorological events', warns Damien Riquet, 'is likely to increase in the future due to the impact of climate change' (2012: 8). Consequently, Bangladesh stands foremost in the Climate Change Vulnerability Index 2011 (Maplecroft 2014).

One of the most critical climate change issues for Bangladesh is the rising sea levels, since most of the country's topography is extremely low and flat (less than ninety metres above MSL), and two-thirds of its land area is less than five metres above MSL. It is estimated that a sea-level rise of one metre will impact on 13 million people in Bangladesh, and 6% of the national rice production will be lost. Further, the rise may also influence the extent of the tides and alter the salinity quality of both surface and groundwater (Yu et al. 2010: 17). Already, the threat is palpable in the Sundarbans – a UNESCO World Heritage site that is also the largest forest of Bangladesh, and the country's last stronghold of the Bengal tiger. Recognizing the gravity of the situation, the Government of Bangladesh has framed a climate management strategy, 'which prioritizes adaptation and disaster risk reduction, and also addresses low carbon development, mitigation, technology transfer and the mobilization and international provision of adequate finance' (MoEF 2009: xvii). In order to address the impacts of climate change, the government set up Bangladesh Climate Change Trust Fund from its own resources in 2010 (Khan et al. 2013: 9), and, in the same year, it also established Bangladesh Climate Change Resilience Fund by joining hands with the development partners and the World Bank (BCCRF 2014). However, the two funds, along with all other donor contributions, are too little for the Bangladesh state to deal effectively with the disastrous impacts of climate change. As Raillon observes:

> [The state's] current strategy is undermining all resilience strategies for dealing with climate crises at the national level. In the 1990s, the structural adjustment policies that were more or less directly promoted by the international economic institutions, the World Trade Organisation, the International Monetary Fund and the World Bank, called for less state [intervention], while economic liberalism steadily dismantled all national and international regulation. (Raillon 2014)

Clearly, the last item of the climate management strategy of Bangladesh, adequate finance, pinpoints the irony of the crisis prompted by climate change: 'that populations with the most fiscal and political power have the greatest ability to avoid the sorts of environmental harm that pragmatically necessitate an immediate and comprehensive response' (Kretz 2012: 9–10). So for example, although both Bangladesh and the Netherlands are low-lying deltaic countries, 'the Netherlands has the financial, scientific, and technological capacity to build higher sea walls, whereas Bangladesh does not' (Huq 2001: 1617). Poverty operates in a vicious circle, for poverty generates further poverty in exponential terms as an account book that has written off the bad debts incurred by the colonizers and slave traders. In a world spurred by the neoliberal proposition that 'the market is in human nature', to which Bangladesh has been well-integrated since the first half of the 1990s, the impending disaster posed by climate change can only mean immense profit-mongering opportunities for finance capital.

In this context, a non-profit body of non-state actors known as Rupantar has set its mission as, inter alia, to '[r]esuscitate, develop and foster folk cultural forms and methods to sensitize grassroots people' and to '[b]uild peoples' capacity to cope with the impacts of climate change and natural disaster and to conserve natural bio-diversity' (Rupantar 2014a). Refusing to be trapped by what Amartya Sen (1999: 3) identifies as 'narrower views' that identify the notion of development with 'the growth of gross national product, or with the rise of personal incomes', Rupantar asserts that 'culture and sustainable development are closely connected' ('Popular Publications' n.d.: 13). Recognized as an NGO by the Government of Bangladesh in 1997, the organization runs development programmes that affect the lives of approximately 26% of the entire population of

Bangladesh, and its development messages reach an additional 7.7% of the population (Rupantar 2012: 5–6). These programmes are funded by the Government of Bangladesh, as well as inter-governmental organizations (IGOs) and international non-governmental organizations (INGOs). In the year that ended on 31 December 2012, Rupantar received tk. 231,316,724 (over US$ 2,825,000), equivalent to 92.26% of its total income from these sources (Rupantar 2012: 39).

When executing its development programmes, Rupantar unfailingly mobilizes theatre to effect change in Bangladesh. Pot Gan is one of the forms of theatre Rupantar mobilizes, and indeed, it has been the most popular, innovative, and successful among all the forms employed. The organization proudly claims a rich harvest of Pot Gan productions on issues related to gender and women empowerment, democracy and governance, and climate change ('Rupantar Method' n.d.: 6–7). The Pot Gan that Rupantar produces and performs today is the result of a long process of re-creation, restoration, and adaptation of the indigenous theatrics of Potuya Gan, which is entirely religious in content and objective. The scroll of the indigenous Potuya Gan performances (usually about 55 cm wide) is painted in small panels, and is displayed vertically with a stand by the *gayen* (the lead narrator) or is unrolled by him/her with one hand (see Figure 8.1). S/he is accompanied by one or two musicians cum choral singers, and the music is monotonous. Rupantar's process of adaptation, restoration, and re-creation began on 5 June 1996, when it performed its first Pot Gan production titled *Bachao Sundarban* (translated as 'Save the Sundarbans'). Today, its performance is presented with nine to thirteen performers, who sing and dance to music that has variety, and borrows heavily from popular folk music that is unrelated to indigenous Potuya Gan performance.

The libretto of Rupantar's Pot Gan is composed in rhymed couplets with seven accented syllables in each line. The plot-structure of the libretto is adapted from European dramaturgy, signalling that the 'indigenous' theatrics adopted by Rupantar is in fact an assimilation. The first stage of a Pot Gan plot serves as introduction, the second generates 'rising action', the third produces the climax, the fourth, the 'falling action', the fifth, the conclusion, and the sixth, the 'call to action'. Rupantar has also abandoned the painting style seen in the scrolls of the indigenous Potuya Gan performances, and instead has adopted the popular style of painting seen on the backboards of rickshaws in Bangladesh. The entire performance is choreographed meticulously following 'Western' principles of direction, usually by Swapan Guha, who was once an active member of the

Figure 8.1. A performance of indigenous Potuya Gan on Pir Gazi. Photo: Syed Jamil Ahmed.

mainstream theatre of Bangladesh, and is now one of the executive directors of Rupantar. The method of displaying the scroll is entirely Rupantar's
innovation. By having an 11-metre-long scroll unfurl horizontally by two
scroll-bearers standing on two sides, and by increasing its width to 1.2
metres, Rupantar today has successfully adapted and recreated the indigenous theatrics of Potuya Gan – so much so that by July 2014, it had
produced 137 productions, which have been performed 10,396 times for
nearly 10.7 million spectators (Nisha 2014: 6).

Performing and devising Pot Gan: Rupantar challenges climate change

It was the morning of 14 February 2014. At the compound of Fine and
Performing Arts Academy in Khulna city, about 500 schoolchildren, along
with a few dignitaries of the city, sat in front of a proscenium-arch stage.
Rupantar was to present a performance of Pot Gan as a part of their celebra-
tion of the Sundarbans Day. Eight musicians and choral singers dressed in
fatua and pantaloon (males) and sari (females) sat on the two sides of the stage:
a male harmonium player with three female choral singers on stage-right and
two female choral singers with two male musicians (violin and *dotara* players)
on stage-left. As they commenced playing orchestral music, five more performers appeared from off left-stage area, dancing to the rhythm of the music:
two male performers carrying on their shoulders a scroll rolled around two
spindles, a *nachiye* (female dancer) playing a 'hollow' (skin-less) tambourine,
a male *bayen* playing a double-ended drum (*bangla dhol*), and a female *gayen*
(lead narrator) carrying a red baton. The *nachiye*, accompanied by the
drummer, moved downstage centre to execute a vigorous and entertaining
dance number. At the same time, the bearers placed the scroll upstage centre
by holding the two spindles vertically and unrolled one of the spindles to
reveal the first panel showing the 'front matter' (the title of the performance
and the credits): Bon Surakshar Pot Gan (Jungle Protection Pot Gan),
composed by Elias Fakir, scroll painted by Debashish Sardar, and directed
by Swapan Guha. When the *nachiye* and the drummer ended their introductory dance, the *gayen* was ready to begin (Figure 8.2).

The scroll was divided into eight panels, one each for the 'front matter'
and the 'back matter' (containing Rupantar's name as the producing
organization), and one panel for each of the six stages of the plot. At the
beginning of each stage of the performance, one of the scroll-bearers
unrolled his spindle along its vertical axis while the other bearer rolled
his up, in consequence of which the scroll travelled horizontally, each time

Figure 8.2. Performance of Bon Surakshar Pot Gan (stage 1) by Rupantar, at
Shilpakala Academy, Khulna city, 14 February 2014. Photo: Syed Jamil Ahmed.

revealing a panel. Except for the first, which displayed a composite image,
each of the five panels of the scroll that illustrated the plot was further
divided into four sub-panels. Each time the change of the panels took
place, the *nachiye* and the drummer moved downstage to execute an
entertaining dance, so as to draw the attention of the spectators away
from the action of the scroll-bearers.

The performance proceeded in six stages, each of which was visualized in
one of the six panels of the scroll. The *gayen* sang the libretto of each stage,
moved to the rhythm of the music, and pointed to the relevant panel of the
scroll to visually emphasize her argument. In the first stage, the *gayen*
praised Allah, the Forest Goddess, and the saints for creating the wonder
that is the Sundarbans. In the second stage, she described the forest in the
past when it was rich in biodiversity, the traditional resource users thrived
by harvesting natural resources of the forest and farmers cultivated their
farmland outside the forest, reaping a bountiful harvest. However,
a gradual rise in salinity disturbed this balance. The custom of the traditional resource users of the past, as the *gayen* reminded the spectators in the
third stage, pursued a set of locally evolved practices underpinned by religious
dictum that protected the Sundarban from over-exploitation. In the fourth
stage, the *gayen* gave examples of how traditional harvesters of honey and
timber would harvest the forest resources by following the indigenous

knowledge system and cultural practices. But with the rise in population, the number of resource users of the Sundarbans increased, as the *gayen* pointed out in the fifth stage; in consequence, the forest users today are driven by greed and completely disregard the indigenous knowledge system and cultural practices. In the sixth stage, the *gayen* called on the people to change their practices of exploitation, the government to apprehend the culprits, and for all to rise and save the Sundarbans. The performance of Bon Surakshar Pot Gan ended with the panel containing the 'back matter'. The panel displayed a slogan at the top ('In order to save the future generations, you too need to save Sundarbans, a world heritage site') and a credit line at the bottom ('presented by Rupantar in collaboration with Bangladesh UNESCO Commission'). Finally, the performers exited in the reverse order of their entrance.

The mode of presentation of Pot Gan followed by Rupantar is similar for all productions. The performances hold the spectators' interest, and the performers are highly skilled in music and dance. Ideally, before such performances are produced, Rupantar engages in a devising process that begins with field-level research conducted at the area where the Pot Gan performance is to serve as an awareness campaign. Rupantar development workers assigned to the given project gather detailed information from the area, such as the mental makeup of the people, their economic condition, and existing social, human, and environmental problems. This is supplemented with further data obtained from government and non-government organizations. Based on the information gathered, the needs of the region are determined. In the next step, the director, the composer of the libretto of the Pot Gan production, the performers, and the field-level development workers investigate the past, the present, and the future state of the selected issue. From this research, they develop the message to be imparted through the performance. Once the 'why' of the performance is determined, the composer of the libretto begins his work. Composed in six stages, the plot-structure of the libretto proceeds to fulfil the following functions: (Stage i) thematic exposition; (Stage ii) exploration of where the problem is located, and its cause; (Stage iii) elucidation of how the problem proliferates; (Stage iv) explication of the consequences caused by the initial problem; (Stage v) formulation of how the problem can be overcome; and (Stage vi) articulation of what needs to be done (Mondal 2009: 123). For the musical score, popular folk tunes are usually chosen from the target region, and then either the libretto is set to these tunes or vice versa.

At the same time as the composer sets to work, the director, the performers, and the painter of the scroll start to visualize the six stages of the plot on paper. This process follows the principle that each of the six parts of the plot should be illustrated with four images. The entire production team discusses the merit of each visual with the field-level development workers assigned to the project, and they select those that are thought to serve best the intended 'why' of the project. Once the images are finalized, the performers begin their initial rehearsal with parts of the libretto that have, by that time, been set to music, and the painter sets off to execute the images on a scroll. By the time the scroll is ready, about a week later, the libretto has also been set to music, and the performers have completed their initial rehearsal with music. It is now time for full rehearsal with the director, a phase of work that lasts about four or five days. During this period, it is the director who determines the visual composition, choreography, and movement of the *gayen*, the *nachiye*, and the *dhuli*. After conducting run-throughs to check the performance rhythm, followed by necessary 'polishing' as final touches, the production is presented as a 'test' show to the opinion leaders, public representatives, government officials, eminent citizens, artistes, and the public of the region where the project is to be materialized. With the feedback received from the spectators of the test show, further amendments are made to the performance. When this is over, the production is ready for public performances.

Slippage of Rupantar's theatrics: emergence of applied theatricks

If part of Rupantar's mission is to '[b]uild peoples' capacity to cope with the impacts of climate change and natural disaster and to conserve natural bio-diversity' (Rupantar 2014a), then it seeks to effect *rupantar*, that is, transformation, through a top-down and 'banking' process. In this process, there is no room for Freirean 'dialogue ... as the practice of freedom' (Freire 1972: 65). But perhaps this is not surprising, for Rupantar states quite unambiguously that one of the ways in which 'culture and sustainable development are closely connected' is that 'culture can be used as a means for *building awareness* among people, especially among *illiterate* people' ('Popular Publications' n.d.: 13–14, emphases added). Hence, according to its process, it is Rupantar's development workers who conduct field-level research and gather necessary information and it is the production team that develops the message to be imparted through the performance. The performance team disseminates necessary information and instructs the spectators as to what is to be done. In this process, even post-performance feedback from the spectators is not deemed necessary. In actuality, then, the entire process of ascertaining the 'why' of the production is confined to the parameter set by the project's aim and objectives. In turn, these objectives have been determined by the donor or tailored to fit to the donor's agenda. In most cases, Rupantar's development workers play no part in gathering information from the people of the project area, and there is hardly any investigation by the production team on the selected issue. Consequently, Rupantar has to fit its Pot Gan production to the needs of the donors.

Consider, for example, the case of Jalabayu Paribartan Pot Gan produced by Rupantar as a partner of Care Bangladesh, which implemented the Canadian CIDA-funded project 'Reduction of Vulnerability of Climate Change (RVCC)' (Rupantar 2005: 1). The goal of the project was 'to increase capacity of communities in the southwest region of Bangladesh to adapt to the adverse effects of climate change' (Chowhan et al. 2005: 1). It attempted to fulfil its goal by means of a three-pronged approach of awareness, action, and advocacy. Jalabayu Paribartan Pot Gan produced by Rupantar was a part of the awareness-building campaign of the project and was implemented from December 2002 to March 2005 in three administrative districts (Rupantar 2005: 2). A study was indeed carried out on 'Knowledge, Attitudes and Behavior (KAB) related to climate change to set a baseline for awareness activities' (Chowhan et al. 2005: 1), but Rupantar had no part to play in it. It was 'entrusted' only with the task of implementing the 'specific component of awareness' (Rupantar 2005: 2). Confined to the parameter set by INGOs, Jalabayu Paribartan Pot Gan served the donor by disseminating information on climate change and preparing the 'target audience' to adapt to it. As only a cog of a giant 'development' machine built and run by the INGOs to urge people to adapt to climate change, the Pot Gan had nothing to say regarding the action and advocacy components of RVCC.

Consequently, even the top-down banking process that Rupantar deems necessary for devising the Pot Gan performances is hardly ever executed in practice. As a result, the plot structure conceived as proceeding in six stages, in which each stage is to fulfil a specific objective, is never actuated. Consider, for example, the Bon Surakshar Pot Gan. The third stage, which is supposed to elucidate how the problem proliferates, informs spectators how the customs of the traditional resource users of previous times protected the Sundarbans from over-exploitation. Instead of presenting an account of the consequences caused by the initial problem, the fourth stage provides further information on the customs of the traditional harvesters of honey and timber. As Swapan Guha ruefully acknowledges, donor intervention and imperatives dictated by availability of funding hardly ever make it possible to devise a Pot Gan 'as we would ideally like to' (personal communication, 11 July 2014).

Because the Pot Gan productions serve only as cogs of giant 'development' machines run by its donors, it does not follow that the cogs do not have important functions to serve. Consider the case of Jalabayu Paribartan Pot Gan. It urged the people not to be worried or blame themselves for their fate, but live with the disasters arising out of climate change by adjusting to them (Stage vi). However, by focusing only on adaptation to climate change in human systems, and in the process, completely forgetting to remember the notion of mitigation of climate change, Jalabayu Paribartan Pot Gan is crafted as a biopolitical tool that, in the last instance, serves the neoliberal drive for personal responsibility and self-care, by representing all actors 'as entrepreneurs of himself [sic]' (Foucault 2008: 226). This tool is most clearly evident in the slogan displayed on the back matter: 'let us take initiatives to adjust ourselves to these disasters'. What the Pot Gan elides is that the initiative of the people 'has a "price-tag"' in that they as individuals 'have to assume responsibility for these activities and the possible failure thereof' (Lemke 2001: 202).

As part of this, Jalabayu Paribartan Pot Gan makes no mention of 'the historical burden placed on poor countries by industrialised countries, which have not only been the main contributors to the existing stock of anthropogenic GHGs [greenhouse gases], but which also continue to emit at per capita rates that are manifold that of a poor country' (Kapur et al. 2009: 36). One year before the RVCC project was implemented, that is in 2001, Bangladesh was emitting less than 0.1% of global greenhouse gas, compared to 24% by the United States. Nevertheless, it was already 'taking steps to reduce its future emissions through the development of renewable energy and the use of (relatively clean) natural gas' (Huq 2001: 1617). Surprisingly, the Pot Gan maintains silence on this fact, and instead lays the blame of climate change squarely on the Government of Pakistan, which had built embankments, sluice gates, and polders in the 1960s (when Bangladesh was a part of Pakistan), to save the region from flood. At the same time, it maintains silence on the Kyoto Protocol to the United Nations Framework Convention on Climate Change, according to which the developed nations had pledged to reduce emissions by an average of 5% by the period 2008–12 (BBC 2013). The silence is understandable because Canada renounced the protocol, and its main trading partner, the United States, ever intended to ratify it. Hence a CIDA-funded project finds it useful to lay a major part of the responsibility of climate change on Pakistan (a 'valuable' villain since the Liberation War of 1971) and relegate the Kyoto Protocol to the shadows.

Jalabayu Paribartan Pot Gan speaks explicitly not only by what it visibly and audibly articulates but also implicitly by the silences that it maintains and the shadows that are cast around it. Once again, the Pot Gan performance bares its actual intent of operating as a neoliberal apparatus that relegates 'areas of social responsibility [to] a matter of personal provisions' (Lemke 2001: 201).

By cautioning spectators that the environment is changing, that natural disasters are increasing, and that these disasters cannot be resisted, Jalabayu Paribartan Pot Gan plays up the fear factor that developed countries often mobilize against under-developed countries in climate change negotiations: 'that the most adverse effects of climate change will be on developing countries and, therefore, it is in the *interest* of developing countries to negotiate some kind of deal on climate change since it is their future that is most at risk' (Kapur et al. 2009: 36, emphasis added). Unsurprisingly, CIDA can safely play up the fear factor, for 'North America [is] a locale with nations financially well-situated to avoid the worst of climate change harms for the longest duration through financial buttressing' (Kretz 2012: 9). At this instance, a transparent neoliberal agenda is made manifest as a political project, for what is at work here is 'a new mode of "governmentality", a manner, or a mentality, in which people are governed and govern themselves' (Read 2009: 29). By seeking to 'conduct' the people of south-western Bangladesh by conducting Rupantar through CARE Bangladesh, Canadian CIDA 'governs', that is, structures the possible field of action of those people by working through the interest generated from the fear factor. It is thus that the 'Western' donors, INGOs, and national NGOs 'create the context for the emergence of new forms of neoliberal governmentalities that are transnational' (Cotoi 2011: 121).

If Jalabayu Paribartan Pot Gan is an example of how Rupantar sought to challenge climate change in 2003 (when the Government of Bangladesh was yet to devise a strategy and action plan), then the Bon Surakshar Pot Gan, produced in 2013, can serve as an indicator as to how it challenges the issue a decade later. Conceived with the goal of '[s]ustainable conservation of the Sundarbans through indigenous knowledge and culture promotion' (Rupantar 2014b: 3), Bon Surakshar Pot Gan was funded by the UNESCO and performed ten times in Khulna region for over 5,600 spectators (Nisha 2014: 1; Rupantar 2014b: 10–11). Although the Pot Gan admirably urges the people to respect and return to indigenous knowledge and culture that conserved the biodiversity of the Sundarbans in the past (Fakir 2013), it nevertheless fails to examine how climate change has affected the economic infrastructure of the region, which in turn has forced the people of the region to adopt practices that are currently destroying the biodiversity. Once again, the Pot Gan places the responsibility on the people to change their practices of exploitation, and once again, it is subsumed by the biopolitical tool that serves the neoliberal call for 'personal responsibility' and 'self-care'.

It is not surprising, therefore, that Bon Surakshar Pot Gan, which speaks so passionately about protecting the Sundarbans, relegates the proposed Rampal Power Plant project into the shadows by remaining silent about it. The power plant, a coal-fired joint venture of Bangladesh Power Development Board (BPDB) and National Thermal Power Corporation (NTPC) of India, is to be constructed at Rampal, located 14 km north of the Sundarbans (Rahman 2014). When completed in 2020, the plant is expected to produce 1,320 MW electricity. Rampal Power Plant project has stirred the environmental activists in Bangladesh to protest against it by contending that 'water diversion to the plant, coupled with air and water pollution and heavy coal barge traffic, could leave the Sundarbans . . . an increasingly degraded ecosystem, potentially threatening the livelihoods of some of the half-million people who depend on the great mangrove forest' (Hance 2013). They have observed that the project not only violates the Environmental Impact Assessment Guidelines for Coal-based Thermal Power Plants but also refuses to obtain Environmental Clearance from the Department of Environment, which stipulates that 'such projects should be outside a twenty-five kilometre radius from the outer periphery of any ecologically sensitive areas' (Kumar 2013).

However, the Prime Minister of the Government of Bangladesh believes that the environmental activists, in opposing the power plant, are conspiring against development and has promised that the government 'will not do anything harmful for world's largest mangrove forest' (Asif 2013). Rupantar, too, argues against the environmental activists, and that more than the detrimental effect of the Rampal Power Plant, the mangrove forest is threatened by human misuse of the forest resources. To prove both the parties wrong, and as if by divine intervention, an oil-tanker carrying 350,000 litres of furnace oil sank at the Sela River of Sundarbans on 9 December 2014. In eight days, the oil slick spread to a second river and a network of canals covering an area of over 350 km^2. At the time of writing (January 2015), only 70,000 litres of oil have been cleaned up.

Rupantar may remain silent regarding the Rampal power plant, and the government may insist the plant will actually develop the region, but what may actually be at work in and around Rampal is what Naomi Klein calls 'disaster capitalism', that is, the 'orchestrated raids on the public sphere in the wake of catastrophic events, combined with the treatment of disasters as exciting market opportunities' (2007: 6). It is not accidental that Rampal, which lies in Mangla sub-district under Bagerhat administrative district, was severely affected by the category-4 tropical cyclone Sidr on 15 November 2007. Eighteen months later, on 25 May 2009, the region was hit once again by a category-1 cyclone named Aila. Not surprisingly, eight months after Aila, Bangladesh and India agreed to build a coal-fired power plant at Rampal. Two years later, on 29 January 2012, BPDB and NTPC signed a contract to build the plant as a joint venture, involving US$ 1.5 billion as capital cost.

Encouraged by the Rampal Power Plant project, finance capital began to flow to Rampal and its vicinity, a 10 km^2 area stretching from Sapmari in Rampal to Jaymani, the last human settlement before the Sundarbans, located a few hundred metres from the forest. Its objective is to buy land cheaply from the local population traumatized by impending climate change threat manifested by Sidr and Aila and launch industrial projects such as shipyards, liquefied petroleum gas bottling plants, and ready-made garment factories, which would be hazardous for the Sundarbans. The entrepreneurs backing the projects are influential politicians who possess enough social capital to override clearance of the Department of Environment.

Indeed, the 'gold rush' of finance capital to Rampal-Jaymani recalls a similar rush of foreign investors and international lenders to the tsunami-devastated coastline of Sri Lanka, to build large resorts (Klein 2007: 9). As Read comments, neoliberalism 'claims to present not an ideal, but a reality: human nature' (Read 2009: 26). Hence, such an outcome is expected in an economic system 'where impersonal relations and objects [*Versachtlicht*] replace personal relation of dependence, and where the accumulation of capital becomes an end in itself and, by and large, irrational' (Löwy 2002: 77). More importantly perhaps, the rush of finance capital to Rampal-Jaymani brings home an important transformation to the familiar postcolonial binary of the 'West' and the Rest, for the finance capital at work in the region is from Bangladesh and India. But then, national markers are immaterial here, for the neoliberal *homo economicus* 'as entrepreneur of himself [sic], being for himself his own capital, being for himself his own producer, being for himself the source of [his] earnings' (Foucault 2008: 226), unceasingly spurred by cost–benefit calculations and market criteria, is liberated from all markers – race, gender, nation, and more. Be that as it may, Rupantar's silence on Rampal-Sapmari does render quite hollow its claim to a mission to '[b]uild peoples' capacity to cope with the impacts of climate change and natural disaster and to conserve natural bio-diversity' (Rupantar 2014a).

From the local to the global: what the doing of applied theatre does

Well-crafted and popular Pot Gan performances that Rupantar have been performing since 1996 may be actively engaged in 'change', but the 'change' acts for neoliberal systematicity. Consequently, the performances slip as applied theatricks by serving as localized assemblages of governmental technique that attempt to produce hybridized and crystallized local specificity of neoliberal 'entrepreneurs of the self, engaged in self-interested conduct as personal investment' (Dilts 2011: 139). The slippage is not an exception but appears to be a general trend among the NGOs in Bangladesh. As Uddin (2013: 207) has shown, 'the much lauded micro-credit organizations [such as Grameen Bank and BRAC] push neoliberal ideologies onto rural borrowers' by means of microcredit, because these financial instruments 'can be regarded as a form of governmentality that is exercised via a generalised control over people's behaviour and over their beliefs, and by spreading the values of entrepreneurship with the "market" as the solver of all ills'. Importantly, it is not what an applied theatre process *stands* for in terms of its constitutive elements (indigenous or otherwise), but what it *acts* for, in this case neoliberalism, that defines its ethical contour. For example, the process followed by Winter/Summer Institute (WSI) in Theatre for Development, launched by the coordinated effort of four universities from the United States, the United Kingdom, South Africa and Lesotho, ostensibly seeks to 'challenge[. . .] participants to create issue-based, aesthetically provocative, entertaining theatre' in the rural mountain villages of Lesotho (WSI 2014a). Developing productions in Lesotho, such as *It's Just You and Me . . . and My Wife and Your Boyfriend* (2008), involves gathering and discussing information from experts, NGOs active in the field, medical personnel, community activists, and so on, then devising a theatre piece by employing Boalian techniques, followed by 'testing' the production to a local audience. Finally, the production is presented to remote villages in Lesotho that would be unlikely to have been exposed to theatre or information on HIV/AIDS, and then WSI engages the villagers in a five-day workshop in order to transfer the theatrical knowledge necessary for them to produce such plays by themselves.

Although WSI's theatre-making processes may be participatory, both in the devising phase and in the post-performance phase, they are often marked by deep divide between the TfD practitioner ('we') and the 'target' population ('they'), As Maurya Wickstrom (2012: 98) observes from first-hand experience of a workshop exploring HIV/AIDS conducted by WSI in 2010, the 'we' hypocritically disavows, without the slightest self-interrogation or ethical qualm, that it is necessary to question if any of its members ('we') could be infected, agree to the need to be tested, or disclose their HIV status, before it sought, as in its work conducted in Lesotho in 2008, to urge the 'target population' ('they') to come out in the open and get tested for HIV (WSI 2014b). More importantly, by insisting the complex relationship between economic poverty and HIV/AIDS is bi-directional, 'in that poverty is a key factor in transmission and HIV/AIDS can impoverish people in such a way as to intensify the epidemic itself' (Drimie 2002: 7), WSI performances bare their neoliberal underpinnings that relegate social responsibility to self-care. This argument is unequivocally supported by Ansell's findings that the responses to AIDS in Lesotho, a country that has the third highest HIV prevalence in the world, 'are hybrid products of local and global discourses, [and] the power relations underlying them are such that they, often unintentionally, serve a neoliberal agenda by depicting young people as individuals in need of saving; of developing personal autonomy or of exercising individual rights' (2010: 1).

Ironically, impervious to the process whereby applied theatre inevitably slips under neoliberalism to emerge as applied theatricks, self-aggrandising applied theatre practitioners, imbued with uninterrogated self-righteousness and obligatory instrumentalism, believe that applied theatre, as 'the agency of intervention', can force 'its way into *closed* worlds', 'to alter the dynamics of a *static* situation' (Prentki 2009: 181, emphasis added). Practitioners working within this paradigm fit their work into the para-meter Epskamp sets for Theatre for Development, that is a 'development support communication device' (2006: 5) deployed '[t]o inform and per-suade people to adopt certain behaviours and practice beneficial to them' (2006: 109). They believe colonialism and its legacy of neo-colonialism induce passivity in the static situation of the closed world. Hence, they argue, it is necessary to mobilize 'the external involvement of a decolonising agent such as the facilitator of an applied theatre process' (Prentki 2009: 182). Faced with such assertions and arguments, one can only refer back to Rupantar in Bangladesh and WSI in Lesotho and agree with Foucault that '[p]eople [read applied theatre practitioners] know what they do; they frequently know why they do what they do; but what they don't know is what they do does' (qtd. in Dreyfus and Rabinow 1983: 187).

When 'what they do does' is pointed out, they premise their counter-argument with *a priori* knowledge that 'in a world where war, famine, poverty, globalization, and the curtailing of human rights will be insidious features for some time yet, development in its various guises *will be a reality*' (Preston 2004: 230, emphasis added). They assert with self-righteous zeal that the 'guise' (defined as 'an external appearance of presentation typically concealing the true nature of something' by the Oxford English Dictionary), which they are committed to, is that of 'play[ing] a radical role in transforming [the] dominant discourses through liberating, transformative agendas' (Preston 2004: 230). With such ideological underpinnings, often hidden and at other times quite explicit, applied theatre practitioner Jane Plastow (2007) launches herself to Eritrea to undo the effects of an education which serves 'inevitably to alienate children from their home communities, [and] inculcate in them a sense of inferiority towards more dominant cultures' by means of two three-day-long workshops (2007: 345). At the end of the stipulated period, she had effected a magical transformation: the 'dumbstruck pupils, who spoke only in tiny voices, from behind their hands, and with much nervous giggling', had grown 'enormously in confidence' (Plastow 2007: 353). And then there is the example of Velda Harris and her second-year BA students, who parachute in to a remote Azeri camp for displaced people to run TIE programmes for large groups of children (up to eighty or even 100). Without 'setting up consultancy and communication networks with teachers in the camps' (2005: 105) and without any form of follow-up activity, she confidently claims that she and her students had turned into pebbles in a pool, and the resulting ripples of change 'will continue to spread' (2005: 106). Stuck with outmoded and dysfunctional analytical tools, the TfD/Applied Theatre practitioners fail to comprehend that despite being mauled by colonialism, the world of the colonial and the post-colonial has hardly ever been static, or its people, 'potatoes in a sack' (Marx 1977: 317). Rather, it has been and is, as Fanon passionately asserts, a 'zone of occult instability' with its 'hidden life, teeming and perpetually in motion' (1968: 227, 224). Today, when subaltern farmers in countries such as Bangladesh, Vietnam, China, and India own mobile phones and use them to connect with agents and traders to estimate market demand and the selling price, and when 50% of these farmers make arrangements for sale over the phones (Halewood and Surya 2012: 39), how can the world of these farmers be passive and closed? As I have argued elsewhere, the subaltern inhabiting a world thought to be static, and closed, engages in the infrapolitics enacted through discreet strategies and disguised efforts, which are all aimed at minimizing or thwarting attempts at material appropriation of labour, production, and property by the dominant classes (Ahmed 2009: 73).

With the best of intentions, many applied theatre practitioners, forgetting to remember that we all live in a globalizing world where the neoliberal project is increasingly the norm, blindly assume that a divide exists between the capitalist 'West' and the victims of colonialism, neo-colonialism, and imperialism in the Rest. They fail to comprehend that the neoliberal *homo economicus*, who is unceasingly accumulating capital, spurred only by impersonal and abstract logic of cost–benefit calculations, erased of all identitarian markers, is at work in both the 'West' and the 'Rest'. Already, China, India, Russia, and Brazil have emerged as the second, third, sixth, and seventh largest economies in the world, respectively, and although the New Development Bank set up by the BRICS economies signals a serious challenge to the IMF and the World Bank, it is not a sign of a new financial world order (Hartley 2014). It is thus that the world economy is moving by the logic of *matsyanaya* ('justice in the world of fish') as described by the ancient political treatises of South Asia, where any 'big fish' (in this case, a large financial capital) will buy out or attempt to outmanoeuvre those lesser to it in size. Because the capital, which determines the size of these 'fishes', is a collective product, we all are implicated in the worldwide dealings of finance capital with which the neoliberal institutions ply the globalized market – by the goods and services that we all buy or sell. There is no denying that capital is not only personal but also a social power. However, the process by which Marx and Engels believed that change in the social character of capital will inevitably convert it 'into the property of all members of society' (2010: 23) has already been largely subverted by the neoliberal project of 'encoding the social domain as a form of the economic domain', such that 'cost-benefit calculations and market criteria [are being] applied to decision-making processes within the family, married life, professional life, etc.' (Lemke 2001: 200). And if this political project of neoliberalism succeeds, there will be no 'discrete and identifiable firms, producers, households, consumers, fathers, mothers, criminals, immigrants, natives, adults, children, or any other, fixed category of human subjectivity'; there will only be 'heterogeneous human capital, distinct in their specific attributes, abilities, natural endowments, skills' (Dilts 2011: 138).

Cognizing the world with archaic and incapacitated analytical tools, applied theatre practitioners sometimes fail to notice, unlike Wickstrom

(2012: 99), that their assumed divide between the 'West' and the Rest 'makes it the precondition for TfD work'. Charged with jihadi interventionist agendas that attempt to impose development, applied theatre practitioners ceaselessly working today to dismantle the distance between the 'West' and the Rest are impervious to the actuality that they have to constitute the distance itself in 'the attempt at suppressing the distance' (Rancière 2007: 277). Consequently, interventions devised by agents such as Rupantar in Bangladesh (and other agencies, including WSI in Lesotho) can only fashion a process of political action which, in the last instance, acts for the neoliberal project.

Instead of seeking to intervene in non-existent worlds that are static and closed, I urge applied theatre practitioners to radically shift their epistemological perspective and invite them to apply their artistry and skill in theatre as 'storytellers', by adopting the ambiguous and liminal attributes of the trickster, 'the spirit of disorder, the enemy of boundaries' (Kerényi 1972: 185). As tricksteresque storytellers (sans their development and intervention baggage), they should engage in 'play', operating, as it were, as 'a "shadow warrior", or Kagemusha', recognizing that both storytelling and play retain 'a dangerous harmlessness' (Turner 1986: 32), for neither knows fear. Because the tricksteresque play of the applied-theatre-practitioners-turned-storytellers could seek to subvert the neoliberal project of 'encoding the social domain as a form of the economic domain', by working as Kagemushas alongside the subaltern classes, to 'tell' stories so that self-care can be re-visioned as social care. I see great promise here because, of all the art forms, it is theatre that can create a tangible sense of community in the act of its shaping and performing. This, then, is my fairy tale of the twenty-first century!

References

Ahmed, S.J. 2009. 'Performing and supplicating Manik Pir: Infrapolitics in the domain of popular Islam'. *TDR: The Drama Review* 53.2: 51–76.

Ansell, N. 2010. 'The discursive construction of childhood and youth in AIDS interventions in Lesotho's education sector: Beyond global–local dichotomies'. *Environment and Planning D: Society and Space* 28: 791–810.

Asif, S. 2013. 'PM backs coal-based power plant at Rampal' http://news.priyo.com/2013/11/13/pm-backs-coal-based-power-plant-rampal-91196.html. Last accessed 16 July 2014.

BBC. 2013. 'A brief history of climate change'. www.bbc.com/news/science-environment-15874560. Last accessed 15 July 2014.

BCCRF (Bangladesh Climate Change Resilience Fund). 2014. 'Bangladesh Climate Change Resilience Fund'. http://bccrf-bd.org/. Last accessed 19 July 2014.

Chowhan, G., Barman, S.K. and SAFE Development Group. 2005. *The Reducing Vulnerability to Climate Change (RVCC) Project: Reflecting on Lessons Learned*. Dhaka: CARE Bangladesh.

Cotoi, C. 2011. 'Neoliberalism: A Foucauldian perspective'. *International Review of Social Research* 1.2: 109–124.

Dilts, A. 2011. 'From "entrepreneur of the self" to "care of the self": Neo-liberal governmentality and Foucault's ethics'. *Foucault Studies* 12: 130–146.

Dreyfus, H.L. and Rabinow, P. 1983. *Michel Foucault: Beyond Structuralism and Hermeneutics*. Chicago: University of Chicago Press.

Drimie, S. 2002. *The Impact of HIV/AIDS on Rural Households and Land Issues in Southern and Eastern Africa, a background paper prepared for the Food and Agricultural Organization, Sub-Regional Office for Southern and Eastern Africa*. ftp://ftp.fao.org/docrep/nonfao/ad696e/ad696e00.pdf. Last accessed 16 January 2015.

Epskamp, K. 2006. *Theatre for Development: An Introduction to Context, Application and Training*. London: Zed Books.

Fakir, E. 2013. 'Pot Song on Jungle Protection' (Unpublished translation of *Bon Surakshar Pot Gan*). Rupantar Theatre Archive, Rupantar, Khulna.

Fanon, F. 1968. *The Wretched of the Earth*. New York: Grove Press Inc.

Foucault, M. 2008. *The Birth of Biopolitics: Lectures at the Collège de France, 1978–79*. New York: Palgrave Macmillan.

Freire, P. 1972. *Pedagogy of the Oppressed*. Harmondsworth: Penguin Education.

Halewood, N.J. and Surya, P. 2012. 'Mobilizing the agricultural value chain' in *Information and Communication Development: Maximizing Mobile*. Washington DC: World Bank, pp. 31–43. http://siteresources.worldbank.org/EXTINFORMATIONANDCOMMUNICATIONANDTECHNOLOGIES/Resources/IC4D-2012-Report.pdf. Last accessed 28 July 2014.

Hance, J. 2013. 'A key mangrove forest faces major threat from a coal plant'. *Environment 360*, 29 October. http://e360.yale.edu/feature/a_key_mangrove_forest_faces_major_threat_from_a_coal_plant/2704/. Last accessed 17 July 2014.

Harris, V. 2005. 'Parachuting in: Issues arising from drama as intervention within communities in Azerbaijan' in Billingham, P. (ed.) *Radical Initiatives in Interventionist and Community Drama*. Bristol: Intellect, pp. 85–107.

Hartley, J. July 28 2014. 'The BRICS bank is born out of politics'. *Forbes* www.forbes.com/sites/jonhartley/2014/07/28/the-brics-bank-is-born-out-of-politics/. Last accessed 28 July 2014.

Huq, S. 2001. 'Editorial: Climate change and Bangladesh'. *Science*, New Series, 294.5547: 1617.

Kapur, D., Khosla, R. and Mehta, P.B. 2009. 'Climate change: India's options'. *Economic and Political Weekly*. 44.31: 34–42.

Kerényi, K. 1972. 'The trickster in relation to Greek mythology' in Radin, P. (ed.) *The Trickster: A Study of American Indian Mythology* (with commentaries by K. Kerényi and C.G. Jung). New York: Schocken Books, pp. 173–191.

Khan, M., Zakir, H., Haque, M. and Rouf, M. 2013. *An Assessment of Climate Finance Governance Bangladesh*. Dhaka: Transparency International.

Klein, N. 2007. *The Shock Doctrine: The Rise of Disaster Capitalism*. New York: Picador.

Kretz, L. 2012. 'Climate change: Bridging the theory-action gap'. *Ethics and the Environment* 17.2: 9–27.

Kumar, C. 24 September 2013. 'Bangladesh power plant struggle calls for international solidarity'. *The World Post*. www.huffingtonpost.com/chaitanya-kumar /bangladesh-power-plant-st_b_3983560.html. Last accessed 16 July 2014.

Lemke, T. 2001. '"The birth of bio-politics": Michel Foucault's lecture at the Collège de France on neo-liberal governmentality'. *Economy and Society* 30.2: 190–207.

Löwy, M. 2002. 'Marx, Weber and the critique of capitalism'. *Logos* 1.3: 77–86.

Maplecroft. 2014. 'New Products and Analysis' http://maplecroft.com/about/ne ws/ccvi.html. Last accessed 19 July 2014.

Marx, K. 1977. 'The eighteenth Brumaire of Louis Bonaparte' in McLellan, D. (ed.) *Karl Marx: Selected Writings*. Oxford: Oxford University Press, pp. 300–325.

Marx, K. and Engels, F. 2010. *Manifesto of the Communist Party*. www.marxists .org/archive/marx/works/download/pdf/Manifesto.pdf. Last accessed 29 July 2014.

MoEF (Ministry of Environment and Forest). 2009. *Bangladesh Climate Change Strategy and Action Plan 2009*. Dhaka: Ministry of Environment and Forest, Government of the People's Republic of Bangladesh.

Mondal, K.U. 2009. *Unnayan Nattya-e Babahrita Nattya Angik Prosongo: Rupantar* (On the Subject of the Theatre Forms Used in Development Theatre: Rupantar). Khulna: Rupantar.

Nisha, A. 2014. 'Prodorshito Pot Gan' (an unpublished report on Pot Gan performances by Rupantar). Rupantar Theatre Archive, Rupantar, Khulna.

Plastow, J. 2007. 'Finding children's voices: a pilot project using performance to discuss attitudes to education among primary school children in two Eritrean villages'. *Research in Drama Education: The Journal of Applied Theatre and Performance*, 12.3: 345–354.

Popular Publications as Development Communication (Brochure). n. d. Khulna: Rupantar.

Prentki, T. 2009. 'Introduction to intervention' in Prentki, T. and Preston, S. (eds.) *The Applied Theatre Reader*. Routledge: Milton Park, Abingdon, pp. 181–183.

Preston, S. 2004. 'An argument for transformative theatre in development: Continuing the debate'. *Research in Drama Education* 9.2: 229–235.

Rahman, M. 2014. '1320 MW Rampal Power Project' www.fairbd.net/Details.php? Id=518. Last accessed 16 July 2014.

Raillon, C. 2014. 'Climate Change and Natural Disasters in Bangladesh: Humanitarianism and the Challenge of Resilience'. www.urd.org/Climate-change-and-natural. Last accessed 12 July 2014.

Rancière, J. 2007. 'The emancipated spectator'. *Artforum*, pp. 271–280 http://members.efn.org/~heroux/The-Emancipated-Spectator-.pdf. Last accessed 27 July 2015.

Read, J. 2009. 'A genealogy of homo-economicus: Neoliberalism and the production of subjectivity'. *Foucault Studies* 6: 25–36.

Riquet, D. 2012. *Review of Development Partners' response to cyclone Aila* (final report commissioned by Disaster Management and Relief Division, Ministry of Food and Disaster Management). www.solutionexchange-un.net/repository/bd/cdrr/update14-res1-en.pdf. Last accessed 21 July 2014.

Rupantar. 2005. 'RVCC Final Report' (unpublished report). Rupantar Archives, Rupantar, Khulna.

Rupantar. 2012. *Annual Report 2012*. Khulna: Rupantar.

Rupantar. 2014a. 'About Rupantar: Rupantar Profile' www.rupantar.org/index.php?option=com_content&view=article&id=90&Itemid=482. Last accessed 5 July 2014.

Rupantar. 2014b. 'Completion Report on Conservation of the Sundarbans (the World Heritage Site) through Indigenous Knowledge and Culture (CSIKC) Project' (unpublished report). Project Management and Monitoring and Evaluation Department, Rupantar, Khulna.

Rupantar Method of Development Communication (Brochure) n. d. Khulna: Rupantar.

Sen, A. 1999. *Development as Freedom*. Oxford: Oxford University Press.

Turner, V. 1986. 'Body, brain and culture'. *Performing Arts Journal* 10. 2: 26–34.

Uddin, M.J. 2013. *Microcredit, Gender and Neoliberal Development in Bangladesh*. Helsinki: Department of Social Research, Sociology, University of Helsinki https://helda.helsinki.fi/bitstream/handle/10138/37948/microcre.pdf?sequence=1. Last accessed 29 July 2014.

Wickstrom, M. 2012. *Performance in the Blockades of Neoliberalism*. Basingstoke: Palgrave Macmillan.

WSI (The Winter/Summer Institute). 2014a. 'Make Theatre: Make a Difference' www.maketheatre.org/. Last accessed 29 July 2014.

WSI (The Winter/Summer Institute). 2014b. 'About Us' www.maketheatre.org/aboutthewintersu.html. Last accessed 29 July 2014.

Yu, H.W., Alam, M., Hassan, A., Khan, A.S., Ruane, A.C., Rosenzweig, C., Major, D.C. and Thurlow, J. 2010. *Climate Change Risks and Food Security in Bangladesh*. Abingdon, Oxon: Earthscan. www.wds.worldbank.org/external/default/WDSContentServer/WDSP/IB/2012/05/24/000426104_20120524164749/Rendered/PDF/690860ESW0P1050ClimateoChangeoRisks.pdf. Last accessed 21 December 2013.

CHAPTER 9

Applied theatre and disaster capitalism
Resisting and rebuilding in Christchurch

Peter O'Connor

Some start with long slow rumbles reminiscent of an approaching underground train reaching a fever pitch deep in the earth below your feet. Others are short sharp jolts that disarm. Some are rolling and sliding quakes that turn the land under your feet to jelly. Others are performances of enormous intensity that seem to sharpen and clear the mind at the same time as they cloud and confuse any sense of safety. Still more are deadly, striking in the hearts of cities, causing grief and sorrow on a scale barely imaginable. Earthquakes perform in different ways. They are all spontaneous, unscripted improvisations of the world as it manipulates fault lines and tectonic plates, and although a major earthquake demands a repeat performance, the encore's timing cannot be guaranteed.

In Catania, Sicily, the earthquakes that rumble as a result of Etna's belligerence are managed through devotion to Saint Agata. Her golden image is paraded annually through the city in colourful pageants celebrating the times she has saved the city. Incan gods in Peru and Chile still ward off the evils that live under the South American mountains. In New Zealand, according to Maori understandings, the god Ruaumoko, still at the breast of Earth mother Papatuunuku, is kept warm by the fires in the centre of the world. The rumblings of volcanoes and earthquakes are made by Ruaumoko as he walks around. His wanderings frighten and pummel humans into spectators, into victimhood. They reduce, by their ferocity, any sense of agency, any possibility of resistance. Media representations of earthquakes enforce this sense of helplessness against uncompromising and relentless gods. Insurance companies routinely describe quakes as 'acts of god', implying that humans cannot be expected to be responsible for what has happened.

In September 2010, Ruaumoko stirred deep within the earth, and the Canterbury region of New Zealand was rocked by a magnitude 7.1 earthquake, which caused considerable physical damage but no deaths.

Awakened again, on the 22nd of February 2011, a magnitude 6.3 earthquake killed 185 people in Canterbury's main city, Christchurch. No one realised at the time that this was the opening act of an ongoing communal and personal trauma that was to last for years. Ruaumoko was to prove restless and tireless, stirring time and time again. He would cause over 13,000 aftershocks, bringing liquefaction, the strange process where the earth appears to turn liquid and bubble through the cracks and floods streets and homes. The silt then dries and turns to a dust that chokes and blinds. Ruaumoko generated earth movements in valleys, triggering 'once every 100 year' floods on a regular, almost monthly basis. Houses were evacuated time and again, then abandoned, then pulled down by the thousands; whole areas of the city and suburbs were bulldozed, the land deemed too dangerous and unstable to be built on again.

An earthquake's unscripted arrival then settles into a largely predictable pattern that is mirrored in nearly every earthquake disaster area. In the days following the February quake, international television played the images caught on inner-city CCTV cameras as a backdrop to its stories. These images are barely distinguishable from those that are used in every disaster representation. They show harrowing images of running, panicked crowds, of uncontrolled screaming, weeping, and devastation. A sense of order amongst the chaos is created by the projection of grim-faced officials in orange vests and hats displaying calm, even as aftershocks literally catch them off guard whilst on camera. Politicians take the opportunity to show themselves standing shoulder to shoulder with their citizenry in helicoptered-in appearances. The Mayor of Christchurch, Sir Bob Parker, was previously a television presenter and his composed, reassuring demeanour was reported as helping calm the nerves of the city. But an event of this magnitude meant the performance of the Christchurch narrative would essentially be driven by central government and in particular the Prime Minister, a former Wall Street commodity broker. Prime Minister John Key had been born in Christchurch. The narrative he was to construct was one that combined appeals for public support with the private pursuit of profitable opportunities for disaster capitalism, built on his enduring commitment to neoliberal economic policies.

Neoliberal reshaping of the land

Peter Freebody argues that it is possible that the term 'neoliberalism' is becoming overused in contemporary critical discourse. As he suggests, 'it is certainly a charged descriptor, widely used by the (many) critics and opponents of the set of arrangements it describes, but rarely if ever by "neoliberals" themselves' (2014: 3). Neoliberal reforms were introduced in New Zealand in 1984 and, according to Rashbrooke, successive governments have used these to radically transform the economy 'profoundly altering not only the economy but the social fabric'. Rashbrooke suggests that in the two decades since the introduction of neoliberalism in New Zealand, 'the gap between those at the top and the bottom of the income ladder in New Zealand opened up more rapidly than in any other comparable society' (2013: 27). The driving imperative of neoliberalism is to transfer power from the State to private capital and create profitable new markets in public services, including those catering for the basic necessities of life. This privatisation is 'Fuelled by transnational corporate greed that does not pretend to put people ahead of profits and is rationalised by an ideology that shows contempt for the carnage that it leaves in its wake' (Kelsey 2008). The evidence suggests that the reform of New Zealand's Keynesian-welfarist institutions was faster and more extreme than elsewhere, including other 'liberal welfare states' like Australia or Britain (Ramia and Wailes 2006). Although Freebody (2014) warns against an overreliance on blaming neoliberalism for all the evils of the twenty-first century, understanding New Zealand's unique experience of neoliberalism and how this was woven into the government response to the earthquakes is central to understanding the manner in which the earthquake recovery was performed.

Thirty years of these reforms had created new fault lines of class across New Zealand. Christchurch had separated into two cities; an affluent white middle class and a rich landed upper class, with a poor underclass who lived mainly in the eastern parts of the city. By 2011, the east was suffering debilitating poverty. High rates of unemployment, domestic violence, and high crime were to be expected markers of a nation that had embraced a particularly virulent form of neoliberalism since the 1980s. These social fault lines were severely tested in the series of ongoing quakes. As Hawkins and Maurer (2010) suggest, disasters exacerbate and create further vulnerabilities within communities. Alex Lee (2014), in her research in Christchurch after the quakes, concludes that the notion of social capital plays out clearly in disaster situations, that is, those with less often fare poorly and those with more fare better. The earthquakes severely damaged the Central Business District of Christchurch and as if a neoliberal god was running the show, the earthquakes smacked hardest into the impoverished communities of the east. As Gould suggests, 'even in developed countries, disasters have a knack of finding the poor and vulnerable' (2008: 169).

The experience of the earthquake was felt very differently across the city. Although many, regardless of class, suffered from badly damaged homes and significant personal and economic costs, the distinction between the rich and poor became apparent afterward. The rich were able to pack up and go elsewhere, either nationally or internationally, short term or long term. Of course, the poorest rarely had this opportunity. They were there for the duration. The damage in the East was also made worse as a result of human intervention. Expert warnings of the potential for major earthquake damage in the flat eastern suburbs had been ignored when the new suburbs were built in the late 1980s and early 1990s. Sir Kerry Burke, former chairman of Environment Canterbury (ECan), a regional council body, told the *Star Canterbury* only weeks after the February 22nd quake that property developers had successfully lobbied to develop on land that they knew was prone to liquefaction. Burke said, 'One of the lessons of the earthquake is perhaps we should pay more attention to science rather than to legal arguments from guys with deep pockets' (NZ Herald 2011). The neoliberal shaking and shaping of Christchurch had contributed to the disaster of the earthquake but the class fault lines were to be further deepened by government policy following the disaster.

Naomi Klein defines 'disaster capitalism' as 'orchestrated raids on the public sphere in the wake of catastrophic events, combined with the treatments of disasters, as exciting market opportunities' (2007: 231). She documents how the combination of social disorientation, and the justification of disaster response, created ideal conditions for right-wing economic reform and a reduction in civil rights in New Orleans post Hurricane Katrina. Klein's argument is that there is a growing, worldwide trend to use the disaster to accelerate the undemocratic transfer of public wealth and resources to private hands. Not surprisingly, given New Zealand's deep and long-term commitment to neoliberal policies, the earthquakes in Christchurch provided a similar opportunity. The great financial crisis had already been used to justify austerity measures and had sharpened the class divide in Christchurch. Sweeping law changes then opened up the region to disaster capitalism, which subsequently has had an even more radical impact on the landscape of Christchurch than the initial quakes. While the public faces of the disaster recovery spoke of 'leaving no one behind' and a united and unified country, in the weeks following the February quake John Key met with fifty corporation CEOs to devise a plan for rebuilding Christchurch. Sweeping laws to create the government quango Canterbury Earthquake Recovery Authority (CERA) soon followed. The legislation, enacted in great haste, allowed CERA to 'obtain information from any source; enter and demolish, remove or build land or structures; "require co-operation" between adjoining landowners; and suspend, amend or revoke plans, policies, resource consents, existing use rights or Certificates of Compliance' (Canterbury Earthquake Recovery Act 2011). The NZ Human Rights Commission has since reported that the legislation demonstrated a fundamental disregard for Cantabrians' right to political participation (Joint Submission EQ Impacts [EQI] 2013).

With the government providing the means to circumvent democratic oversight in Christchurch, publicly listed corporate giants Fletcher Construction, Downer, and McConnell Dowell were bonded into the NZ$40 billion rebuilding. The plans for the rebuild included convention centres, new shopping malls and a NZ$500 million rugby stadium and its focus on the city centre left many people in East Christchurch feeling they had been abandoned and forgotten. In the east, 10,000 homes have been bull-dozed as residents have fought insurance companies for compensation. They have nowhere to lodge complaints or to seek redress for the changes wrought on them, not by the earthquake, but by the rebuild process itself. As in New Orleans, the disaster also prompted a neoliberal review of the schooling across the city, with many schools in the east closed, providing ripe ground for the government's wider ambition to further privatise education provision.

Applied theatre in disaster zones

Five actors sit on stage; the West side and East side actors divided by Dante.

Dante stands. A title appears: Dante Bower Ave, February 2012.

Dante takes a swig from the beer in his hand then turns and slowly revolves as he looks around the city.

DANTE: *C-Town. Christ-church. The Gar-den City. Rubble and dust, dust and struggle, struggle and dust, dust and rubble. Crackers getting their panties in a bunch about a cathedral when some people still can't shit in their own houses? Damn, son. Bet Bob Parker shits in his own house. Bet Gerry Brownlee shits in his own house. Bet Gerry Brownlee's got a big fat toilet cos Gerry Brownlee's got a big fat ass. That Jabba the Hutt motherfucker couldn't fit on a chemical toilet even if he was on Survivor going for immunity. 'They' say the quakes have brought us all together but 'they' don't know what the hell they're talking about. It's all a West Side Story, yo. People need to open their eyes: rubble and dust, dust and struggle, struggle and dust, dust and rubble.*

DANTE pulls out a spray can and a stencil, graffitis on the side of the portaloo. It's a stencil of Gerry Brownlee having a shit.

DANTE: Yeah-ya. East-Side, rep-re-SENT!
The opening scene from *Aftershocks* by Victor Rodgers (2013).

The above extract comes from a devised play put on in community halls in the most quake-affected parts of the city. Its highly politicised dialogue is one of the many shapes and forms applied theatre takes within disaster zones. James Thompson, in his study of theatre and performance in war-torn Sri Lanka, writes of the 'multiple performance responses to war, forms that have intersected with therapeutic activities, ritual practices or political demonstrations' (2005:7). Theatre takes place across a broad spectrum of performance, 'connecting it with the wider forces of ritual and revolt that thread through so many spheres of human culture' (Kelleher 2009). Drawing on this notion of the interconnectedness of performances on theatre stages and performances that occur in other sites of the social landscape, and following Thompson's example, I include a wide range of performance practices in my consideration of theatrical responses to the earthquakes in Christchurch. In seeking to reveal a range of performative contexts within the public performance of life in Christchurch after the earthquakes, I recognise that to 'drive an analytic wedge through these initiatives, partitioning them between the social and non social, would deny their delicate and complex relation to their particular contexts and to their troubled but undeniable interconnectedness' (2005: 240).

John Key, in a nationally televised address the day after the February quake, unwittingly spoke a series of truths about the earthquakes. He said, '[t]here is no reason that can make sense of this event. No words that can spare our pain' (Key 2011). In recognising that 'words weren't enough to spare our pain', artists became a vital part of the recovery process for Christchurch. Socially engaged dance, music, traditional Maori performance rituals and processes featured alongside individual art therapies with some of the most traumatised. Much of the work was interdisciplinary and cross disciplinary, echoing the collapse of the city boundaries between art forms disappeared or were reconstructed. Foremost amongst the arts activities were multimedia performance events that existed outside the traditional theatres that had been destroyed in the quakes. Some of these performance events seemed to arise organically from the city, generated out of the rubble and ruin. Other events were state sponsored or came from outside Christchurch. Increasingly these new theatre forms in the city moved beyond a desire to make sense of what was happening, to highlight the senselessness of government responses, or to question government narratives about the rebuild of the city.

Disaster literature often presents the overlapping steps involved in human response to disaster as involving Risk management, Response, Recovery and finally Resilience (see, for example, Myers and Zunin 2000). These Rs are used to inform thinking of both physical and social scientists engaged in disaster research. In applied theatre in disaster zones, the Christchurch experience suggests, however, a different set of 'Rs' that provide a taxonomy of most if not all the applied theatre work I either witnessed or was part of in Christchurch following the quakes. The taxonomy refers to the intentionality of the performances discussed. These are: Rallying, Reflecting, Reclaiming, Relief and Resisting. The boundaries between these classifications are not fixed and questions as to the intentionality of any performance event can and should be interrogated.

Rallying and reflecting

> Today, in the aftermath of this tragedy, and reminded of life's fragility, we come together to share in the unbreakable strength of the ties that bind us. The ties that bind the community of Christchurch, and that bind us as citizens of New Zealand and of the world. Above all we remember those who lives were abruptly taken because they were in the wrong place at the wrong time. There is no justification for their deaths. (John Key 2011)

Over 50,000 people came to the inner Christchurch's Hagley Park for the National Memorial Service held only three weeks after the deadly February 22nd earthquake. Speeches were given by civic and national leaders and Prince William, visiting from the United Kingdom. Stirring Maori haka, massed singing and videos of the city in ruins played on giant screens framed the event. The performances also provided opportunity for a more participatory space where people could find lost friends and share impromptu stories of survival, of loss, of luck, of heroes. The communal sharing of grief was reported as cathartic for a population renowned for its emotional closeness. And many wept as they remembered family and friends who had died and reflected on the events only three weeks before. A ten-minute video showing the cordoned-off areas of the inner city was shown for the first time so that people might see what had happened there. The live televised screening of the service, for those of us watching elsewhere in New Zealand, showed a stilled and silently weeping audience as they gazed at the images on the big screens. The stirring words of Prime Minister John Key were reminiscent of a wartime speech, almost Churchillian in tone, except for the Prime Minister's unfortunate ability to mangle the most simple of sentences. It was designed to rally national and international concern for the plight of the victims of the quakes. The experience of the quake was reflected on in the relatively safe space and framing of a theatrical event for 'in art, trauma is not viewed as an individual, private, or pathological experience, but as shared experience, appropriate to a public forum' (Reisner 2002: 16).

Reisner co-ordinated theatre in Kosovo after the Bosnian conflict. Two years after the war he directed a play that used a traditional story about the death of a bridegroom. He describes this moment when he was approached by an older man in Kosovo after a performance:

> He looked at me, his eyes red, his voiced choked. He spoke, and the translator translated: 'I have seen now more than I ever thought I would see in my life. I went back to my village after the fighting stopped. The villagers dug up a grave and lined up thirty corpses. My neighbors. My friends. My cousin. I didn't cry. I saw many terrible things, and I did not cry. But today I am crying. Why? Why? Before now I couldn't cry. But today I am crying. Why – Why???' I was shaken up, and gave an answer that I can only hope was improved by the translator. But the answer I wish I had given would be, 'Before, there were no tears because, before, tears were not enough to express what you were feeling'. (2002: 27)

Reisner recognises that theatre provides a space for the communal sharing of grief, but perhaps this needs to be understood within the wider political framing of the theatrical event. One anonymous blogger on a government website wrote about the event: 'I looked across the park and reminded myself, when I shook, you shook. When I was woken in the middle of the night, you were too. When I was afraid, I was not alone. "We are all in this together"' (Quake Stories 2012). Another Christchurch blogger was somewhat more suspicious about the memorial event: 'The New Zealand government cynically used a memorial service last Friday, featuring Britain's Prince William, to smother rising discontent over the grossly inadequate relief given to those whose homes have been damaged or who have lost their jobs as a result of the earthquake that hit Christchurch, the country's second largest city, on February 22. While praising the "resilience" of Christchurch residents, none of the speakers mentioned the desperate situation still facing thousands whose houses have been ruined and who have spent weeks without basic services such as water, sewerage and electricity' (Worldwide Socialist Web 2012).

Other State-organised theatrical events that have occurred in the four years since the start of the quakes have provided the opportunities for mass ritualised outpourings of grief. They have also provided the space for a communal catharsis – which some in Christchurch have seen as designed to dampen and quieten political agitation. The rallying calls of these performances, with their deliberate appeal to patriotism and the communal good, gave room for Gerry Brownlee, the minister responsible for the rebuild, to respond to those who complained two years later that they still didn't have proper sanitation: 'I'm sick of these people carping and moaning', he said. 'The constant suggestion that somehow we've abandoned these people or forgotten about them is just the most insulting thing they could possibly say' (Dally 2012). Right-wing blogger Cameron Slater, whom the Prime Minister contacts on a regular basis, was referring meanwhile to the residents of Christchurch East as 'useless pricks and scum who vote Labour' (Slater, in Hager 2014). A week after these claims by the minister, a group convened a Christchurch 'whingers and carpers' party where the advertised event online said, '[c]ome along to our Party. You can write down your troubles when you arrive and post them in our "Worry Box" and leave your worries at the door while you sing and dance the night away.'

There are a number of ironies in this first and the other memorial services held in the years following the Christchurch quake. One is that the same government which fractured the city on class lines prior to the quake, and has perpetuated and deepened those divides with its neoliberal policies since, has also successfully manipulated local and national sentiments through these highly staged performative events. These performances act to unite superficially and simultaneously silence large sections of the community. The public launch of the plan for the city rebuild in July 2012 was a very different performance, where again the Prime Minister was the main actor. At this event, Key was chief businessman rather than people's leader. Business luminaries and the Prime Minister gathered for a televised dinner and revealed plans for convention centres, cafes, restaurants and other business opportunities in the inner city. The video released that night began: 'There is an unprecedented opportunity in the South Island' (Bayer 2012). The people of the eastern suburbs and their 28,000 damaged homes, left untouched since the quakes, were not part of the plan. Mirroring the typical disaster capitalist script, shared public sacrifice was replaced by private and privatised individual gain and opportunity.

The co-option of performance events is not unusual for governments determined to present a unifying narrative in disaster zones. My first engagement with earthquakes and how theatre practitioners worked in communities to make sense of what had happened was in China following the Szechuan earthquakes in 2008. I was invited by a Chinese theatre company to work with theatre companies who had recently returned to Beijing after extended stints in Szechuan immediately after the quake. The groups were genuinely dissatisfied with their efforts and they asked me to reflect on what they had done and consider how they might work differently when they returned to the quake zones. What became clear as we talked about their work was that they felt the role-play techniques they had been using had hindered rather than helped communities understand the implications of what had happened. There was a sense that the replaying of the actual earthquakes had done little more than retraumatise communities rather than provide a space for dialogue that the companies sought. We looked for ways in which we might use other theatre forms to disrupt the naturalistic flow of role-play. As a result, one theatre company returned to Szechuan using traditional acrobatic dance forms, another used dream sequencing and yet another company used forum theatre. Central to the story of the earthquakes in Szechuan was the way in which thousands of children were killed in poorly built schools. Theatre companies were told by the Chinese government that they could continue to work in the earthquake zones if their focus was on telling the story of the State's management of the rebuild rather than create any opportunity for criticism of the government's complicity in the deaths caused by the quality of the school buildings. None of the theatre companies I worked with continued to work in the earthquake zones after this policy was made clear to them.

The anti-democratic impulse in the New Zealand context is clearly at a different level and scale. I remember being worried for the freedoms of the theatre workers in China if they were to continue to work against the rallying demands of the government. In New Zealand, where active democracy is also under constant threat under a neoliberal agenda, this plays out within a largely hidden agenda of corporate profit and a public demeaning of the suffering and genuine concerns of the poor. Theatre companies in the Christchurch context searched for ways to disrupt and resist the homogenisation of the government narrative.

Reclaiming

As jobs, livelihoods, the homes that people lived in and then whole
neighbourhoods disappeared in the months that followed the initial
memorial service, artists became increasingly involved in reclaiming the
physical and spiritual landscape of the city. The most celebrated of the
artistic reclaiming was done by an arts grouping called Gap Filler. Gap
Filler describes itself as offering 'site-specific projects which can help us
celebrate, mourn and criticise all that we've lost; can help us play,
experiment and toy with ideas for the future; can make otherwise
empty areas active; and can ultimately pave the way in the revitalisation
of the city (without using pavement)' (Gap Filler 2011). Gap Filler started
immediately after the September 10th earthquake when an empty site
brought about by the demolition of a badly damaged and very popular
restaurant was transformed by a loose collective of artists into a space
which hosted a temporary garden café, petanque, live music, poetry
readings, outdoor cinema and more. The space operated for two weeks
and became a focal point for hundreds of residents to gather. The artists
involved were at this time voluntary. By the end of 2014, Gap Filler had
established numerous sites across the city and had grown to a paid
organisation with six staff members. Projects included the ironically
named *Stand Your Ground*, described as a 're-inhabitation of urban
space. Three artists re-imagined and overwrote rock piles and monu-
ments in an arresting cross-disciplinary collaboration between video art
and contemporary dance' (GapFiller 2011). As part of a related project,
co-founder of Gap Filler, Ryan Reynolds, coordinated the *Transitional
City Tour*. This project offered locals and visitors to the city alike the
opportunity to explore part of what was once the CBD on foot. The tour
links selected sites, buildings, and landmarks – both notable and
obscure – into a trail that takes participants around a central city loop.
Reynolds said, 'The motivation for this project came from a group of
people who were keen to explore and demonstrate their shared interest in
the Transitional City, and a desire to critique the top-down, "Master
Plan"/Blueprint process.' The project brought together people involved
in fine arts and creative arts disciplines, geography, planning, architecture, and landscape architecture from CPIT, Lincoln University, and the
University of Canterbury. This stood in marked contrast to other tours of
the Central Business District, which were coordinated through the
government and were largely designed for business entrepreneurs to
consider the marvellous opportunities an earthquake can provide.

A further example of the use of theatre to reclaim the landscape was Gap Filler's *The Pallet Pavilion*, created in 2013 as a temporary performance space as all the purpose-built theatres had been destroyed in the quakes. Following the model of sustainable architecture projects or 'Palletecture', such as the Paletten Haus in Vienna, the pavilion at the Nordic Alpine skiing world championships in Germany, Jellyfish theatre in London, and projects by Avatar Architettura in Italy, Pallet Pavilion was built entirely by volunteers using shipping pallets. It is promoted on its website as 'built by the community/for the community' (Gap Filler 2013). From 2013 to 2015, the venue hosted a range of performance and visual art events, some spontaneous, others highly organised. Coralie Winn, another founder of Gap Filler, commented at the time: 'We speak the language of Performance Studies, which actually is the same language as urban design and architecture, it's how people interact with and move through space, and how space performs and how it causes you to perform' (cited in McCaffrey 2013). Gap Filler's reclamation of spaces made ugly by the earthquakes or the legion of bulldozers that destroyed the city's rich architectural heritage echoes debates about the importance of beauty in applied theatre work. The desire to beautify the city, not in a commodified sense but to spread visual and aesthetic pleasure, is based on an under-standing of the vital connection between hope and beauty. As Veronica Baxter suggests, beauty in applied theatre 'can make a difference, create an aspiration for doing good, or even a moment with renewed courage to continue of life's path' (2015: 184).

Resistance

Norman Denzin suggests, 'performance is an act of intervention, a method of resistance, a form of criticism, a way of revealing agency. Performance becomes public pedagogy when it uses the aesthetic, the performative, to foreground the intersection of politics, institutional sites, and embodied experience. In this way performance is a form of agency, a way of bringing culture and the person into play' (2003: 209). Theatre, which always exists in the intersection of the aesthetic, the performative and the political can, be seen ultimately as an act of public performed resistance. In post-disaster capitalism dominated by geopolitical forces creating the unseen, the unheard and the dismissed as whole classes of people, one of the central roles of theatre might be to disclose the stories, the lives of those who exist within or beyond the margins. It is an active resistance to this form of silencing and stilling of people, to again create a form of theatre that sits at the heart of democracy.

Theatre in Christchurch increasingly became involved in contesting the space between the public rallying of government and the neoliberal disaster capitalism that was playing havoc with people's lives across the city. This contestation was about disturbing and unsettling the narratives of a patriotic and selfless Christchurch seeking opportunities at every corner and replacing it with a troubled and more nuanced sense of the city.

The examples of applied theatre chosen to illustrate these ideas are only some of the projects that began to proliferate across the city. Each example shows how different forms and processes engaged communities in different ways to disrupt, challenge and resist government narratives of the rebuild.

MATTHEW: *We live in the Soap Opera of the Christchurch recovery*
BEN: *Heroes, villains, intrigues, cliff-hangers,*
ANDREW: *greedy landlords, people living in sheds and cars,*
PETER: *schoolchildren going hungry, charter schools, education cuts, social services cuts,*
REBECCA: *a state of exception in which anything can be justified in the name of the earthquake*
CAROLINE: *This is a book by Naomi Klein.*
JOSIE: *We are living in the Soap Opera of the recovery clinging on from episode to episode never quite sure when we will learn who is really in charge, what the next twist will be, or even who we really are or when we will be written out*
MATTHEW: *To help Christchurch recover John Key took power away from Bob Parker and the Council*
BEN: *Bob Parker is not so busy doing interviews any more so he has had time during the recovery to write a book*
ANDREW: *Christchurch This is Your Disaster*
MATTHEW: *John Key put Gerry Brownlee as Minister in charge of the disastrous recovery*
PETER: *Sorry the disaster recovery*
JOSIE: *There are no women leading the recovery of Christchurch because it is man's work and you need a hard hat*

The above extract is from *The Lonely and The Lovely: A Different Soap Opera* (2013), which was devised and performed by the members of Different Light Theatre Company, an ensemble of performers perceived to have intellectual disabilities. It troubled and questioned the government narrative of opportunity, of the equally shared trauma of the city. It was a political counter to the government line, that all was well except for the moaners and carpers, the 'pricks and scum' of East Christchurch.

The play troubled notions of a city disabled not by the earthquake but by deliberate government policy. The biting humour provides an insight into how theatre in resisting the neoliberal might 'model ways of critically engaging with it, eluding it, critiquing it, repudiating and ridiculing it, and seek and model ways of being which preserve principles of social collaboration and interdependence' (Harvie 2014: 193), for although John Key might have wondered about how what had happened in Christchurch during the earthquake was interpreted, Different Light highlighted the senselessness and destructiveness of much of his government's response. The play highlights the uncaring nature of the government response and playfully positions it within a soap opera format where the prime minister plays the arch villain intent on maximising the business opportunities of the city at the expense of the poor in the city. The disaster recovery is revealed for what it has been, a disaster for the poorest and most vulnerable in the city.

Different Light Theatre Company, however, found themselves at odds with Gap Filler. Invited to present at the Pallet Pavilion, it became apparent that people in wheelchairs were unable to access the stage. Different Light artistic director, Tony McCaffrey, wrote:

> What was, however, communicated clearly by the presentation, was a lack of consideration for accessibility in the urban regeneration of Christchurch. It was assumed that wheelchair users would not be occupying the stage, or this was just not thought about – this at a time when large sections of the city needs to be redesigned and reconstructed from the ground up. (2013: 6)

McCaffrey goes even further in questioning the agenda of the Gap Filler project:

> Another assumption that the evening exposed was that 'community' is composed of like-minded, like-bodied, flexible urbanites, who are adaptable to changing pop-up projects, transitional structures and gap filling solutions. The flexibility of this community suits the neoliberal agenda. There is a danger that the artpreneurs of the transitional do the work of the neoliberal National and local government for them and the transition is extended, the 'professionals' as Gap Filler refer to them or big government never arrive and leave everything to 'big society'. (2013: 8)

McCaffrey's argument suggests that the success of Gap Filler, at one level, is an excellent example of disaster capitalism at work. It was an enterprising start-up business which took the opportunity to create a niche market to meet the needs of the disaster economy. It builds into a profitable business and becomes mainstream. By 2012, Life in Vacant Spaces (LIVS), an independent Trust, acts as an umbrella organisation working on behalf of Gap Filler and many other groups and individuals to manage privately owned property for landowners. It finds short- and medium-term uses for the countless vacant sites and buildings of the city. LIVS advertises its services to artists as 'a low cost means to test drive a brand and get their name known. It's a means of collaboration and healthy competition between innovators as ideas are shared and synergies are found' (LIVS 2014). Gap Filler is commodified and then claimed by the government to sell its narrative of a successful rebuild of the city, the success of the arts, and the success of the Christchurch spirit. Gap Filler is sold by its government funders as: 'Crucially, business leaders recognise these transitional projects are improving the economic health of the city. Gap Filler's work has supported existing businesses, attracted start-ups and redefined Christchurch as a place to invest or test out new, small-scale ideas' (Creative New Zealand 2015). Instead of Gap Filler acting as a form of resistance, government simply co-opted the critique and passion of Gap Filler to present a public image of Christchurch that is incongruent with the ongoing private lives of its citizens.

Other theatre acts have resisted the co-option of government desire to reframe resistance as creativity, largely because of the one-off community base in which the theatre work originates. Performance artist Mark Harvey facilitated a series of group projects. Harvey's *Productive Promises* in one of the most effected parts of East Christchurch provided practical measures to raise spirits and confidence, including the removal of rubbish accumulating on vacant lots in the mall through a working bee, shifting it from private sites to public space for council staff to collect. In response to requests from residents, Harvey also coordinated a street march declaring: 'We Love New Brighton', manifesting the feelings of residents experiencing a sense of ongoing neglect from civic leaders for a suburb in which earthquake damage and liquefaction had seen significant population flight and the planning for the permanent evacuation of suburbs like Bexley. Harvey was also keen to highlight that there were other ways to conceive of measuring productivity rather than economic rewards, which dominates the government discourse surrounding recovery.

As a neoliberal education agenda descended on the city with the mass closures of the schools which had served as centres for the recovery in the eastern suburbs, the University of Canterbury's *Place in Time's Freeville Project* was a collaborative undertaking between Tim Veling and David Cook, involving school students from Freeville School. At the time of the project, there were plans to abandon Freeville School in 2016, with classes and staff integrated into North New Brighton and Central New Brighton schools. This project considered how the Freeville School's location might appear many years from now. Veling provided students with basic tuition in photography and composition, documenting the school's buildings and playing fields, and enlarging the images and cutting and pasting drawings of how they imagined a future for the site, into their work. These were displayed over two adjacent walls in New Brighton mall, acting as installation, public work of art and checker-board response by numerous individuals to events in their community. At a time when decisions about the future of their community had been taken away from them, Freeville Project actively engaged the community in imagining alternatives.

Applied theatre: speaking to the gods

The manner in which the earthquake story has been performed since that early morning in September 2010 suggests that the newly minted god of disaster capitalism has colluded with Ruaumoko in wrecking a tragic wasteland on large parts of the city of Christchurch. Performance events have made sense of the disaster in government terms and perpetuated the narratives of a united city recovering together. Theatre originally designed to critique has been co-opted into the message of business as usual. Theatre in these years has not provided opportunities to transform or change the lived experiences of those hardest hit by the quakes and government neglect. It would be naïve to think it might be able to do so. But some theatre has also provided a space to reclaim and resist the rallied forces of crisis capitalism. It has done it with a desire to puncture the language of the market that sees in disaster only business opportunity and profit. In reclaiming the voice of the eastern side of the city, theatre has attempted to animate the ruins with more democratic, more human responses to the old and new gods. That the voices are not heard or listened to as the business barons reconstruct the city to meet their own ends does not detract from the value of the theatre work. Finding ways to live amidst the rubble caused by neoliberalism is a challenge for many faced with the steady encroachments of globalised capitalism. The two-fingered salute given by some theatre makers in Christchurch, the collective struggle they reveal, are pointers to ways in which we might act amidst the pervasive and wearying pressure of all that conspires to rob us of our humanity.

References

Baxter, V. 2015. 'Imazamo Yethu-our efforts to engage through theatre' in Prentki, T. (ed.) *Applied Theatre: Development*. London: Methuen Bloomsbury, pp. 169–184.

Bayer, K. 2012. *Christchurch rebuild plan revealed* [Streaming video]. www.nzher ald.co.nz/nz/news/article.cfm?c_id=1&objectid=10823289. Last accessed 23 March 2015.

Creative New Zealand. 2014. www.creativenz.govt.nz/en/arts-development-and-resources/advocacy-toolkit/case-studies/gap-filler. Last accessed 23 March 2015.

Dally, J. 2012. 'Brownlee fed up with moaning residents' www.stuff.co.nz/the-press/news/christchurch-earthquake-2011/7656654/Brownlee-fed-up-with-moaning-residents. Last accessed 17 July 2015.

Denzin, N. 2003. *Performance Ethnography: Critical Pedagogy and the Politics of Culture*. New York: Sage Publications.

Freebody, P. 2014. *Controversies in Education: Orthodoxy and Heresy in Practice and Policy*. New York: Springer.

Gap Filler. 2011. www.gapfiller.org.nz/about. Last accessed 23 March 2015.

Gap Filler. 2011. *Stand your ground (improvised dance performance)* www.gapfiller .org.nz/gap-3b-276-colombo-street-beckenham/. Last accessed 23 March 2015.

Gap Filler. 2013. palletpavilion.com. Last accessed 23 March 2015.

Gould, C. 2008. 'The right to housing recovery after natural disasters'. *Harvard Human Rights Journal* 22: 169–204.

Hager, N. 2014. *Dirty Politics: How Attack Politics is Poisoning New Zealand's Political Environment*. Wellington: Craig Potton Publishing.

Harvie, J. 2014. *Fair Play: Art, Performance and Neoliberalism*. Basingstoke: Palgrave Macmillan.

Hawkins, R. and Maurer, K. 2010. 'Bonding, bridging and linking: Social capital operated in New Orleans following Hurricane Katrina'. *British Journal of Social Work* 40:177–193.

Joint Submission EQ Impacts. 2013. *Joint stakeholder submission: The human rights impacts of the Canterbury earthquakes for the universal periodic review of New Zealand* (submitted 17 June 2013; for 18th Session of the Human Rights Council: January 2014) www.pacifica.org.nz/wp-content/uploads/2010/07/CHC-Branch-Joint-Submission-17-June-final.pdf. Last accessed 15 July 2015.

Kelleher, J. 2009. *Theatre & Politics*. Basingstoke: Palgrave Macmillan.

Kelsey, J. 2008. 'Regulatory responsibility: Embedded neo liberalism and its contradictions'. *Policy Quarterly* 6.2: 36–41.

Key, J. 2011. John Key's Full Speech. www.stuff.co.nz/national/christchurch-earthquake/4694016/John-Keys-full-speech. Last accessed 20 July 2015.

Key, J. 2011. Transcript: John Key's Memorial speech. *New Zealand Herald*, March 11th www.nzherald.co.nz/nz/news/article.cfm?c_id=1&objec tid=10713388. Last accessed 20 June 2015.

Klein, N. 2007. *The Shock Doctrine: The Rise of Disaster Capitalism*. London: Allen Lane.

Lee, A. 2014. 'Casting an architectural lens on disaster reconstruction'. *Disaster Prevention and Management* 22: 5: 480–490.

LIVS. 2014. http://livs.org.nz/home/. Last accessed 23 March 2015.

McCaffrey, T. 2013. *The city disabled; performance retarded: Responses to the earthquakes in Christchurch in performance by people with intellectual disabilities* Paper given at PSi 19, Performance Studies International Conference at University of Stanford, Stanford, CA.

New Zealand Government. 2011. *Canterbury Earthquake Recovery Act* http://www.legislation.govt.nz/act/public/2011/0012/latest/DLM3653522.html. Last Accessed 12 December 2015.

New Zealand Herald. 2011. 'Predictions of liquefaction ignored' http://www.nzherald.co.nz/nz/news/article.cfm?c_id =1&objectid=10711617. Last accessed 25 July 2015.

Quake Stories. 2012. www.quakestories.govt.nz/504/story/. Last accessed 23 March 2015.

Rashbrooke, M. 2013. *Inequality: A New Zealand Crisis.* Wellington: Bridget Williams Books.

Ramia, G. and Wailes, N. 2006. 'Putting wage-earners into wage earners' welfare states: The relationship between social policy and industrial relations in Australia and New Zealand'. *Australian Journal of Social Issues* 41.1: 49–68.

Reisner, S. 2002. 'Staging the unspeakable: A report on the collaboration between theatre arts against political violence, the associzione culturale altrimenti and 40 counsellors in training in Pristina, Kosovo'. *Psychosocial Notebook* 3:9–30.

Thompson, J. 2005. *Digging up Stories.* Manchester: Manchester University Press.

Thompson, J. 2009. *Performance Affects.* Basingstoke: Palgrave Macmillan.

World Wide Socialist Web. 2012. www.wsws.org/articles/2011/.../eqnz-m22.sht. Last accessed 23 March 2015.

Zunin L.M. and Myers, D. 2000. *Training Manual for Human Service Workers in Major Disasters,* 2nd edn. Washington, DC: Department of Health and Human Services, Substance Abuse and Mental Health Services Administration, Center for Mental Health Services; DHHS Publication No. ADM, 90–538 www.mentalhealth.org/publications/allpubs/ADM90-538/tmsection1.asp. Last accessed 20 July 2015.

PART III

Poetics and participation

CHAPTER 10

Applied theatre and participation in the 'new' South Africa
A possible politics

Mark Fleishman

In the words of political scientist, Lawrence Hamilton, the majority of South Africans post-apartheid continue to live in a state of what he refers to as 'unfreedom' – they have acquired freedom in terms of the law but do not have the power to benefit from it (2011: 355). This chapter explores the extent to which participatory performance projects, particularly among those sectors of society that remain 'unfree' in South Africa today (and among the youth in particular), might intervene to counter perceptions of a 'neo-liberal squeeze on democracy' and the weakening of active citizenship in a context in which:

> The dream of a people's democracy has been shrunk from the triad of strong representative, associational and participatory democracy to a form of weak representational democracy. (Satgar 2012: n.p.)

The chapter will engage with questions that arise from participatory theatre practices that work in alliance with more established and resourced organisations, and the possible politics they might give rise to in particular with regard to the notion of authority. In order to ground these ideas, the chapter will focus on two long-term participatory performance projects with marginalised youth conducted by Magnet Theatre, a company I founded together with Jennie Reznek in 1987, with strong links to the University of Cape Town (UCT) where I have taught since 1991.

The first project, the Clanwilliam Arts Project (2001–ongoing), based in the small town of Clanwilliam 300 km north of Cape Town, is an eight-day arts residency for rural school learners free for all who wish to participate on a voluntary basis. It is based on stories from the Bleek and Lloyd Collection, the most extensive and important archive of San (particularly /Xam) culture. These stories were narrated to linguist Wilhelm Bleek and his sister-in-law, Lucy Lloyd, in the mid-nineteenth century and transcribed in more than 13,000 notebooks now housed in the UCT library. Each year the project 'frees' one story from the archive and reinserts it into the landscape from which it originated. The project involves 500–700 school learners from the town each year and about forty facilitators are involved from various creative disciplines: lecturers and students from the UCT Drama, Music and Fine Art departments and trainees on the Magnet Theatre Training Programme under the direction of the Magnet Theatre creative team.

At the beginning of spring each year (for the past fifteen years), the project runs workshops in storytelling, dance, music, the visual arts, lantern-making and fire performance over a week – during school hours in the local primary school and after school hours outside the school – drawing on themes and iconography from one of the stories told to Bleek and Lloyd. Then, on the final evening, on the eighth day, we assemble at a designated site, along with parents, grandparents and other members of the community, now numbering in the thousands, to participate in a lantern parade and performance in which the learners share what they have learnt with the community through a multi-disciplinary telling of the selected story from the /Xam tradition, not as the /Xam would have told it, but recast for our time.

Over the fifteen-year history of the project two further extensions have emerged: a locally based community arts initiative (COMNET) run by older participants who grew up in the annual arts project and wanted more intensive and ongoing arts involvement (including the possibility of employment); and a more recent farm school project that attempts to reach learners at poorly resourced farm schools who have not had access to the annual arts project previously.

The second project, the Community Groups Intervention (CGI) and Culture Gangs Project (2002–ongoing), initiated by my colleagues Mandla Mbothwe and Jennie Reznek, emerged out of a request for mentorship from existing community drama groups in the township of Khayelitsha on the outskirts of the Cape Town city centre. It consisted primarily of mentorship from theatre fieldworkers who assisted in the development of plays that had been devised by these drama groups and skills development workshops given by theatre professionals. An additional component was taking participant drama groups to as much theatre in Cape Town as possible in order to develop the groups' awareness of a range of performance styles. The drama groups would also showcase their work at the end of each year at a day-long performance festival organised by Magnet Theatre in Khayelitsha which ended with an inter-generational discussion between parents and their children, and between participants from different groups, based on what had been performed and experienced during the day, and the outcomes from and possibilities for the project going forward into the future.

The work continued over a period of six years, working intensely with the more serious theatre groups. It became obvious over time that some participants were intent on growing their skills so as to become employable in the professional theatre industry while others (the majority) saw theatre as a recreational activity, and this ushered in the need to provide two streams of work by 2008. The first stream is the Magnet Theatre Training and Job Creation Programme for aspiring theatre makers and performers from a broader region than just Khayelitsha. The second stream, the Culture Gangs Project, is aimed at those who expressed a wish to continue with recreational theatre activities. The latter involves activities similar to those that made up the original CGI project and intends to support gangs engaged in cultural activities rather than gangs engaged in criminal activities. Through the CGI or Magnet Training Programme a number of individuals have been able to bridge the divide between school and higher education, and many have graduated from the UCT Drama department.

The examination of these two projects that follows is divided into three sections that deal with collective participation, the redistribution of authority and active citizenship, respectively. Together, they argue for a 'possible' politics of participatory performance practice.

Collective participation

Theatre and performance more broadly are commonly understood to be collective practices in which a community of some kind is brought into being albeit for a limited period of time. This community is typically divided between a part that is on the stage, participating by acting/dancing/singing (the performers), and a part that is off the stage, participating by watching (the audience). Both, it can be argued, are performing but differently and both are indispensable. In fact, most definitions of theatre activity would require at the very least someone doing *something* while being watched by someone else. In the projects I discuss here, however, the distinction between those on-stage performing and those off-stage watching is fluid. There is no obvious audience separated from performers; there is only one community and it is brought together through collective participation in a range of performance or performance-related events. To make the claim that collective participation produces a community

requires a little time to unpack these two terms: collective and participation – exploring how they are understood in this context and how they
operate to produce particular effects.

Magnet's projects attempt to activate the participants in three ways: by
making them producers of the event rather than consumers of a pre-
prepared spectacle; the ceding of at least some authorial control to the
participants allowing them to play within predetermined structures but
always with the possibility that their play might break apart the structure;
and the possibility that participation in the collective event can for
a limited period repair the disintegrating social fabric by restoring the
social bond. In this way the dramaturgy leads us off the stage and
into the social realm. But what does 'social' mean in this context?
In *Reassembling the Social* (2005), Bruno Latour suggests that because
'[t]he sense of belonging has entered into a crisis' and in order 'to register
this feeling of crisis and to follow these new connections, another notion of
the social has to be devised'. This new conception of the social:

> has to be *much wider* than what is usually called by that name, yet *strictly
> limited* to the tracing of new associations and to the designing of their
> assemblages. [. . .] [T]he social not as a special domain, a specific realm, or
> a particular sort of thing, but only as a very peculiar movement of re-
> association and reassembling. (2005: 7, emphasis original)

This suggests two things. First, for Latour the social is much less of a thing
or a 'special domain' than it is a fluid process or medium in which many
elements are mixed. In such a mixing, there are moments of separateness
and other moments in which it is difficult to separate one element from
another. Yet despite this fluidity, the social remains robust and does not
easily or readily collapse. Second, Latour insists that we need to expand the
social to include those elements that are usually excluded. In other words,
the social involves the 'momentary association' of human and other-than-
human actors 'into new shapes', new forms of assembly (2005: 65) that
Latour suggests be called 'not a society but a *collective*' (14, emphasis
original). And such a collective is never a given, it is always having to be
'made, or re-made' (2005: 34).

The linking of expansion and ongoing and active assemblage outlined
here resonates with Jacques Rancière's notion of the 'distribution of the
sensible' discussed in his *The Politics of Aesthetics* (2000): 'The distribution
of the sensible reveals who can have a share in what is common to the
community based on what they do and on the time and space in which this
activity is performed' (2000: 12). According to Gabriel Rockhill, the

'distribution of the sensible is the system of divisions and boundaries that define [...] what is visible and audible within a particular aesthetico-political regime' (2004: 1) and that 'divides the community into groups, social positions and functions [...] implicitly separat[ing] those who take part from those who are excluded' (2004: 3). The participants in both case-study projects suffer a multiplicity of exclusions that are economic, cultural and geographical – while they are no longer denied citizenship on the basis of race, they are marginalised on the basis of class, silenced on the basis of language and dislocated in peri-urban or rural peripheries where they are in effect rendered invisible. But most importantly for our purposes, they are excluded from open and active participation in the sensible organisation of the society, denied a share in practices of 'doing and making' on the basis that they lack the capacity or interest to participate in these fields (even while continuing to participate in forms of such activities that remain hidden from general view and hearing).

For Rancière, 'the essence of politics consists in interrupting the distribution of the sensible' (Rockhill 2004: 3) through 'modes of doing and making' that involve those who are usually excluded from participation. This opens up spaces of possibility that are also the 'space[s] of appearance' invoked by Hannah Arendt (1959: 178). For Arendt, the space of appearance 'comes into being wherever men (sic) are together in the manner of speech and action' (1959: 178). For Arendt '[t]he *polis* [...] is the organization of the people as it arises out of acting and speaking together, and its true space lies between people living together for this purpose, no matter where they happen to be' (1959: 198). But the space of appearance:

> does not survive the actuality of the movement which brought it into being, but disappears not only with the dispersal of men [...] but with the disappearance or arrest of the activities themselves. Wherever people gather together, it is potentially there, but only potentially, not necessarily and not forever. (1959: 178)

So any 'space of appearance' is temporary and fragile, and it must be continually recreated through the actions and speech of individuals who have come together to undertake some common project. This coming together to undertake a common project is what Arendt calls 'power': 'What first undermines and then kills political communities is loss of power and final impotence; and power cannot be stored up and kept in reserve for emergencies [...] but exists only in its actualizations' (1959: 178).

With this in mind, it might be important to stress at this point that any sense of a community that is brought into being through acts of collective participation in art practices is not based on the politics of identity – on a pre-existent myth of belonging. Any kind of provisional 'we' that might emerge through Magnet's participatory projects, 'come[s] into being fleetingly' and are in Irit Rogoff's terms 'momentary shared mutualities [that] do not form a collective heritage' (2005: 123). What they can do, according to Rogoff, is 'provide the short-lived access to power described by Arendt, not to the power of the state [the interruption of which is the politics of performance according to Rancière] but to the power of speech' (2005: 123) – the ways in which people describe themselves as subjects. As Slavoj Žižek puts it: 'those magic, violently poetic moments of political subjectivization in which the excluded [. . .] put forward their claim to speak for themselves' which can work to 'effectuate a change in the global perception of social space, so that their claims would have a legitimate place in it' (2004: 69).

How does this come about? How do the participants in the case-study projects speak for themselves? Central to both the projects under scrutiny here, I would argue, is the idea of storying. While a story is a particular category or form of artistic or cultural expression defined by a set of stylistic conventions or norms, storying is the process of 'making and doing' with stories, which involves, variously but not only, composition, construction, playing, performance, listening, watching and responding.

Storying allows possibilities for participants to reflect their own concerns and agendas, concerns and agendas that often run counter to dominant narratives. In a 2004 article, the members of the Retort collective argue that under neo-liberal forms of democracy, the state displays 'a relentless will to control the minutiae of appearance' and to 'micro-manage the means of symbolic production' (2004: 5) by controlling the production and distribution of images. The primary vehicle for this process in South Africa post-1994 has been television and, as I have argued elsewhere, the production of narrative drama on television over the past twenty years has produced a particular version of 'reality' that is more aspirational than it is reflective of the everyday life of ordinary people and as a result, 'present challenges facing the majority like increasing poverty levels and the increasing wealth gap, high unemployment and crime have in effect been rendered "unspeakable"'(Fleishman 2015: 6). It is my contention that low-tech art forms like theatre offer the possibility of an alternative space for the production and distribution of 'other' images and stories that are more reflective of reality for the 'unfree' majority, and particularly for the youth, and participatory networks, such as those operating in the case studies examined here, facilitate the sharing of these 'other' images.

The anthropologist Michael Jackson argues that stories provide 'strategies and generat[e] experiences that help people redress imbalances and correct perceived injustices [. . .] so that in telling a story with others one reclaims some sense of agency, recovers some sense of purpose' (2002: 36). In this respect, stories are in the interest of their tellers. However, this is not only because they serve their worldly interests but also because, as Hannah Arendt indicates, 'in the word's most literal significance' interest means 'something which *inter-est*, which lies between people and therefore can relate and bind them together' (1959: 162, emphasis original). And while stories are usually about some 'worldly objective reality', they can also lead to what Arendt calls 'a disclosure of the acting and speaking agent' (1959: 162–163). This 'comes to the fore where people are with others and neither for nor against them – that is, in sheer human togetherness' (1959: 160), which is a feature of oral storytelling because, as Jackson reminds us, stories are 'commonly *lived through* as a physical, sensual, and vital interaction between the body of the storyteller and the bodies of the listeners, in which people reach out toward one another, sitting closely together, singing in unison, laughing or crying as one' (2002: 28, emphasis original). It is also a feature of the micro-community created in each of the case-study projects, which reflects what sociologist Georg Simmel refers to as 'sociability': 'A feeling for, [or] a satisfaction in, the very fact that one is associated with others and that the solitariness of the individual is resolved into togetherness, a union with others' (1997: 121). This is captured in a description of a CGI Showcase event in 2005 as recorded by Gay Morris:

> The relative youth of the perhaps 300 people present, the air of excited playfulness and enjoyment amongst all those present, the easy inclusivity of audience and performers who mingled together – and in many cases were one and the same – and the investment in the morning's theatrical event, not only from the Magnet Theatre team of leaders and fieldworkers but from all who were present, brought to light community engagement, participation and playing through a theatrical event. And yet all those present took the work seriously. The performers were not 'showing off'. They were communicating through performance on subject matter in which they were personally invested because they had chosen it. They had made the plays in self-selected theatrical forms, and in many cases demonstrated levels of skill, creativity and particularly team coherence that was thrilling [. . .]. (2010: 15)

What comes across is a sense of fun and excitement at being part of – participating in – a collective and an event bigger than themselves as individuals, a sense of sociability. But at the same time there exists a feeling that all are engaged in serious work (making good theatre) and with serious issues (that need to be spoken about because they are un(der) spoken elsewhere). There is a sense of serious playfulness at the heart of the event.

Play is an essential element of storying, aesthetically and politically, connected as it is to two fundamental storying moves: the un-making and re-making of stories (and conceptions of reality). According to Nigel Thrift, 'play is a process of performative experiment', a field of speculative endeavour in which possibilities are acted out (2008: 119). For Victor Turner, play 'reveals to us [. . .] the possibility of changing our goals and, therefore, the restructuring of what our culture states to be reality' (1983: 233–234). Yet as Richard Schechner notes, play is 'dangerous' too and we counter this by suggesting that play is fun and that we do it voluntarily. For Schechner, 'the fun of playing, when there is fun, is in playing with fire, going in over one's head, inverting accepted procedures and hierarchies [. . .]' (1993: 27).

To 'play with fire' is to engage in a risky activity, and this is true in the Clanwilliam project on a literal level (participants actually do play with fire). It is true on a social level too where the risk involves disrupting the given situation, the social order, and proposing a new way of speaking and acting and of being together. It is true on a personal level where individuals risk doing things they have not done before, and are unfamiliar with, things that might make them look strange, different and funny in the eyes of their peers. But it is also risky because it affords the possibility for what Schechner calls 'dark play':

> Dark play may be conscious playing, but it can also be playing in the dark when some or even all of the players don't know they are playing. [. . .] Dark play subverts order, dissolves frames, breaks its own rules, so that the playing itself is in danger of being destroyed. (1993: 36)

For example, there have been times during the parade in Clanwilliam when the entire event risks spinning out of control as some participants change the game to one of violent destruction. Groups of young boys who have not been centrally involved throughout the week infiltrate the parade and, operating as a kind of fifth column, grab lanterns from the hands of younger children and use them as weapons, indiscriminately hitting other participants on the head or back with the lanterns they have stolen as the parade proceeds on its way. This introduces first an uncertainty (What kind of playing is this? Should I play along?) and then panic among those who are fast becoming victims. Or, as another example, when real-world violence impinges on a group making theatre in the CGI project and a participant is killed by members of the gang he is trying to free himself from (as was the case one year). In other words, there is a very real chance that playing will be replaced by something altogether more sinister and any political effect that storying of this kind might present can very quickly and without warning be turned into something ungovernable and quite counter-productive or shockingly useless in the face of real-world violence.

Redistributing authority

I have argued that in both projects what is created is a collective, a micro-community, albeit a short-lived, fragile and in some respects 'imaginary' one. This collective comes together through participation in an assemblage of performance activities over an extended period of time – in excess of ten years in each case. These activities include making and doing performance, participating in skills workshops, watching theatre, and importantly, contributing to an ongoing discourse about performance and the ways in which it is being experienced. In both cases, the collective is made up of young people – male and female and under the age of thirty – living in difficult socio-economic conditions on the margins of society, engaged in or having had compromised basic education, and with limited prospects of employment or further education opportunities. In other words, the participants are among those whom Hamilton has described as 'unfree' twenty years on from the advent of democracy in South Africa, as cited at the opening of this chapter. Over the extended time period of the projects participants come and go in a mutable state of flux, forming a more consistent core and a changing periphery of participation.

However, this shifting collective is anchored to, and in many ways dependent for its ongoing existence as a collective on, an outside organisation – Magnet Theatre. Magnet is outside in the sense that it cannot be said to be 'unfree' in the same way as the other participants are and yet in other ways Magnet can also be considered to be inside, a constituent part of the collective community. This is partly because Magnet as an organisation is heterogeneous: while representatives of the politically, economically and academically dominant classes (both socially and in terms of the theatre) run the organisation, many of its facilitators are in fact part of the same communities that the participants in the projects come from who having benefitted from these self-same projects have gone on to acquire further education and training themselves. In any event, whether seen as inside or outside the community of participants, Magnet offers the participants a framework for continuity that they might alone fail to maintain, and access to knowledge, skill, status, structure and experience that they would struggle to access on their own.

Magnet has always made theatre rather than staged works written by playwrights. In this making process, there has always been an emphasis on participation: of the whole ensemble. While different participants participate differently, there is at least a commitment to allow everyone to have their say. This emerges from a history of workshop theatre in South Africa, but this idea of workshopping or collaborative playmaking has evolved over time from a sentimental idea of democracy in which everyone has an equal say to a consensual democracy in which while everyone participates, not everyone participates equally (Fleishman 1991). At the forefront of this work is a philosophy and practice of facilitation, which in turn might be understood as an interfacing 'between different holders of authority' (Wakeford and Pimbert 2013: 69). In this case, the authority of the theatre experts connected to Magnet Theatre and the authority of the organic or grassroots participants derived from a particular kind of life experience.

Magnet's facilitators do not undergo some kind of course to prepare them to work with the groups. There is no 'off-the-shelf' set of ready-made techniques and procedures to be employed or followed by the facilitators. Most of the facilitators have been exposed to Magnet's way of collaborative theatre making and to some extent this serves as a kind of apprenticeship but when they get into the field they operate as bricoleurs using whatever comes to hand in an immediate and responsive engagement with what the groups are doing. The fieldworker is granted authority by virtue of her connection with Magnet but that authority is always temporary and up for negotiation. If the facilitator pushes too hard or is too prescriptive, the authority can be withdrawn and the facilitator and her advice challenged and/or ignored.

I would suggest that the relationship between Magnet Theatre and the participants in the case-study projects can be defined as an 'authoritative power relationship' (Blencowe 2013: 9). In other words, the participants engage with Magnet because Magnet embodies 'authority' in the performance field. For Claire Blencowe authority is 'a type of power' that is traditionally tied to a sense of hierarchy and 'refers to things anti-democratic, inegalitarian and cruel', but, following Arendt, she also suggests that it can be 'a very positive term' (2013: 12). For Arendt, '[a]uthority implies an obedience in which men (sic) retain their freedom' (1977: 105). This is because it manifests as what Blencowe describes as 'the force of "wise" or "in the know" counsel' (2013: 10) that can be, at least theoretically, ignored. Authority is not about a command issued by those who have the power that must be executed by those who lack the power, it is rather 'a mere advice, needing neither the form of command nor external coercion to make itself heard' (Arendt 1977: 123). Blencowe reframes Arendt's ideas on authority, suggesting it is also attached to an idea of objectivity understood as 'the essential outside of experiential knowledge [. . .] a position outside of particular perspectives (the outside of the community), and outside of the subjective realm of interpretation' (2013: 15). In other words, the authority that Magnet provides the participants is a knowledge that exists beyond the experiences they can glean on their own from their immediate environment (their community) and beyond what they can understand and experience for themselves through their own existent capacities and capabilities. It thus has the potential to open up new ways of thinking and new ways of acting and to launch the participants into an alternative realm of possibility (defined in terms of skills, ideas, forms and styles and modes and materials) to which they would not otherwise readily have had access.

Blencowe goes on to argue that:

> There is something fundamentally collaborative about authority. Authority is to some extent in the hands of all participants in an authoritative relationship – it has to be granted by those who are subjected to its constraint. (2013: 13)

The participants in the two case-study projects agree to grant Magnet the 'authority' and to subject themselves to the constraints and limitations that this implies. And yet following Arendt, Blencowe argued that it is precisely these limitations that 'pluralise the possibilities of politics' and create 'spaces of freedom that are more (potentially) inclusive' despite an obviously unequal relationship. In this sense the politics of the projects is not based on equality – 'the condition of freedom in the extraordinarily exclusive Greek *polis*' – but on authority – 'the condition of politics (equality and freedom) among *un-equals* in the much more inclusive and diverse Roman *civitas*' (2013: 14). However, the authority relationship is not static; it shifts over time. As skill levels and experience have grown, so many participants have begun to gain authority both within the projects and outside. Some participants have become facilitators within the projects and others have become leaders of new projects in other spaces both in the townships in which they live and outside in other institutions such as the Baxter Theatre's *Zabalaza* community theatre festival or the *Kasi-to-Kasi Public Arts Festival* in Gugulethu, a township on the outskirts of Cape Town. Recently, Magnet initiated an alumni conference to provide a platform for those who have been involved in the projects over the years to discuss and engage with issues and challenges they face in the industry. While the idea arose with Magnet and Magnet provided some logistical support, it was the young participants themselves who organised the event, curated the programme and determined the direction of the conversation.

According to Blencowe, '[d]emocratisation is about the dispersal of authority throughout society' (2013b: 37). It allows ordinary people, those who are often not visible or heard precisely because they are considered to have no authority, to garner sufficient authority 'to make political demands, to hold people to account, to be taken seriously' (2013b: 37). For Blencowe, there is a direct 'link between democracy and dignity', and this is tied to whether people are considered to have authority or not. '[T]he dignity and self-respect of ordinary, economically excluded people' (2013b: 41) is undermined when a perception is produced that they lack authority (expert knowledge in a particular field or insight gained through real and valued experience in the world), and this makes it extremely difficult for such people to express a point of view or to make any political demands that they believe will be taken seriously. In other words, their capacity for political action, for acting as empowered citizens in a supposed democracy, is dependent on a sense of authority, which is tied to a sense of dignity and self-respect. Blencowe argues that '[p]articipatory practices can be technologies for redistributing authority' (2013b: 41) by widening participation through expanding access to those groups who are often excluded on the basis of a lack of expertise or experience and furthermore, by opening up what might constitute our notion(s) of reality and what value or respect should be accorded to what version of reality. It is my contention that the kinds of participatory processes and projects that Magnet Theatre engages in contribute to the redistribution of authority on both scores. First, they widen participation – in theatre itself and then by extension in the political process – by increasing access to experiences and expertise. Second, they help participants to reconfigure the perception of what constitutes 'reality' – in the aesthetics and content of theatre practice and in terms of how life is lived and experienced – by facilitating the production and reception of stories and images with those who are most often ignored.

Active citizenship

In the first section, I argued that through collective participation in a range of performance projects a kind of 'political subjectivization' (Žižek 2004: 69) occurs through which the participants 'disclose themselves as subjects'

(Arendt 1959: 163) and that in the process a community comes into being between the participants and Magnet Theatre, however temporary or loose that community might be. In the second section, I argued that the relationship between the participants and Magnet Theatre can be defined as an authoritative power relationship and that the projects redistribute authority so as to widen democratic participation. It now leaves me to argue in the final section for a connection of the above to the notion of citizenship in the new democratic dispensation in South Africa and particularly to countering the idea of weak citizenship and replacing it with an active citizenship.

According to Kymlicka and Norman (1994), citizenship can be understood in two ways: the first is 'citizenship-as-legal-status, that is as full membership in a political community' with particular rights and responsibilities attached to such membership; the second is 'citizenship-as-desirable-activity, where the extent and quality of one's citizenship is a function of one's participation in that community' (1994: 353). The young participants in the projects under discussion here have attained the first kind of citizenship as a consequence of the successful struggle against apartheid. The constitution of the new South Africa guarantees them this status as an extension of its founding values, which can be summarised as the pursuit of human dignity, the achievement of equality and the advancement of human rights and freedoms in a non-racial and non-sexist society with universal adult suffrage in a multi-party system of democratic government. However, as Jürgen Habermas argues, 'the institutions of constitutional freedom are only worth as much as a population makes of them' (1992: 7). There is therefore no guarantee that the attainment of citizenship as a legal status will lead automatically to an active, participatory citizenship. On the contrary, this has clearly not been the case in South Africa post-1994, which is why Satgar argues that democracy in South Africa has been shrunk 'from the triad of strong representative, associational and participatory democracy to a form of weak representational democracy' (2012: n.p.). It is my contention that participation in performance projects such as those discussed here is an attempt at strengthening democracy by reinvigorating its associational and participatory aspects.

The question that arises from this contention is: how best to encourage or facilitate a meaningful sense of participation as active citizens? According to political theorist Michael Walzer, for example, 'the civility that makes democratic politics possible can only be learned in the associational networks of civil society' (1992: 104). In my understanding, the community that arises through each of the projects we are discussing here is such an 'associational network' and it is characterised by the following features:

1. Participation is voluntary. Participants choose to become involved. They are not involved by virtue of a law that demands involvement. In the Clanwilliam project, participants choose to participate on an individual basis (with more or less information as to what it is they are getting involved in). In the Culture Gangs Project, however, participants become part of the association by virtue of belonging to particular existent drama groups who have chosen to be part of the association.

2. In cases where the participants are part of the association because they belong to groups, these groups remain separate entities – separate from other similar groups and from Magnet. In this sense the associational network is a plurality not a singularity. In this regard, Michael Oakeshott distinguishes between two types of human association: '*societas* and *universitas*' (1975: 199, emphasis original). *Universitas* defines an association that comes together to engage in a common project in order to achieve a common goal or result based on common interest. Such an association he describes as 'a partnership of persons which is itself a Person' (Oakeshott 1975: 203). In other words in coming together the association formed becomes like a single person in its own right – a singularity. *Societas* on the other hand is described as a 'civil association' that comes together because those who make up the association recognise that they have things in common with one another and as a result they are loyal to one another and wish to express a solidarity with one another.

3. The participants and/or the groups remain free to belong to other groups and associations in pursuit of other goals and purposes. In other words, Magnet and the groups are united in a loose assemblage rather than a rigid and exclusive structure, and as an assemblage it is determined by relations of exteriority rather than interiority. As De Landa points out, the components that make up the assemblage are not essential to the identity of the whole; they could be replaced by other components (De Landa 2006). There is nothing essential that determines membership. Any number of different parties could enter into such an assemblage, and the assemblage does not collapse as soon as some party decides to leave or breaks off. It is also not something predetermined and given for all time. It is something that needs to be

continually practised if it is to exist at all and the terms of this practice are constantly negotiated over time and as a result are always mutable and shifting. As Mouffe describes it, it is 'a community without a definite shape or a definite identity and in continuous re-enactment' (1992: 233).

4. The association is more than a simple alliance between different existent groups as if there was no power differential between the groups in the given situation; it takes into consideration the need to identify the power differences in the given situation and to move to change them.

5. The association and its activities operate in the public domain and have a particular spatial dimension. In other words, the association mediates between the private space of the home and the space of the state and the concerns of the association are not determined by private preference but emerge in a public space through ongoing deliberation and debate and through 'practices and activities that are characteristic of that space' and its institutional parameters (Arendt in Passerin d'Entrèves 1992: 153). In this public space these concerns are articulated, negotiated and distributed.

Now if a group wants to participate in the association and derive benefits from the relationships it affords, it would have to agree to play by the rules or 'norm[s] of conduct' (Mouffe 1992: 233) of the association. Such norms serve as the 'grammar' of the participants' conduct in the shared social practices of the association. Mouffe with reference to Michael Oakeshott describes this as:

> a complex of rules or rule-like prescriptions, which do not prescribe [. . .] actions to be performed but 'moral considerations specifying conditions to be subscribed to in choosing performances'. (Mouffe 1992: 232, citing Oakeshott 1975: 182)

Oakeshott and Mouffe are not concerned with performances here in the way that theatre and performance scholars might be. Nonetheless, I think that this conception does apply to performances in the theatrical sense in the current case. For example, in the beginning of our work with these groups, by far the majority of productions we saw the groups making were concerned with the violence that is so prevalent in the communities from which they come. However, in many cases what concerned us was that the violence was being glorified. The plays were full of guns wielded with a sense of bravado and even pride, the most popular characters were gangsters, and the stage was often littered with dead bodies. While this was understandable given that gangsters were perceived to be empowered in communities in which most felt decidedly disempowered, and the gun was a means of attaining power, we moved quickly to change this predominance. It became a rule of our association that while we did not determine the subject matter of the plays in general, there were to be no guns (a gun-free zone in all respects) and no gangsters. The result of this was fascinating because it immediately changed so much about the performances the groups made, both in terms of content (a much wider range of themes and characters) and styles (a need to find more interesting and challenging ways of engaging the audience when one could not simply rely on the popularity of a particular set of characters). This rule was based on a set of values that came from Magnet and could hold sway because of the authority Magnet holds in the relationship, and there is no sense that these values are universally shared by all members of all groups. Within the network there is no 'value homogeneity' or 'value consensus', and there is no ultimate desire for harmony or for unanimity. So what participants do outside of the collective practice of making plays and sharing in performances as part of the associational network might not change – individual participants might and do have very different ideas of what constitutes the good – but the rules of behaviour and the consequent products have changed *within* the context of the association itself.

I would argue that an associational network is a particular form of what Arendt calls 'the political community'. However, I would suggest that we define it as *a* political community, one among many in a plurality of differentiated political communities. For as Chantal Mouffe explains it: '[t]he way we define citizenship is intimately linked to the kind of society and political community we want' (1992: 225). If our goal is to ensure a democracy that is both radical and plural, that ensures that the principles of equality and justice are extended across the widest set of social relations, then there is a need to recognise a plurality of political struggles within that society that are understood to be equivalent. There is no one overarching sphere of struggle more important than all the others as was the case when the struggle against apartheid superseded all other struggles such as the rights of women or minorities. In other words we recognise that politics and political participation operates at multiple levels in any society and that these levels are integrated to some extent at least. The political becomes a distributed concept not confined to representative politics only and the value of our citizenship is to a large extent determined by our participation in such politics. In other words, as Mouffe puts it, we cannot conceive of our citizenship 'independently of our insertion in a political community' (1992:4) or many such communities simulta neously. And with reference to the discussion above, Blencowe points out that political community is constituted through authority:

> To feel the force of authority, is to feel the reality of a community, to belong . . . to that community. To affirm, exercise or recognise authority is to affirm the reality of, and invest in, a particular community. [. . .] Authority offers its bearer a sense of communal support when facing the potentially paralysing agonies of decision making. (2013: 13)

Furthermore, following Rancière, we can only really describe a community as political when it is characterised by 'dissensus' and not 'consensus'. As Gabriel Rockhill explains in his glossary of technical terms in Rancière's *The Politics of Aesthetics*:

> A dissensus is not a quarrel over personal interests or opinions. It is a political process that [. . .] creates a fissure in the sensible order by confronting the established framework of perception, thought and action with the 'inadmissible'. (2004: 85)

The 'inadmissible' is that which has been excluded and Rancière refers to this as the *demos*, the Greek term for those who have no right or power – those 'who have no share in the communal distribution of the sensible' (2004: 84). The *demos* is opposed in Rancière to the *ochlos*, the Greek term for 'the multitude' or 'a throng of people' which is a community obsessed with its own unification at the expense of excluding the *demos*. In this conception democracy can only be possible when the *demos* disrupts the consensual drive of the *ochlos*.

In the title of this chapter, I proposed a possible politics for participatory performance practices in South Africa. The politics is 'possible' first because the relationship between theatre/performance and politics cannot any longer be taken as given or obvious. Writers such as Baz Kershaw and Alan Read have worried this relationship to great effect elsewhere (Kershaw 1999; Read 2008). Second, it is a 'possible politics' in the sense that it is close to hand and achievable. It is not impossible; it does not operate in a sphere beyond the grasp of the young participants, both in the sense of their comprehension of what is at stake and in the sense of actually doing something actively to change their circumstances. And third, it is a 'possible politics' because participatory projects and the networks they give rise to, bring into existence 'a new topography of the possible' (Rancière 2008: 49). For Rancière, we need 'to loosen the bonds that enclose [. . .] possibility within the machine that makes the "state of things" seem evident, unquestionable' (Rancière in Carnevale and Kelsey 2007: 261). It is my contention that the active participation and the shifting authority in the projects under consideration here do exactly that.

References

Arendt, H. 1959. *The Human Condition*. New York: Doubleday.

Arendt, H. 1977. *Between Past and Future*. Harmondsworth: Penguin.

Blencowe, C. 2013. 'Biopolitical authority, objectivity and the groundwork of modern citizenship'. *Journal of Political Power* 6.1: 9–28.

Blencowe, C. 2013b. 'Participatory knowledge matters for democracy' in Noorani, T. Blencowe, C. and Brigstocke, J. (eds.) *Problems of Participation: Reflections on Authority, Democracy and the Struggle for Common Life*. Lewes: ARN Press, pp. 37–47.

Carnevale, F. and Kelsey, J. 2007. 'Art of the possible: Fulvia Carnevale and John Kelsey in conversation with Jacques Rancière'. *Artforum* 45.7: 256–269.

De Landa, M. 2006. *A New Philosophy of Society: Assemblage Theory and Social Complexity*. London and New York: Continuum.

Fleishman, M. 1991. 'Workshop Theatre in South Africa in the 1980s: A Critical Examination with Specific Reference to Power, Orality and the Carnivalesque'. Unpublished MA thesis, University of Cape Town.

Fleishman, M. 2015. 'Lapsing into democracy: Magnet Theatre and the drama of "unspeakability" in the new South Africa' in Luckhurst, M. and Morin, E. (eds.) *Theatre and Human Rights after 1945: Things Unspeakable*. Basingstoke: Palgrave Macmillan.

Habermas, J. 1992. 'Citizenship and national identity: Some reflections on the future of Europe'. *Praxis International* 12: 1–19.

Hamilton, L. 2011. 'Collective unfreedom in South Africa'. *Contemporary Politics* 17.4: 355–372.

Jackson, M. 2002. *The Politics of Storytelling: Violence, Transgression and Intersubjectivity*. Copenhagen: Museum Tusculanum Press.

Kershaw, B. 1999. *The Radical in Performance: Between Brecht and Baudrillard*. London and New York: Routledge.

Kymlicka, W. and Norman, W. 1994. 'Return of the citizen: A survey of recent work on citizenship theory'. *Ethics*, 104: 352–381.

Latour, B. 2005. *Reassembling the Social: An Introduction to Actor-Network-Theory*. Oxford: Oxford University Press.

Morris, G. 2010. 'Own-made in the (post-) new South Africa: a study of theatre originating from selected townships in the vicinity of Cape Town'. Unpublished PhD thesis, University of Cape Town.

Mouffe, C. 1992. 'Democratic citizenship and the political community' in Mouffe, C. (ed.) *Dimensions of Radical Democracy: Pluralism, Citizenship, Community*. London: Verso, pp. 225–239.

Oakeshott, M. 1975. *On Human Conduct*. Oxford: Oxford University Press.

Passerin d'Entrèves, M. 1992. 'Hannah Arendt and the idea of citizenship' in Mouffe, C. (ed.) *Dimensions of Radical Democracy: Pluralism, Citizenship, Community*. London: Verso, pp. 145–168.

Rancière, J. 2000. (trans. G. Rockhill 2004). *The Politics of Aesthetics*. London: Continuum.

Rancière, J. 2008. (trans. G. Rockhill 2011). *The Emancipated Spectator*. London: Verso.

Read, A. 2008. *Theatre, Intimacy & Engagement: The Last Human Venue*. Basingstoke: Palgrave Macmillan.

Retort. 2004. 'Afflicted powers: The state, the spectacle and September 11'. *New Left Review* May/June(27): 5–21.

Rockhill, G. 2004. 'Translator's introduction: Jacques Rancière's politics of perception' in Rancière, J. *The Politics of Aesthetics*. London: Continuum, pp. 1–6.

Rogoff, I. 2005. 'Looking away: Participations in visual culture' in Butt, G. (ed.) *After Criticism: New Responses to Art and Performance*. Oxford: Blackwell Publishing, pp. 117–134.

Satgar, V. 2012. 'The neoliberal squeeze on post-apartheid democracy: Reclaiming the "South African dream"'. *Global Research*, January 2, n.p. Available: www.globalresearch.ca/the-neoliberal-squeeze-on-post-apartheid-democracy-recliaming-the-south-african-dream/28453. Last accessed 6 October 2014.

Schechner, R. 1993. *The Future of Ritual: Writings on Culture and Performance*. London and New York: Routledge.

Simmel, G. 1997. (ed. by D. Frisby and M. Featherstone) *Simmel on Culture: Selected Writings*. London: Sage.

Thrift, N. 2008. *Non-representational Theory: Space, Politics, Affect*. London and New York: Routledge.

Turner, V. 1983. 'Body, brain and culture'. *Zygon* 18.3: 221–245.

Wakeford, T. and Pimbert, M. 2013. 'Opening participatory democracy's black box: Facilitation as creative bricolage' in Noorani, T., Blencowe, C. and Brigstocke, J. (eds.) *Problems of Participation: Reflections on Authority, Democracy and the Struggle for Common Life*. Lewes: ARN Press, pp. 69–82.

Walzer, M. 1992. 'The civil society argument' in Mouffe, C. (ed.) *Dimensions of Radical Democracy: Pluralism, Citizenship, Community*. London: Verso, pp. 89–107.

Žižek, S. 2004. 'Afterword: The lesson of Rancière' in Rancière, J. *The Politics of Aesthetics*. London: Continuum, pp. 69–79.

CHAPTER 11

Staging Labour Rites

D. Soyini Madison

This chapter presents a political and poetic inquiry into performance's relationship to the existential ubiquity of labour, examined here through an exploration of the staging of a public performance. The intersections of affect, materiality, beauty, and futurity are discussed as theoretical reference points in staging labour as an activist performance that offers alternative narratives and imaginings for what it means and how it feels to labour.

I will pause here to enumerate how I am defining labour. My aim is not to be complete or definitive but descriptive and generative of labour's many manifestations. First, to clarify the distinction between 'labour' and 'work': by labour I mean work *and* the nature, ontology, philosophy, and politics of work as well as work's metaphorical, poetic, and symbolic imaginings; the work of the brain and body constitute the infinite temporalities, materiality, and power dynamics of labour. Second, to clarify the distinction between 'a job' and 'labour': labour both entails and exceeds 'a job'; by labour I mean *both* a job *and* its resonances in working in/on a job, that is something that one must get done with and for others including the job's emotional affects, material structures, shared context and belonging that give it form – a *space* to work – and make our choice to have and access to a job a human right. Third, labour includes the physicality and procedures of the job and the ontology of work entailed, while expanding the discourses about these physicalities and procedures as well as their possible futures. Labour becomes the overarching rubric across the domains of the job and the work that the job demands – labour encompasses the felt-sensing experiences, histories, and symbology of job and work. Fourth, labour includes the future and imagining the utopic (the here, the now, in this place, in an everywhere, or a nowhere place) to guide and inspire formations of freedom and the actions required to attain those formations; labour encompasses a great effort – work and working a job – and imaging a new materiality, that is a plausible or realizable future.

The question becomes: How are these descriptions of labour and their implications staged relative to the day-to-day actions of our lives, both locally and globally? What do these descriptions look like in performance? How do we access those defining stories that labour generates? I am interested in the spectacularity of labour across existential suffering and resistant acts, both mythic and real. These are the small stories – the Davids and their slingshots against the Goliaths and their massive power – of those who order, dictate, discipline, and punish the bodies and dreams of those who are cast out as small and their courage underestimated. Performance enters and becomes the possible rupture, the framed symbolic alternative, the persistent otherwise in how we can re-imagine labour. I want to add to the offering of performance as political action and provocative witness to labour and its future imaginings.

Materiality

Labor matters. It cuts and cuts into matter ... the mother of all. To labor is to affirm life which begins with labor ... Inasmuch as the fact of labor is that with it life begins and goes on, the truth of life is that labor defines, that is, makes finite, much of what we do and are in life, that labor, having always and already begun, survives its own manifold articulations, including all that seeks to negate it ... The transition from one type of labor to another thus not only brings a change in the forms of life in which one finds oneself, it also demands a change of the lenses through which one views the history that is just past and one's own place in the history that is now unfolding. (Chang 2010: 90)

Chang's quote reminds us that all life is constituted by labour. Existence begins and is sustained, transformed, and threatened through unending and epochal forms of labour. Labour is our blessing and our curse; therefore, labour, in all its local and global epochs, shapes our past, present, and future as temporality is composed of infinite formations of labour. If matter is 'the mother of all' and if subatomic particles and cosmic star stuff birthed the world (and all of us) into being, it follows that the connective tissue of all that is material – of all that is something and everything – must reckon with how this materiality is then variously categorized, arranged, disciplined, perpetuated, destroyed, sustained, and determined. Because the immateriality of consciousness, emotion, and ideology are influenced by the overarching materiality and political

economies of how our lives are situated and placed, I turn to how these
political economies of space, time, bodies, objects, nature, and capital
generate our activist projects. If activist performance is to show, tell,
and shake up processes of economic production, distribution, and
exchange as well as how we imagine and feel about these economies
and, moreover, how they imagine and feel about us, it follows that we
must then make art that beckons collective attention and participation.
Referring to art and narration, Toni Morrison states that art, 'should try
deliberately to make you stand up and make you *feel* something profoundly [...] to weep and to cry and to accede or to change and to
modify' (1994: 494). She goes on to refer to the effective and affective
resonances of art, stating that art

> should be beautiful, and powerful, but it should also *work*. It should have
> something in it that enlightens; something in it that opens the door and
> points the way. Something in it that suggests what the conflicts are, what the
> problems are. But it need not solve those problems because it is not a case
> study, it is not a recipe. (1994: 494)

Morrison makes a call for political, beautiful, and communal art that
causes us to 'stand up' and to feel, think, and move towards paths that
need followings and doors that need openings. Activist theatre-makers are
part of an enduring legacy that conjoins social justice and economies of
matter to both effect and affect the hearts and minds of civic life, community formations, and global citizenry.

Embodied narration

Because performed narratives illuminate those micro moments of life
experience otherwise unseen and unheard, or too far away to grasp, and
because staging them creates a space for reckoning with the inseparability
between private life and public structures, social justice theatre has used
narration to explicate and make connections between private and public
domains as well as the formations of power that are both spectacular and
hidden in plain sight while influencing the 'multiple structures and relationships where individuals are immersed' (Sliep et al. 2013: 85). Much has
been written about how life experiences are constructed and deconstructed,
through narrative performance, to reveal how reality is ordered and comes
into being as it pertains to a particular consciousness and context (ibid.:
88). Understanding that narratives are always already constructed, we may
turn to the many ways they can be deconstructed for the 'greater good'.

Drawing on Walter Benjamin's description of the storyteller, Helen Nicholson states: 'the social role of the storyteller ends with the claim that the storyteller is allied to goodness' (Nicholson 2014 [2005]: 65). Nicholson goes on to note, 'The storyteller's gift [. . .] is to use experiences of life to offer practical wisdom, finding narratives and metaphors which make connections between life as it is, and life as it might be' (2014 [2005]: 66). Nicholson asserts that good storytelling is less a reportage of facts and information, but an event where body, gesture, and craft form expressive moments of sharing and exchange; therefore good storytelling 'combines aesthetics and ethics, an act of generosity' (2014 [2005]: 66). It is storytelling as an act of embodied generosity, as an act that invites a shared space for more tellings, that unmasks revelations of power where the frictions – deadly or enlivening – between the private and the public blur and bleed. It is in this spirit of narrative performance and generosity where, in this instance, labour enters.

This performative convergence of labour and narration is exemplified in excerpts from *a free public performance* I adapted and directed with a diverse group of students at Northwestern University, United States, in 2012 to tell the story of labour activism in the United States against the contemporary backdrop of the International Occupy Protests as well as using ethnographic interviews I conducted with local labour leaders. The aim was to involve students across racial, transnational, and other identity formations in a performative process of staging moments in the rituals and rights of human labour. As I began the directing and adaptation process, I aimed for the focus to be as much or more about the rehearsal and workshop experience and embodying what we collectively learned and felt in our shared effort towards a pedagogy of labour and creating activist performance. I wanted the performance to effectively and affectively inspire our audiences, but my primary focus was to inspire the students in a mutual process of creation and labour awareness, moreover, in understanding how and why labour matters both as materiality and as a passionate cause or a cause for passion. The performance, entitled, *Labour Rites*, combined comic satire, myth, dramatic monologue, oral history, digital imagery, dance, symbolic movement as well as projected imagery and sound installations from the history of the international labour movement's rich music tradition and visual archive, all forming theatrical trajectories of labour activism.

Scene

A single performer enacting a sweatshop worker's monologue expresses the paradox and cruel contradictions of the global economy, and intimate and affective desires within the micro spaces of an international market-driven, economic order.

The stage is empty and dark. A woman enters and stands centre. She reads a letter from the other side of the world.

Dear Anna

Today the Americans came to visit their factory. They traveled far. The American company must prove they do 'fair labour practices'. Today [...] no one was called a bad name. No woman sent to back room. Nobody worked behind locked doors late into the night. The small ones could go home. The day before the Americans came, the bosses made us clean everything: scrub floors, wash machines, take locks from doors and windows, put away garbage, the chemicals, the dyes ... They told us to dress up nice and to look neat and pretty and smile a lot. We smile. We don't want to get fired. The bosses told us if the Americans ask us any questions, we must be happy and tell them how much we love the factory. We must tell the Americans our bosses are good to us and they love America. We are to tell them we work so we can be prosperous like Americans. We are to tell them that we are grateful to America for this factory. We are to tell the Americans that the factory has given us a better way of life. We are to say 'Thank you for giving us work and making us free' ... We tell them this, but the Americans know that none of it is true. They know. We tell them what they want to hear. They do not want to feel bad. They want to stay rich and be happy. And, we want the factory. We don't want to be poor, we don't want to eat garbage off the street.

We have heard the call: sweatshops keep the poor from starving! Yes? No? In whose interest and to whose material benefit do sweatshops become the only or best alternative to poverty? Activist performance, with its polemics and advocacy, where the 'message' guides its measure of effect, is too often criticized for 'telling audiences what to think'. James Thompson urges us to 'focus on affect rather than effect' (Thompson 2011: 111). The emphasis on 'effect' is too often overrun by didacticism where the affective and persuasive potential of performance is, instead, a didactic harangue rather than a compelling moment of deep interest that beckons our lively attention. Toni Morrison, turning her attention to beauty, expresses concern when affect and effect are disconnected: '[t]he Problem comes when you find harangue passing off as art. It seems to me that the best art is political and you ought to be able to make it

unquestionably political and irrevocably beautiful at the same time'
(Morrison 1994: 497). In staging *The Letter* scene, the method was to
engage with the political economy and its politics of materiality through
the poetics of a compelling story. I adapted the story from various
newspaper and archival accounts to form a composite experience of
a sweatshop worker. Activist performance is constituted by enlivening
subjects, each with a story to tell, circulating in an empirical world across
complex realms of global citizenship, local communities, social and
political collaborations, and the belongings of family and extended
families. These realms hold infinite stories that evolve into embodied
narratives of material consequences and affects that we, as performance
makers, struggle to stage and to make present to others in a shared
poetics of experience and personhood. However, I am also aware that
not every story is a spoken story. There is also the agency of silence and
the powerful resistance of the unsaid and the refusal to speak. There are
alternative stories that are wordless and full of motion and sound.
In conducting fieldwork in Ghana, West Africa, for example, there
were revelatory moment of human rights activism where what became
known and felt was not expressed in story, but in dance, song, musical
rhythms, realms of adornment and dress, and in the everyday moments
of gestural codes and ceremony (Madison 2010). This is akin to what
Barbara Ehrenreich calls 'collective moments of joy' (Ehrenreich 2007).
There were also those moments too painful and less amenable to the
logics of words, but nonetheless storied, intelligible, and impassioned.
To return to James Thompson: 'there is a tendency to create a binary
between speaking and silence that forgets that both are part of processes
that many engage with at different times in their histories' (Thompson
2011: 67).

From story to expressions of silence, and believing in the multiple
dimensions of activist performance, I will turn from 'matter as the mother
of us all' to what appears to be its opposite: myth. Although matter
connotes substance and myth connotes the ethereal, my argument here is
that moving from matter to myth is less of an oppositional move and more
of a complementary one. Matter conjures economies of substance and
myth conjures economies of the imagination. They are an enlivening and
persuasive pair in activist performance. Myths are made into breathtaking
stories as they can be beautifully staged, adding symbolic and metaphoric
power to the message.

Myth of Sisyphus

> Myth functions as an affirmation of self that transcends the temporal
> [...] myth shows us that it is possible to relate ourselves to the grand
> and mysterious universe that surrounds and informs our being: it
> makes us aware of other orders of reality and experience and in that
> awareness makes the universe our home [...] Myth, then, is an
> expression of the tendency to make stories of power out of the life
> we live in imagination. (Allen 1994: 549)

Myths are performance pedagogues, archetypes of the senses, transhuman
feelings, and epochal histories of timeless questions. In *Labour Rites*, we
sought to bear witness to myth's questions as they reflect the trajectory of
human consciousness, play, and reason. We experienced how the virtuosic
performer and the virtuosic story can transport an audience to an otherwise
place, providing a glimpse of alternative futures. Our hope was that people
came into the performance space expecting to believe the performance, in
this instance, to believe the true lessons of myth and to think, feel, and act
our way past what we, as audience members, believe we already know. This
might be understood as a communicative experience of timeless propor-
tions that can both construct and deconstruct the present. The use of
myths is a beautiful tactic and a most effective performative for staging
social justice, because with performative intrigue and authentic complexity, cultural myths re-enact formations of power, public tensions, and
private intimacies; they shame and implicate grand authority through
vernacular pedagogy; they play with and magnify dichotomies; they embel-
lish the dramas of invention and conventions of signification; they unveil
the coding, encoding, and decoding of what is believed to be the wicked
and the virtuous; they untangle formations of desire. For us, myth and the
praxis of activist performance were a profound coupling. An example of
myth serving labour activism can be found in our performance of the myth
of Sisyphus.

Scene

Sisyphus and his selfish desire to live forever locked death into a cave for all
eternity. Since death was no longer active in the world, nothing died. Time
passed and Sisyphus realized that without death life was miserable and
chaotic: the cycles of life ended and with it nature fought for space; humans
struggled to remember the preciousness of love, family, and friendship; all
that was once of primordial reverence was forgotten; knowledge was

without wisdom and invention. Without death everyone and all living organisms suffered.

ACTOR 1: *Sisyphus bore witness to the tragic mess that he created.*

ACTOR 2: *His selfishness made him weary and ashamed.*

ACTOR 3: *He could no longer carry the weight of so much guilt. He was sorry.*

ACTOR 4: *He was very, very, very sorry.*

ACTOR 5: *Sisyphus opened the cave and freed Death from the iron shackles. Death told Sisyphus:*

ACTOR 6: *'You may have played the greatest trick by locking me into the cave, but you have committed the greatest crime against all living things.' Death turned to Sisyphus without mercy: 'I will grant you the mortality that you so desperately want, and that mortality will be the very curse of your existence'.*

ACTOR 7: *Sisyphus looked into Death's face and saw the truth.*

ACTOR 8: *'For this punishment', said Death, 'You will wish you were dead, because it is the most insufferable punishment for any god or mortal.'*

ACTOR 9: *Sisyphus, still looking Death in the face, saw the truth, again.*

ACTOR 10: *'You, Sisyphus', said Death, 'Are condemned to an eternity of hard labour. I will turn this cave, where you imprisoned me, into an enormous boulder that you must carry, with the greatest toil and exertion, up to the very top of the mighty mountain. And when you lift this giant boulder to the summit of the mountain, it will roll back down to the bottom where you must, again, lift it to the top. And you will carry this giant rock up the mountain for eternity, for every time it reaches the top it will roll to the bottom where you must endlessly start again [. . .] This is your immortal punishment of which there is no escape. You are condemned to the unending hell of repetitive labour'.*

ACTOR 1: *And so it was. Sisyphus must carry the boulder, with all his strength and sweat, mile after mile, up the tall mountain again and again and again and again in dreadful, purposeless, repetitious labour.*

ACTOR 2: *But with the passing of time, the heart and mind of this trickster that we call Sisyphus began to change.*

ACTOR 3: *He began to remember the magic of his one eye that saw under the tongues of liars.*

ACTOR 3: *He began to remember living in trees and singing to the night.*

ACTOR 4: *He remembered when he made life good for the good and bad for the bad.*

ACTOR 5: *He began to remember karma.*

ACTOR 6: *Seconds turned into minutes, minutes into hours, hours into days, days into months, months into years, and after years and years of climbing up the mountain [. . .] Sisyphus began to think new thoughts. 'I have been punished enough.' Peering deep into the boulder [. . .] He, now, saw himself – the strength of his arms, the sweat of his brow, but most of all, there in the stone of the boulder, he saw reflections of truths waiting under his own tongue – truths that reached higher than the mountain and carried more weight than the boulders: in every bead of his sweat/in every pore of his muscles/in every grasp of his breath there is boundless life, infinite lessons to be learned, metaphors still and forever to be made. Plots to be played – plays to be plotted. Each time the rock rolled down the mountain, Sisyphus – with his ancient determination – carried the boulder victoriously to the top. Each day was a new opportunity to say 'NO' to his destiny, to say 'Yes' to his imagination. A new thought and a different effort. When Sisyphus journeyed down the mountain [. . .] he reimagined his labour and he made it so. With our immortal trickster's self-determined will, every walk down the mountain became a newly imagined act of freedom.*

We brought Sisyphus to stage as a 'choreopoem', and our aim was to engage the sensual experience of dramatic action, unfolding across a narrative journey of compelling fantasy and lyricism, in the service of labour justice.[1] For *Labour Rites*, this ancient story spectacularized through costumes, lighting, vocality, colour, and movement showed the interdependency between life, death and labour. Here, the hope and prayer for long life is inflected with the paradox of death as a saving grace. And death ultimately serves life; life ends to create beginnings. For Sisyphus, the only existential tragedy greater than death is a life without it (without endings!). It is at this point that labour as work enters the story, in relation to endings. Death opens the connections between labour and endings at two levels. First, labour as unending drudgery is constituted by the hope that it will soon end, making the condemnation of unending labour an archetypal nightmare. This is what makes the Sisyphus myth so compelling. Therefore, when re-visioning the myth, I did not negate his destiny of

Figure 11.1. 'Don't Ever Cross a Picket Line'. Dance transition from sweatshop scene. Choreography by Joel Valentin-Martinez. Photo: Rafi Letzter.

unending labour. This approach of changing the plot or ending to fit our message is sometimes too easy and side steps the interpretive work required to excavate the deeper resonances and implications below the surface of the original story. It was not the *actions* of the plot or ending I felt at liberty to change, but how they could be otherwise interpreted. The intention was to excavate an alternative interpretation of labour, by placing Sisyphus in possession of his own body and destiny and in communion with others and with nature. As a result, Sisyphus's work did not end, but Death's power over his destiny did. When Sisyphus realized that his endless labour on the mountain also held the endless labours of living multitudes, he realized he would never labour alone. Sisyphus came to know that as these multitudes exist in their infinite belongings and procreations of life, love, labour, and story – and that he was with them body-to-body and dream-to-dream – each day was an offering of infinite renewal. The intervention was to deconstruct Death's punishment of labour's unending drudgery to that of labour's unending relations to be narrated and witnessed – nature and all its multitudes are renewed each day by their connectedness. Each day is guaranteed another tomorrow because of this blessed union. Our revision of Sisyphus departs from that of Albert Camus (2005 [1942]) in that Sisyphus is not resigned to the absurdity of his destiny, but finds his strength in the multitudes who struggle, resist, and labour together in the reclamation and possession of their own bodies and dreams.

Utopian futurity and labour

> Perhaps part of the desire to attend the theatre and performance is to reach for something better, for new ideas about how to be and how to be with each other. (Dolan 2005: 520)

In our utopian re-visioning of the myth, Death was defeated in deluding Sisyphus that he was of limited capacity. Sisyphus imagined his body and mind exceeding Death's condemnation, and he made it so. Sisyphus was not alone on the mountain, but in union with multitudes in regenerative labour. Our mythic Sisyphus had the same ending, but a different future. In making this activist performance, we asked ourselves, 'what is most needed beyond this "presentness"?' The question begs for an alternative future than what is now in the present. Jose Munoz states that the hope is for 'something that should mobilize us, push us forward' (2005: 9). He then describes utopia relative to futurity by stating that the 'utopian is not prescriptive; it renders potential blueprints of a world not quite here, a horizon of possibility, not a fixed schema' (2005: 225). Citing Theodor Adorno and Herbert Marcuse, Munoz reiterates: 'utopia is primarily a critique of the here and now, it is an insistence that there is, as they put it, something missing in the here and the now' (2005: 226). If utopia is within a present that 'pushes' us towards a multiplicity of possible futures – alternatives and potentialities – then this becomes a hope for a better world. Munoz goes on to state, 'but in this instance, I dwell on hope because I wish to think about futurity; and hope, I argue, is the emotional modality that permits us to access futurity, par excellence' (2005: 226). For Gilles Deleuze and Felix Guattari art can function as a 'line of flight' – a signifying and material unending force that both traverses and combines individual and collective subjectivities and desires, challenging common sense and normativity as it pushes it to the limit in its combinations and reconfigurations (1987). The connective, expansive, and de-territorializing character of lines of flight, as artistic praxis – conjures a politics of the utopia – a critical utopia that 'fuels the political imagination' and therefore enacts a politics of futurity. In taking up futurity, I move from excerpts representing the global economy of a sweatshop, to Sisyphus' labouring multitudes, to enter 'this present' and a utopic ending for labour.

Moving from the mythic to the here and now of daily life when making this performance, we remembered how many of us are still happy when we 'get off work'. We are relieved when work 'ends' and it is vacation time again. Retirement is associated with age, the accumulation of work, and the good fortune and freedom to retire from it. However, the end of labour is variously felt: there is the feeling for labour *not* to end while embracing the fulfilment of our labour; there are the devastating consequences when the opportunity to labour disappears and our security is threatened; there is the love of labour as an act of unending generosity and reciprocity to the earth and others; there is the owning and exploitation of other people's labour that diminishes their freedom, mobility, and so much more. Labour is a matrix of feelings and consequences where rights and justice are implicated at every turn. In uniting an ethics of labour with performance, the final scene culminated in questions around the ontology and (de) valuing of labour, while combining the mythic with the ethnographic.

Scene

In the final scene, reading from their journals, the actors covered the stage in colourful T-shirts performing excerpted quotes from interviews

I conducted with US labour leaders. The quotes were a mixture of philosophical remembering and reportage of labour union activism. Two large screens upstage projected varying images and video footage from the International Occupy Movement as words of American labour leaders were performed downstage. Towards the end of the scene, there was a brief moment when the actors re-enacted the Sisyphus dance while naming other tricksters from world mythology. The play ends with an alternative future for labour with new and culminating questions: can we envision the end of work? Can we envision universal base pay and a six-hour workday? These were the penultimate questions that came before the dance honouring the International Occupy Movement. Juxtaposed above the dancers were looming projections of striking images, from various Occupy protests across the globe, to underscore labour rights, in the present moment of the performance, as a universal cause.

VOICE 14: *My grandmother taught me a lesson I will never forget. My mother would send me to my grandmother's house during the summer. My mother was a hillbilly. She was so poor she would put paper on the walls to keep the wind from coming in. My mother hitchhiked to Chicago that's how she got here and that's how I ended up here.*
    (Actors change position on stage)

VOICE 1: *One day I heard my grandmother talking on the phone about a union. I was very little so I asked her 'what is a union?' She pulled out a piece of rope then she started to tease the rope out so you could see all the threads. She said: You see this right here? It is one thread. It represents one worker. Now, look at all the many threads, well, that is the company. But look at the way it's threaded right at the top and the way these threads are holding them all together – well that's the union, that's the unity.*
    (Actors change position on stage)

VOICE 2: *I never forgot that. The power is the unity: 'What holds those threads together'.*
    (Actors reprieve the following excerpt from the Sisyphus dance)

ACTOR 1: *Anansi,*

ACTOR 2: *Coyote,*

ACTOR 3: *Loki,*

ACTOR 4: *Red Boy,*

ACTOR 5: *Kokopelli,*

ACTOR 6: *Brer Rabbit,*

ACTOR 7: *Maui,*

ACTOR 8: *John the Conqueror,*

ACTOR 9: *Puck!*
    (Actors move about the stage in multiple directions and the Occupy images and videos are projected upstage)

VOICE 3: *A six-hour workday to Re-Imagine Life*

VOICE 4: *Base Pay over wages to Re-Imagine Mountains, Boulders, and Creation*

VOICE 5: *A six-hour workday and base pay to Re-Imagine how we Re-Imagine*

VOICE 6: *We will Re-Imagine Labour. When work consumes your life the whole spirit of your community is broken. Jess Kadjo*

VOICE 7: *Imagine: What holds those threads together. Buddy Bronier*

VOICE 8: *Why make life more difficult for children because you worship at the alter of ideological opposition to the union! James Thindwa*

VOICE 9: *Imagine: This strike wasn't about wages, working conditions, benefits [. . .] no it was about respect and dignity on the union floor! Edward Flowers*

VOICE 10: *A six-hour workday to Re-Imagine Life*

VOICE 11: *Base Pay over wages to Re-Imagine Mountains and Creation*

VOICE 12: *A six-hour workday and base pay to Re-Imagine how we Re-Imagine*

VOICE 13: *Utopiaaaa*

VOICE 14: *Necessiteeee*

VOICE 1: *Imagine. It's not just wage theft, but it's denying a human being the ability to flourish. Jess Kadjo*

VOICE 2: *The only consistent and stable person in the lives of some of these children is their teacher. James Thindwa*

VOICE 3: *Re-Imagine. If nobody keeps the embers burning the fire will burn out. Buddy Bronier*

VOICE 4: *We need to be in sympathy with them and show solidarity. Edward Flowers*

VOICE 5: *Throughout history the greatest organized force for change has always been about labour. Harold Rogers*

CLOWN 1: *Re-Imagine. Six-hour day*

CLOWN 2: *Base pay*

GIRL: *Utopiaaa*

ALL: *Necessiteee [in variations]*

Weaving the re-imaging work into the labour leaders' quotes and the final reprieve of Sisyphus, with the idea of a six-hour day and universal base pay, was to introduce and stylize (rather than demand and make explicit) a utopian future for labour. The hope was to leave the audience with the idea that a six-hour workday and base pay are worthy alternatives for reimaging work. In other words, a six-hour day and base pay are both utopian projections as well as hopeful realities for the future of labour. The performance claimed it, said it out loud, and aimed to set it in motion for further dialogue and thought experiments. For example, Thought One: Some have argued that to think about work as a naturalized or evitable activity is to depoliticize it. Is the real liberation of labour, the liberation from labour? (Weeks 2011). Thought Two: It has been said that capitalism not only puts us to work but also makes us want to be put to work, because labour is a naturalized existence that is right, just, and moral; even in a 'post-revolutionary world', we can't imagine a world without a job.

Figure 11.2. Lucy Parsons consoles her husband, Albert Parsons - wrongly accused and executed for the murder of police officers during the Chicago Haymarket Riot in 1886. Photo: Rafi Letzter.

Thought Three: Can we not worry and ponder over 'post-work' but instead clarify the logics of a universal basic income for all? (Konczal 2013). Thought Four: Can we imagine how a basic income compensates for the private appropriation of the common good, those goods we owe to each other that should never be commodified – our natural resources, education, health care, a secure retirement?

Concluding reflections: beauty as affect and futurity

> Of life's two chief prizes, beauty and truth, I found the first in a loving heart and the second in a labourer's hand. (commonly attributed to Kahlil Gibran, source unknown)

As adapter, director, and teacher my own labour was focused on making *Labour Rites* beautiful primarily for and with a diverse group of students and then for the audience. I was influenced here by the long philosophical tradition that aligns beauty with truth, justice, and futurity. The quote from Gibran reflects this diverse philosophical trajectory and also reflects where labour and performance came together in *Labour Rites*, referring to the magnificence of making beauty and the grand alchemy across acts of creation that labour beauty into being. Contemporary theorizations of beauty relate it to social justice and art practice. James Thompson, for example, underscores the power of affect and the value of artistic expression that is beyond discourse and 'outside a framework of utility and purpose' (Thompson 2011: 123). These voices, from their varying places, times and perspectives, add to the chorus of thinkers and activists across the globe who honour the relevance of beauty for making a just world. It was with this sentiment that we staged *Labour Rites*.

As performance makers, within the realms of embodied technique and symbolic processes there are political demands for performative beauty. We learn and get better, as performance practitioners and activists, in sharing more and different examples of our aesthetic methods and their contexts. As I share moments from an example of where labour and performance conjoin, I focus on the weight and substance of beauty, because in making activist performance politics and passion may feel ineffable and their excesses too painful or incoherent for speech and discourse alone. James Thompson states that silence is its own form of 'defiance' and that 'not speaking might also be the most rewarding place for a person or community to occupy at a particular time' (2011: 68). If silence is contextual and manifest in forms of resistance, and if local culture shapes the forms and acts of silence, then when performance honours local context and its embodiments, beauty may overlay pain through the use of metaphor, symbol, or gesture. Not to make pain disappear in plain sight of the audience (or to make the pain less political) but to make the contexts and causes of pain more intensely felt and more radically charged towards alternative actions and futures. Within this troubled present, art provides the coherence of metaphor and symbol to imagine alternative possibilities. If art is unforgettably provocative and breathlessly beautiful in its joyful and tragic expression, we discover that this expressive offering is not only a transcendent moment but also an invitation to newly formed futures. Art as performance activism also requires that practitioners pay deep and abiding attention, that we keep quiet and be still for a moment to stand in courageous love with what we do and with whom and for whom we do our work. The call here is to examine how we work towards the politics of symbol-making to unleash the hidden abodes of materiality and its structures of power for the sake of utopic love and futurity. Our passion for making the ordinary so stunningly extraordinary and for stretching social justice towards metaphor and embodied narrative demands that we respect how beauty and political action interact.

James Thompson's theorization of beauty, relative to applied theatre, emphasizes the importance of affect. Offering Deleuze's assertation that '[i]t is only in affect that the force of art can be understood', Thompson points to how art and affect are conjoined (2011: 124), and his comprehensive exploration of beauty, affect and theatre might be usefully mapped onto my project here. Attending to affect allows us to honour embodied ways of engaging worlds of experience that exceed meaning, interpretation, and conceptualization. This means the exclusive domain of cognition and disembodied paradigms of knowledge production must now recognize the power and intensity of felt-sensory ways of knowing and the emotional intelligence of bodily sensations invoked by experiences of beauty and the pleasure it brings. Thompson states that 'affect is the bodily sensation that is sustained and provoked particularly by aesthetic experiences. It is the force that emerges from attention to pleasure and beauty' (2011: 135). Because beauty is the 'intense affect' that we feel in our bodies, yet is invoked by a phenomenon located outside the body (2011: 145), we experience beauty as both an internal affect and simultaneously as an external object or experience. Thompson not only draws here on Elaine Scarry's discussion of beauty (1999), but also extends this discussion by addressing the 'intimate politics of sharing' (Thompson 2011: 155) in performance, and here the very act of replicating the beautiful is an act of communication, an invitation to share in the pleasure of the object or event. This is a relational engagement with greater possibilities for collaboration and sociability and here 'it is not necessarily a vision of equality that is understood but more basically a sensation of goodness: that there is something better than the feelings associated with the absence of justice' (Thompson 2011: 152). As such, the labour of making a beautiful thing, including the social and collaborative work of making *Labour Rites*, lets loose a 'sensation of goodness' that makes all involved in this labour political actors 'making claims of the new, better, more beautiful worlds that they want to linger as an ongoing inspiration for social change' (2011: 159).

On one of the last days of rehearsal, a cast member expressed his concern that representing the ubiquity, rights, and power of labour at the beginning of the show was contradicted at the end of the show by our advocacy for a shortened workday, and even labour's demise through base pay. We reminded ourselves that the play was not so much about inventing ways to attain more labour, or less labour, or the end of labour, but to illuminate how the world is ordered by labour, by who owns our labour, and by how we act, think, and feel about it. All life with a nervous system requires food, water, shelter, security, and communion with others, therefore they also require labour. But, what does it mean to make labour both (meaningfully) matter and make it into (embodied) matter? The greatest suffering in the world (war, torture, poverty, loneliness) is too often caused, directly and indirectly, by conditions of labour. *Labour Rites* asked: What are and what could or should be our responses to these conditions when materiality, futurity, and beauty are critically conjoined with performance?

References

Allen, P.G. 1994. 'Something sacred going ON out there: Myth and vision in American Indian literature' in D. Soyini Madison (ed.) *The Woman That I Am*. New York: St. Martin's Press.

Camus, A. 2005 [1942]. *The Myth of Sisyphus*. London: Penguin.

Chang, B.G. 2010. 'Forum: Introduction on labour'. *Communication Critical/ Cultural Studies* 7: 90–91.

Deleuze, G. and Guattari, F. 1987. (trans. B. Massumi) *A Thousand Plateaus: Capitalism and Schizophrenia*. Minneapolis: University of Minnesota Press.

Dolan, J. 2005 'The polemics and potential of theatre studies and performance' in D. Soyini Madison and J. Hamera (eds.) *The Sage Handbook of Performance Studies*. Thousand Oaks, California and London: Sage Press.

Ehrenreich, B. 2007. *Dancing in the Streets: A History of Collective Joy*. Great Britain: Granta Books.

Konczal, M. 2013. 'Thinking Utopian: How about a universal basic income'. *The Washington Post*, 11 May 2013.

Madison, D.S. 2010. *Acts of Activism: Human Rights as Radical Performance*. Cambridge: Cambridge University Press.

Morrison, T. 1994. 'Rootedness: The ancestor as foundation' in D. Soyini Madison (ed.) *The Woman That I Am*. New York: St. Martin's Press.

Munoz, J.E. 2005. 'Stages: Queers, punks, and the utopian performative' in D. Soyini Madison and J. Hamera (eds.) *The Sage Handbook of Performance Studies*. Thousand Oaks, California and London: Sage Press.

Nicholson, H. 2014 [2005]. *Applied Drama: The Gift of Theatre*. Basingstoke: Palgrave Macmillan.

Scarry, E. 1999. *On Beauty and Being Just*. London: Duckbacks.

Sliep, Y., Weingarten, K. and Gilbert, A. 2013. 'Narrative theatre as an interactive community approach to mobilizing collective action in Northern Uganda' in M. Balfour (ed.) *Refugee Performance: Practical Encounters*. Bristol, UK: Intellect.

Thompson, J. 2011. *Performance Affects: Applied Theatre and the End of Effect*. Basingstoke: Palgrave Macmillan.

Weeks, K. 2011. *The Problem of Work: Feminism, Marxism, Antiwork Politics, and Postwork Imaginaries*. Durham, NC: Duke University Press.

CHAPTER 12

The micro-political and the socio-structural in applied theatre with homeless youth

Kathleen Gallagher

Applied theatre projects often find themselves caught between individual versus community interests and micro-political interventions versus socio-structural analyses. The ethical and creative trials of applied theatre projects can become most pronounced when practitioners and researchers carry out their work within particular communities, in full view of the tensions inherent in attending to the micro- and macro-political meanings and possibilities of their work. In this chapter, I explore some applied theatre research from a shelter for homeless youth in Toronto (Canada)[1] in which these points of tension were particularly evident. Socio-economic inequality and socio-spatial polarization are realities in many global Western cities. Our interdisciplinary research (including scholarly, community, national, governmental, and non-governmental organizations) is focused on urban inequality and socio-spatial (i.e., neighbourhood) polarization in six Canadian metropolitan areas: Vancouver, Calgary, Winnipeg, Toronto, Montréal, and Halifax. Applied theatre, I argued to the larger cross-disciplinary team, would be both a fitting research methodology and form of socio-artistic engagement to get inside the locality of such macro socio-economic processes and structures. As the interdisciplinary team considered the growing socio-spatial inequality in Toronto, I felt motivated to make a contribution to the larger project in three distinct ways. First, I wished to strongly inject youth voices into the larger study, and conceivably some of the most marginalized youth voices there are: shelter or homeless youth. Second, I wanted to bring a drama methodology to this mixed methods study for its potential to differently discover and articulate qualitative stories, as well as engage in knowledge mobilization practices that draw from theatre's capacity to communicate variability and nuance. Third, I wanted to work closely with specific community partners (a theatre company and a youth shelter) to benefit from our very different experiences with, and understandings of, young people.[2]

In exploratory discussions with Project: Humanity co-founding member Daniel Chapman, we decided to work with Seeking Shelter, a shelter for homeless youth with whom they had a six-year history of work, offering free programming to their residents. This commitment is something Project: Humanity engages in as part of their mandate to make socially engaged theatre and to be responsive to their local community. Working with Project: Humanity, we used drama techniques to explore issues and experiences of spatialized inequality in young people's neighbourhoods. Methodologically, drama would be employed as a means for the youth to give creative expression to their neighbourhood and the negative attributes of localized poverty. A programme of theatre workshops taking place on Friday mornings over a sixteen-week period, deftly facilitated by Project: Humanity members (Daniel Chapman-Smith, Catherine Murray, Antonio Cayonne, and Andrew Kushnir), gave us a deep and sustained engagement with the youth. As researchers, we participated in the workshops, but also stepped back at points, allowing the actors to work more intimately with the youth. In our experience, slow and careful work with young people is essential for building a group and importantly contributes to working relations that make room for unrehearsed conversations and reflections. The relational aspects of drama are one of its strengths, and such work cannot be rushed or truncated. Working with homeless youth, in particular, requires this kind of investment of time as they often have less reason to trust or to engage with institutions or research. This chapter explores our work with one youth shelter population, paying particular attention to the micro-political meanings and macro-structural pressures of such a project.

Placing our approach in conversation with the broader field of applied theatre and homelessness

Acting as an important cautionary tale for us was a study completed by a researcher at Montreal's Concordia University. Hamel's account chronicles an (largely failed) attempt to use applied theatre to highlight the narratives of the homeless population at the time of a heated debate over the relocation of a safe injection site in a downtown Montreal neighbourhood. Hamel writes that she hoped, above all, to deconstruct normative frameworks wherein 'homelessness is often correlated with delinquent behaviour and poor individual choices, rather than being a manifestation of a delinquent State unable or unwilling to ensure affordable housing' (2013: 404).[3] Like us, she documented and analysed her intervention, working in partnership with a local participatory theatre company. In Hamel's case, however, weekly theatre workshops led to the creation of a public Forum Theatre production. In our case, neither Forum Theatre, nor a culminating 'final production' were a part of our project. This is a rather important difference to both the aesthetic and the methodological qualities of our work. In our case, there was never the pressure to take shortcuts in order to produce a final performance, and this meant that we were relieved of the burden to meet another set of expectations. Neither did we feel the adrenaline sometimes experienced as creative energy by those driven by such external expectations. It further meant, importantly, that we could focus on critical dialogue about process, a luxury not always afforded to applied theatre interventions.

Over the course of their workshops, Hamel's participants identified the police as 'antagonists', regularly (and often violently) displacing them, taking their possessions, and incarcerating them. A critique of police and policing practices was also a clear and substantive area of exploration and critique among the young people with whom we worked. In our case, we did not attempt to 'stage' such experiences but rather used Verbatim scenes to re-present back to the youth some of the spontaneous dialogues about the police that had erupted in earlier weeks. We then invited a new group of youth (the constitution of groups changed weekly) to reflect on the articulations of previous groups, on the subject of policing. Project: Humanity actors would create and perform Verbatim scenes from previous workshops and invite the new group to reflect on the ideas represented in the scenes. Here, the scene was really a launching point for further macro- and micro-analyses undertaken with the youth. In Hamel's case, the youth stories of policing practices were crafted by the theatre practitioner ('joker') for the final forum presentation, but she explains that the forum play was regrettably apolitical and individualistic. Also, no homeless community members came to the public presentation of their play; instead, domiciled spectators who intervened in the action and participated in a subsequent dialogue tended to argue that poor individual choices were primarily to blame for the plight of the homeless who would find life much easier if only they were better mannered. Clearly, perpetuating such stereotypes lacking in greater structural analyses was something we wished to avoid and was likely one of the reasons why the practitioners of our study steered away from culminating performances. The Project: Humanity leaders were even reluctant to jump thoughtlessly into dramatized scenes within the workshops. They worked as though the 'aesthetic of talk' (Gallagher 2014) was a very important element in any subsequent creative work.

Hamel's self-critical article constitutes a cautionary tale of how a 'legitimate effort to elicit reflexivity among ... participants in order to ... avoid antagonising audience members' (2013: 406) backfired substantially. It also highlights some of the challenges involved in transplanting 'a third-world aesthetic language of resistance [Theatre of the Oppressed]' (2013: 414) to an individualistic, first-world context, obsessed with its meritocracy myth. The article cites compelling criticisms of the Forum Theatre model and its difficult relationship with broader and politicized conceptions of social relations.[4] Finally, the article highlights the fact that many of these tensions and blind spots are further exacerbated by a 'funding climate predicated on an uncritical colonial model of social inclusion' (2013: 403). Despite being funded by a major national governmental granting agency, we experienced considerable autonomy and we hoped to avoid, or at least be conscious of, such asymmetrical research relations.

Where our work with the Seeking Shelter group may differ from more traditional applied theatre interventions is its foregrounding of social critique rather than individual and community transformation. While there may have been individual therapeutic value for some of the young people, our discussion of the larger project made clear that their work with us was micro-political in the sense of it serving broader structural analyses. Why might young, homeless, people be so interested in structural or political analyses when their immediate survival needs were barely being met? From interviews and discussions, I would note that there was something powerful for the youth about the idea of being able to 'help' other homeless youth who may find themselves, consequently, more conscious of the structural barriers experienced by homelessness because of the insights the youth were examining with us. It was not inconceivable that some young people in the group might also take some therapeutic value from the experience of creating, or the positive and respectful social climate we aimed to create each week, but this was not our primary aim.

The Executive Director of the shelter shared with our research team that she had observed a notable difference between the kind of residents that were commonly showing up at their door now as opposed to even two short years ago, summarizing this difference as 'much more mental health issues now than in the past'. In such a context, individual empowerment would matter, but we clearly explained to the groups that their insights would help us address large issues of structural and social inequality and better equip us to make political and policy interventions. In Neelands' critique of an apparent de-politicizing of applied theatre, he argues that the therapeutic value of applied theatre should not be mistaken for the 'socially transformative' (2007). In our case, we made central the structural analyses of our enquiry and invited the youth to take, with us, such a macro-analytic stance. Our commitment to the broader project helped to keep the social analysis of our experiences together in the foreground of our work and our research, as well as a drama approach which valued the aesthetic of talk and further helped position the young people themselves as theory-builders of their own lives and key players in the task of social analysis, as I have argued in greater depth elsewhere (Gallagher and Lortie 2007).

Taking up a stance more politically and artistically akin to our own and dealing with similar issues (homelessness and the criminal justice system), Jenny Hughes' description of The Men's Room – an arts and social welfare project that works with young men with experiences of homelessness, sex work, and the criminal justice system – draws from Shannon Jackson's work, and offers another perspective. The work describes a collaboration between The Men's Room and the Royal Exchange Theatre in Manchester in 2012. Taking up the idea of *reflecting* rather than *transforming*, Hughes suggests that 'the temptation to identify and fix is replaced [by] an invitation to keep company with, stand alongside, be surprised, and revise preconceptions' (2013: 145). Such efforts to make more symmetrical and dialogical the social relations of applied theatre research do not, however, comfortably settle our ethical obligations. Snyder-Young examines an autoethnographic performance called *Housed and Homeless*, by Minneapolis-based zAmya Theatre, in which she struggles with the best way to honour the story/storyteller but also to offer a rigorous critique of the story and bring it into conversation with a larger social story. She offers three possible ways to analyse an individual story: dramaturgically, contextually, or through a close-text analysis, ultimately deciding that 'there is a need for further study of ethical analytical methods by which they [autoethnographic performances] can be critiqued' (2011: 949). Avoiding appropriation is a serious concern for applied theatre researchers, especially given the propensity of applied theatre to engage with so-called marginalized groups. One of the ways we have found to refine our use of critical tools for analysing self-referential stories of homeless youth is to bring these into conversation with the interdisciplinary, mixed methods discourses of our larger project. Such an engagement does not foreclose the possibilities for a close-text reading but rather asks researchers to make clear what aspects of a story speak to broader issues of structural inequality and what aspects speak more directly to the creative practices or group-specific concerns and cultural discourses at play in the applied theatre group itself. It is not that these aspects never overlap nor that they are always clearly demarcated, but the question itself has helped us to think through some of the ethically troubling issues of witnessing painful stories and aiming to make some greater social good of those stories.

In another example of this precarious and imperfect balance between the personal/individual and the social/structural of applied theatre research, Szeman chronicles the Bucharest Youth Theatre's production of *Home*, a play about youth homelessness in Romania, performed by homeless/orphaned youth alongside professional actors. Szeman argues that *Home* effectively combats '[a] rhetoric of undeserving entitlement and complaints about the benefits distributed to unworthy Gypsies or orphans' (2003: 201). The article devotes substantial space to examining the role of Europe as a rhetorical symbol in the play and to a broader discussion of Romania's history vis-à-vis Europe but offers a comparatively limited analysis of the role of homeless youth themselves in the production. In Szeman's project, the youth themselves were not involved in the writing of the play. They were, however, invited to talk about themselves and their material circumstances in a discussion that followed the performance. Again, the question emerges: to what end is such an intervention working? The article applauds the effort, but reveals less about its effects on homeless Romanian youth or the social conditions affecting them, apart from reporting that the specific applied theatre participants secured housing and honorary diplomas from the National Theatre Academy as a result of their involvement. In other words, the problem was set up as a social-structural issue, but the 'impact' question came down on the side of the particular, local, and individual.

Szeman closes by asserting that *Home* 'is a strong statement about the power of theatre to change reality, as the production manages to reintegrate the young homeless outcasts in the Romanian affective landscape' (2003: 209). I share Szeman's desire for a theatre that might 'change reality', especially given the harsh realities for young people without permanent shelter, and I, too, value the 'affective landscape' and hold out hope for the ways in which large social changes might first enter at the level of popular discourse in order to later penetrate broader social policies and practices. Here, I think, may be an example of applied theatre projects that use the micro-political and the individual to address the structural and the communal, but making that extension of the personal story ought to be built, methodologically, into both the drama work and the research. Questions of impact (usually meaning 'effects' rather than 'affects') remain challenging. The affective impact of theatre, deftly articulated by James Thompson in *Performance Affects* (2009), insists that what reaches us through the senses is foundational to the politics of theatre and performance, eschewing entirely the notion that the affective realm repudiates political action. Thompson's argument resolves to some extent the binaries of individual/personal and social/political presented above through its repositioning of the affective register in theatre as key to both its aesthetic and its political force. Herein also lies the key to methodological sophistication: in blurring the clear lines drawn between social-structural analysis and individual emancipation, or the macro- and micro-political aspects of applied theatre work, the following analysis of our drama work aims to underscore their important mutuality.

The personal and structural collide/collude: a close reading of one workshop

A particularly challenging factor when working with this population was its sheer evanescence. We often only saw particular youth once or twice, maybe three times at the most. Sometimes a young person would be present for two weeks in a row, then disappear for a couple of months, and then return for another week, months later. The turnover was extraordinary. Each week, we were connecting with new people and trying to create a sense of cohesion for those few who were returning. At the end of the workshop each week, our team (myself and two or three research assistants) would interview individuals or small focus groups. I also interviewed two shelter staff. After each session, when we parted ways, we gave the theatre workshop practitioners a recorder to take home during their hour-long car ride back into the heart of the city in order to record their practitioner debriefs. Finally, we recorded our final debrief meeting between the research team and the theatre practitioners. Rather than provide a summary of these data, I will describe one particular workshop to (i) provide a clearer sense of some of the applied theatre and research methods used, (ii) take a closer look at the predominant narrative of policing practices as an especially menacing reality that repeatedly surfaced, and (iii) illustrate how the micro- and macro-political remained alive in the discourse. Here, I offer an examination of one Workshop Day – 2 May 2014 – when the social processes underpinning the criminalization of youth came to light through the subjective experiences of one group. But it also stands in as a clear example of the supple relationship between individual and collective concerns and the vacillating micro-political and socio-structural imperatives at play in applied theatre.

After a warm-up exercise, the facilitators would often initiate a 'value line'. This activity usually focused on a specific research interest (e.g., youth relationships with the police) and created an embodied discussion as a stepping off point for creative scene work. Frequently, when a point of interest emerged, the facilitators would set up an improvisation to see how they might further explore the issues at play. Also, these value lines would in turn create the Verbatim dialogue/scenes for groups to interact with in subsequent workshops, helping to fulfil our research interest in engaging in analysis with the youth themselves. A value line would happen physically in the room, where a facilitator would suggest a given topic and then invite the youth to take up a position on an imaginary line that best represented their perspective on the issue. Dan Chapman, the main facilitator of this activity, introduces the value line, which quickly erupts into a set of stories that launch us into the frames of reference the youth are bringing to the topic:

DAN (WHITE MALE):　We are going to do a police theme, to see what you guys think about the police. So on this side we will have 'police make me feel safe. I feel good around police, they're taking care of me.' And on this side of the line, you have 'police make me feel unsafe, every cop is crooked and they are about to take you down. Police make me feel terrible and paranoid.'

　　[everyone placing themselves on the line, including facilitators and researchers; largest bulk of people leaning towards the 'police make me feel safe' side of the value line.]

JEFF [WHITE MALE]:　I don't hate them, but I don't really like them either.

KAYMAN [BLACK MALE]:　Don't get me wrong, I hate the police. But they make me feel safe. When a police drive by, it's like 'yes!', he's patrolling the area, like 'yes!'. People see the cops like 'oh shit the cops' – not me, I love the police.

DAN:　On this side, Marakesh, where do you weigh in?

MARAKESH [LATINA FEMALE]:　I'm like in the middle. Yeah, they're out to make sure you aren't doing anything wrong. And if you're doing something wrong, you're screwed. But like, as a girl walking around here, I'm like it's late, it's dark, okay a creepy guy [miming walking past people], okay a few more, oh yay police! Alright, I'm safe.

DAN:　[to Keeji] Where do you fit in?

KEEJI [BLACK MALE]:　It depends on the police officer. I've met amazing police officers. I know of certain police officers – I just met one yesterday and he actually did me the biggest solid ever. And there's ones that actually got me in that situation where I was actually really discriminated, where that wasn't necessary. And it really depends on the officer, not just the police. You can't really categorize them as 'the police' . . .

DAN.   So Ramir, you moved [referring to his place on the value line]. What made
    you move?

RAMIR [LATINO MALE]:   Kind of what Kayman said. It's true, if you're walking
    in an area that's kind of bad – 'cause like I had problems with them before,
    the way they treated my mom before . . .

KAYMAN: It's their words against yours under every circumstance. It does not
    matter. And once there's 2 to wit – I've been in situations where they beat
    me up and I've tried to take them to court. It never works . . .

DAN: So let's set up another value line. This side – cops are like a gang, the
    system is totally corrupt, everything the police ever does is messed up. And
    on this side the other extreme – the cop system is perfect, all the systems they
    have make everything safe, the system is amazing . . .
    [some individuals move to different places on the line]

Clearly, the group members had some strong opinions about the police in
this initial introduction to the subject and have also had encounters with
the police that they are drawing from. None of this is surprising given the
ubiquitous criminalization of youth, and particularly racialized and poor
urban youth. It became quickly clear that those of us with cultural capital
and who are white were much less likely to have first-hand negative
experience with the police. Kayman continues:

KAYMAN: I fear nothing but a person. But a man coming to gun me down. If I see
    the cops, I don't care about the cops. They're non-existent to me, even if
    I have something on me. They don't exist . . . If they pull you over, ask them
    'am I under investigation?' If they say no, 'you have yourself a good day'. It's
    because half of the people don't know their rights as civilians. That's why
    when the cops come, they shake them down. Once I give you my ID you can't
    search me. You now know who I am, unless my name is in that system and
    I am red flagged, say 'must search', then you can search me, but if my name is
    not red flagged you can't touch me. You can't go through my bag, you can't
    go through my pockets; I'll call a lawyer right now. Once you lawyer up with
    them, 'okay you have yourself a good day'. I've had many things on me, the
    cops come, 'yo let me just call my lawyer real quick; let me see if this search is
    allowed'. 'Oh no sir, you have yourself a wonderful day!' and walk away . . .

DAN: A quick revert back to this side [the side where the police are seen as totally
    messed up] Do you buy into that, that if you know what you need to do-

KEEJI: Sure, if you know what you're saying. Like the first time I got pulled over
    I failed. He tricked me; 'how's it goin?' And then he was like, 'where you
    going?' and then two seconds later I was being pat down – I didn't know
    what was happening. That's when I was inexperienced.

KATHLEEN: What's the mistake you made that allowed them to do that?

KEEJI: I didn't know. They try to friend you up, you know, 'how's your day
    going?' He slowly gets into the aggressive, and the next thing you know, you
    are being pat down. And then your name's in the system. And that's the

system how they search you, check for things – 'hey you did that, so and so, you volunteered there and there'.

A member of our cross-disciplinary team, Scot Wortley from the department of Criminology at the University of Toronto, has published a great deal on the controversial 'stop and search' practices of Canadian police forces.[5] The even more insidious issue in Canada is that race-based statistics on police practices are officially banned by the government, in the name of official multicultural policy. In other words, such statistics are thought, in themselves, to represent racial bias. Of course, this makes providing evidence of the kinds of racial profiling that has been experienced by so many of the youth with whom we are working impossible to produce as evidence beyond anecdotal experience. Wortley and Owusu-Bempah draw out the implications of an official policy that turns a blind eye to race-based experiences with policing:

> In our opinion, the Canadian government's unofficial ban on the collection and dissemination of race-based criminal justice statistics provides an excellent example of democratic racism in action. At the same time that the police and other criminal justice agencies claim to provide equitable service to all Canadians, they systematically withhold vital information that is essential to the examination and ultimate elimination of any racial disparities that may exist. (2011: 404)

The conversation about knowledge of civil rights continues and I also, with macro-analyses in mind, try to interject some of our research knowledge into the conversation:

DAN: Is that fair that we should expect citizens to know?
KAYMAN: Of course. Especially if you see what's going on in your city. You watch the news, you see how many people are dying, how many people are being pulled over, put in jail. You guys should already know your rights. Go Google the charter of human rights and study that.
KATHLEEN: But, there are policies with the police that override some of those things. One of our researchers is a criminologist and he has spent his career studying those practices of the police and how they disadvantage certain people. You know the 'carding', when they come and say 'show me your ID'? So every time a cop does that to you they have to fill in a little form that they submit with your information. So you give your ID, and you've done nothing, and he says 'great [miming writing something down] good, have yourself a nice day'. You're in the system so that the next time you're pulled over by a different cop, he looks you up, and you know that term 'known to the police' and we always assume when we hear that when a crime's reported that that person's no good? That's all it means. It means that they might have stopped you on your way to a movie and now you're in the system-
KAYMAN: It's deeper than that though.

KATHLEEN: But there's no documentation that says why you were stopped and what the consequence of that was. So any other cop who reads that might be assuming the worst about you.

KAYMAN: They profile us. That's exactly what they do . . .

ILIAS (BLACK MALE, IMMIGRATED TO TORONTO IN 2012):   They stopped me yesterday at Coffee Time. A couple cops. Just like a normal person. I was drinking my coffee; someone came from nowhere and showed me his badge. 'Can I get your ID?' so I tell him 'Why? I'm just drinking my coffee.' So I gave him my ID. He said like, 'you don't look like a gangster or like a bad boy'. He searched me, he's searching my bag, my wallet, everything. And he said if I've seen people around, where I'm from, stuff like this. Like he said the people that have the Blue Jays hat, yeah the blue one, they are Crypts [a known street gang in Toronto]. And he been looking for those people around. I'm like, 'I don't know'.

DAN: And did he record any of your information?

ILIAS: Yeah. He wrote my name and that's it.

KEEJI: The reason they write down your name is that they just throw it into larger investigations around the area. . .

The conversation became decidedly more personal. In particular, Ilias' immigrant status became relevant to the discussion; at one point, Keeji explained, 'Yeah, it's hard for people like him. The cops know that he doesn't know his rights. They prey on people like that.' Ramir, another new immigrant, also interjects with a story in which he describes how the police confronted him in a park near his apartment building and said he 'matched a description' (because he was 'mulatto', as described by the cop) of someone who had just committed a crime. Ramir asked us what 'mulatto' meant. Catherine Murray (another theatre facilitator) explained the etymology of the term from horse breeding and described it as an outdated and derogatory term to describe a person of mixed race. Ramir further explained that the cops demanded that he bring them to his house and show them what clothes he was wearing at the time of the crime. Ramir had to bring the police into his building where his little sister was and into his bedroom where his clothes were. The idea that people don't know what to do when they find themselves in a difficult situation with the police begins to take centre stage. Dan makes a pedagogical decision in deciding to see where improvisation might take us.

Turning to improvisation

DAN: So I wanted to set up a cop training improv. We're going to have an interaction between two people: one person is pulled over by the cops. I'm going to ask one of you to be the cop [pointing to Kayman and Keeji] and the other one to be the trainer, like the side coach.

[Dan explains how the improvisation will work, the trainer coaches the person stopped by the cops in how to respond to the cop]

KATHLEEN: So Kayman, you are coaching the person who has been pulled over. Kayman, you know the rights of civilians?

KAYMAN: I know most of them.

KATHLEEN: Okay, so you have to try to intervene and help the person being arrested.

DAN: Yeah. If I feel stuck, I'm going to say 'need the trainer'.

[improv starts, Dan is playing the person getting pulled over walking from the subway station, and Keeji is the cop]

KEEJI: Hey buddy, come here.

DAN (TO KAYMAN):   Ah, need the trainer.

KAYMAN (TO DAN):   You can talk to him; you have the choice.

DAN: Okay. How's it going?

KEEJI: Where you going?

DAN (TO KAYMAN):   Do I tell the truth?

KAYMAN (TO DAN):   You don't have to. You don't have to tell them anything if you don't want to.

[Dan stumbles]

KAYMAN: [offering the line] Am I being arrested? Am I under investigation?

DAN: Oh. Am I being arrested?

KEEJI: I'm just asking where you're going.

DAN: What do I do now [looking to Kayman]?

KAYMAN (TO DAN):   Am I under investigation?

DAN: I just ask again? [turning to Keeji] Am I under investigation?

KEEJI: I just want to know how your day is going?

DAN: But I want to know if I'm under investigation.

KEEJI: No.

KAYMAN: Now that changes the whole – now you're good. Now you're definitely not being arrested.

DAN: Okay, so I can talk to him now?

KAYMAN: If you want.

KEEJI [OUT OF ROLE]:   You can walk away if you want to.

DAN: Okay, no I'm cool.

KEEJI: See the Raptor's [NBA Toronto Basketball team] game yesterday?

DAN: Yeah. I didn't catch it; I saw the highlights. [out of role turning to Kayman] It doesn't matter that I lied? It was an accident.

[everyone laughs]

DAN: I'm nervous! [to the audience]. I saw the highlights.

KEEJI: Raptors might take it. So, where you get to right now?

DAN: I was just going to go get some beers at the store.

KEEJI: Okay. You have any ID on you right now?

DAN: Yeah.

KEEJI: Can I see it?

DAN: [to Kayman] What do I do?

KAYMAN: If you're not under arrest or under investigation, why does he have to see your ID?

DAN (TO KAYMAN):   Ask him why?

KAYMAN: Yeah.

DAN: If I'm not under investigation, why do you need my ID?

KEEJI: I just want to see it.

KAYMAN: I've heard that so many times! You don't need identification if I'm not under arrest.

DAN: So I can like get up in his face a bit?

KAYMAN: Yes!

DAN: You don't need my ID!

KEEJI: [out of role and obviously taking his 'educating his peers' role seriously] No. Don't do that.

KAYMAN: You would be surprised by the reaction.

DAN: I want to poll the audience; what do I actually do then?

VOICE: (unidentifiable on the video tape) I would not get up in his face like that!

KATHLEEN: I would say 'I'm sorry buddy but I know my rights and I don't have to give you my ID'.

KEEJI: Yeah, that's what I would say.

RAMIR: I wouldn't get all in his face, but I would make him know who you are, that you can't be stepped over.

DAN: Listen, I know my rights, I know you're not allowed to ask for my ID, so I'm not going to show you my ID.

KEEJI: Well, what if you were lying to me? You could be someone else.

DAN: But since I know my rights, I know that it doesn't matter whether I'm lying or not, you're not allowed to – [turning to Kayman] did I make a mistake?

KAYMAN: He already told you, you aren't under investigation, so it doesn't matter who you are.

DAN: So it doesn't matter who I am, I know you're not allowed to ask for my ID.

KEEJI: You're being a bit persistent here and we might have to take you–

DAN: (to Kayman) What do I do?

KAYMAN (TO DAN):   Call my lawyer! Let me call a lawyer to see if you can do this.

DAN: Sorry, I just need to call my lawyer. My brother's a lawyer; I need to call him to make sure–

KEEJI: You know, actually I just got something to do at the office.

DAN: Wooooooooo!!!!!

KATHLEEN [INCREDULOUS]:   Is that how it really happens?

KAYMAN: When you lawyer up, their whole mode switches. 'A call, 10–4, I'll be there right now.' It completely switches. It's actually pretty funny to see them, you know to see a cop like on his toes, and now *he's* nervous and *he's* scared 'cause lawyers make them scared. Lawyers make them scared.

After this first improvisation, there was another that focused on Ramir and Marakesh being pulled over because they 'matched a description' the police were patrolling the neighbourhood with. After these two scenes, Anne Wessels, a research assistant on the project, asked whether the playful improvisation session had helped anyone feel better about how to comport themselves when confronted by the police. We had no way of knowing whether the information shared was accurate even though it was offered with a strong sense of authority. Anne pressed further, worried about those who might not have a lawyer to call and might be caught off-guard at a coffee shop (referencing Ilias' real-life story). Keeji informed the group that there's a legal aid hotline to call where youth can get a twenty-minute free conversation with a lawyer. Dan asks, 'so you just google Legal Aid when you're stopped by police?' Keeji explains that he has it saved in his phone and offers the number to everyone in the room 1-800-668-8258 and offers his final piece of advice: 'Just say I'm calling my lawyer, not legal aid.' Anne looked to Ilias, who quietly explained that he didn't have a phone, but would be getting one tomorrow. The structural becomes personal this time.

The micro-politics of improvisation: personal, structural, collective

From the transcribed debrief session in the car among the Project: Humanity facilitators on the way back into the city, we learned that they had equally felt some discomfort about the 'information' being circulated that day. Their conversation goes on for quite a long while, feeling their way through their ambivalence about what had transpired, both pleased that there was a kind of peer teaching going on but also uncertain about how correct the information was, all the while recognizing the importance and sense of social bonding (not an every-week occurrence) that the sharing of personal narratives had opened up in the space. They also clearly felt conflicted about how possible it is for privileged white people to not have to think so strategically about encounters with the police, our individual differences in full view. The day made utterly clear who is, and who is not, included in the Toronto Police Force's motto 'To serve and protect'.

At one point in their debrief, they turn to a discussion of their methods. Dan asks: 'So in terms of our methods, this is the second week in a row where I really took a huge left turn out of the value line . . . which [isn't] what we talked about doing – having the freedom to go where the discussion goes. But you [to Catherine] being there for both of them, do you feel that that's sort of a successful approach so far?' And after a long conversation about the relative merits of discussion and the relative merits of improvised exploration, Dan asks frankly: 'But . . . what worked today about the improv?'

ANDREW: Well . . . I felt that it was . . . I felt the stakes went up in the room because people were suddenly rapt with this encounter that they either have had or could have. And there was . . . I mean that's where the real peer–peer empowerment happened . . . like that was where you had Kayman piping up and Keeji was offering his insights and you know although less vocal, Marakesh was – I could see her going, 'yeah yeah yeah . . . that's how it goes . . . !' And I think that . . . you know . . . a discussion can get very . . . . I mean what makes it different than them talking in the common room right? Or them talking in whatever context they feel may be comfortable for talking about these things . . . what makes it different is that *we're using drama to make it, in a way, more possible to talk about things* or in a way to not spend the battery . . . .discussion can spend the battery, right? And-

DAN: - And we expand it too, don't we? Because in discussion, don't you only talk about something as long as it's cool? But here, there's a context where we're asking them to expand it as much as they can.

ANDREW: Yeah . . . yeah . . . I think . . . I don't know . . . it's . . . there's a . . . I felt that the improv in that context re-vivified the conversation and I think it also made more concrete what we were talking about. You can hear somebody's story and you can digest that narrative but what the scenes allow, or doing improvs allow, is it becomes a narrative that everybody has access to. Like we're witnessing it first-hand.

My sense is their discussion immediately following the workshop vacillated among their sense of the social goals, the pedagogical responsibilities, and the questions that linger about why or how exploration through drama makes a different contribution to a group's shared understanding of personal experiences and structural systems that they encounter daily. What does the heightened pedagogy of the improvisation offer to the group and to the creative exploration? Aesthetically, these kinds of drama activities are usually neither the most interesting nor the most sophisticated. But in this case, improvisation also became a way to extend the positive relationships that were being forged in the room, a way *to lift the personal into the communal.* There was an aesthetic to the kind of relationship made possible and a careful attention to the qualities of the meta-world the improvisation was building. There was a mentoring between the facilitators and the youth and between the youth themselves that was beautiful to watch. When asked in an interview how he experienced the improvisation activities in the workshops, Riche offered the following:

RICHE (BLACK MALE):   Yes! You have the workers, the team leaders and whatever, they build that communication. You can talk, you can laugh, you feel comfortable saying whatever you feel like saying. There's no certain rules, you know?

ANNE (WHITE, FEMALE RESEARCH ASSISTANT):   How do you think they make everybody feel so comfortable?

RICHE: Mostly, if there is a topic out there you kind of improvise and expand something and just bring it out there and everybody just laugh, you know it's like – these are good people. So you feel comfortable in the sense that yeah, we could talk, you know.

There is a further very important affordance I have observed with the use of improvisation, important to our methodological attempts to make productive the tensions between the personal and the structural: improv can make visible important contradictions (e.g., the police are a threat, but they help us too). Such contradictions get voiced before a more flattening narrative, whether pedagogical or research-based, takes hold of those disparate realities, forcing a coherence on them. As I've observed it, that capacity to keep alive the contradictions of their lives has been one of the most powerful aspects of the improvisation activities. Contradictory realities and feelings co-exist and allow a variety of meanings to circulate, offering the chance for a different reasoning, or a different analysis to emerge from the fog. In other words, doing improv allowed us to keep at bay gross generalizations about 'the system', or macro-political ideas, because the contradictions present in the very personal stories moderated such sweeping generalizations and allowed for a more thoughtful structural analysis.

Conclusion

I could conclude with a list of positive short-term outcomes, like Riche's sense of a growing community, that resulted from that day, or I could take the longer view and move the discussion towards the relationship between dialogue and embodied drama. But, what I am foregrounding in this chapter is how applied theatre practices navigate that vital relationship between large socio-structural systems and individual, personal, experiential narratives; the micro-political work of applied theatre is always challenged by this uneasy asymmetry.

Each week of our applied theatre intervention was its own culmination. Given the transience of the group, we found ourselves looking for small, important moments of an encounter worth having rather than an experience of a group that might result in a final performance that could illustrate the learning, creative and otherwise, of a committed group of young people. Our goals were modest. As an applied theatre intervention, we came to rely on the fleeting weekly moments, a positive exchange, a small sense of social togetherness, an appreciative laugh during an improv, the risk and pleasure of taking on a role, for a moment, and thinking otherwise. Making large structural and political interventions, like our larger policy-relevant research project wishes to do at various levels of government and in the public sector, is another sort of intervention entirely but, I now believe, comes to count heavily on these small qualitative accounts of positive engagement. Change, on a large scale, is a staged process. It is built from micro-encounters that shift the landscape momentarily, make discursive interjections, and together may amount to a different analytic possibility.

I could close by spending time discussing the merits and limitations of working from young people's 'real-life' stories when building plays, improvisations, or structuring applied theatre experiences. Kathleen McCreery's play, *When I Meet My Mother*, is just such an attempt to convey the plight of Brazilian street children to a wide audience, in the context of neoliberalism, urbanization, and ever-increasing wealth disparity. In an article, McCreery introduces the text of her play by characterizing the conditions that lead to the deaths of approximately four street children per day in Brazil as 'an indictment of an economic system that breeds violence and the abuse of children's rights' (2001: 124). McCreery writes that her goal as a playwright is to 'raise awareness' and better enable street children to share their own stories (2001: 126). She adamantly rejects the notion of 'giving voice', writing that homeless youth 'have voices, loud ones, and they can be formidably articulate. The challenge is to persuade people to listen' (2001: 126). The article goes on to include the (seemingly) full text of the play itself, which tells the story of a day in the life of a gang of Brazilian street children and the eventual murder of one of them as she is on her way to a youth shelter. Next, McCreery briefly describes her time facilitating drama workshops with street children in Accra, which resulted in the production of five plays based on participants' life experiences. Reflecting on these Ghanaian workshops, McCreery recalls the initial scepticism of youth, which she says almost invariably gave way to enthusiasm. In our youth shelter, we encountered some of the same initial scepticism, but in

our experience it did not always give way to such unbridled interest.
I remember, on the very first day, a poignant conversation with one
young man who simply did not buy that research could ever change policy
nor influence corrupt politicians. The micro-political, in his view, had
neither rhetorical nor real power in systems and structures. He did not
hesitate to point out what he felt was our naiveté and did not consent to
participate because he would not, on principle, participate in a study that
might be counted as 'education' for élites. For this young man, the micro-
political potential of applied theatre was not worth the cost.

It is also not a given that exploiting such 'personal stories' always makes
for the best drama explorations, but when the larger goal is to use reality-
based qualitative stories in the interest of large-scale, politically invested
social research, it is clear to me that understanding the complexities and
nuances of 'real-life' stories through drama can be a potentially powerful
research approach. And if our goal is to understand their lives, so we can
communicate them ultimately to those policy-makers in a position to make
change in their favour – notwithstanding the understandable scepticism of
the young man we met coupled, at times, with our own doubts – this rather
more creative approach to thinking on their feet about what they know
deeply in their bodies can have a very powerful effect both for the participants and for the researchers trying to listen carefully for the contradictions
and the threads.

Caroline Wake, writing on the Verbatim method of 'headphone theatre', also examines the method of depicting 'real lives' on stage. In her case,
though, the actors depict 'real' research participants through an exacting
replication, or aural authenticity, of non-verbal attributes like coughs,
sneezes, pauses, and hesitations. But what is more interesting about her
article is, like McCreery, her opposition to the notion of 'giving voice' in
favour of what she calls 'granting an audience' (2003: 332). I would like to
take this idea forward with our work and think about the ways in which
homeless youth become 'audience' to their own stories, the stories of their
peers, to a theatre company's ideas about what constitutes good drama
pedagogy, to our narration of research and its possibilities for social
amelioration. This precarious dance between personal story and structural
change remains central to any substantive discussion about the (im)possi-
bilities of the micro-political in applied theatre. For our larger research
project, a final set of interventions lies ahead as we look to create its
different audiences in scholarly, political, and various policy realms.
To be granted an audience is no small thing; to move an audience to
action, the Holy Grail. What I have learned are the significant gains in

keeping personal stories in lively deliberation with structural analyses, that is to say, making productive the tensions we perceive when we find ourselves caught between them. Rather than seeing the personal and structural as competing interests, we invited our research participants into the stimulating labour of probing the micro- and macro-political meanings of our theatre-making.

References

Gallagher, K. 2014. *Why Theatre Matters: Urban Youth, Engagement, and a Pedagogy of the Real*. Toronto: University of Toronto Press.

Gallagher, K. and Lortie, P. 2007. 'Building theories of their lives: Youth engaged in drama research' in Thiessen, D. and Cook-Sather, A. (eds.) *International Handbook of Student Experience in Elementary and Secondary School*. Dordrecht, the Netherlands: Springer Publishing, pp. 405–438.

Hamel, S. 2013. 'When theatre of the oppressed becomes theatre of the oppressor'. *Research in Drama Education: The Journal of Applied Theatre and Performance* 18.4: 403–416.

Hughes, J. 2013. 'Queer choreographies of care: A guided tour of an arts and social welfare initiative in Manchester'. *Research in Drama Education: The Journal of Applied Theatre and Performance* 18.2: 144–154.

McCreery, K. 2001. 'From street to stage with children in Brazil and Ghana'. *Annals of the American Academy of Political and Social Science* 575.1: 122–146.

Neelands, J. 2007. 'Taming the political: The struggle over recognition in the politics of applied theatre'. *Research in Drama Education* 12.2: 305–317.

O'Sullivan, C. 2001. 'The postgraduate short article searching for the Marxist in Boal'. *Research in Drama Education* 6.1: 85–97.

Prentki, T. 2012. 'Fooling with applications' in Prentki, T. (ed.) *The Fool in European Theatre Stages of Folly*. New York: Palgrave Macmillan, pp. 201–225.

Snyder-Young, D. 2011. '"Here to Tell Her Story": Analyzing the autoethnographic performances of others'. *Qualitative Inquiry* 17.10: 943–951.

Stapleton, J., Murphy, B. and Xing, Y. 2012. 'The "Working Poor" in the Toronto Region: Who they are, where they live, and how trends are changing'. Toronto: Metcalf Foundation Report. http://metcalffoundation.com/wp-content/uploads/2012/02/Working-Poor-in-Toronto-Region.pdf. Last accessed 8.12.2015

Szeman, I. 2003. 'Finding a home on stage: A place for Romania in Europe'. *Theatre Research International* 28.2:193–210.

Thompson, J. 2009. *Performance Affects: Applied Theatre and the End of Effect*. Basingstoke: Palgrave Macmillan.

Wake, C. 2003. 'Headphone verbatim theatre: Methods, histories, genres, theories'. *New Theatre Quarterly* 29.4: 321–335.

Wortley, S. and Owusu-Bempah, A. 2011. 'The usual suspects: Police stop and search practices in Canada'. *Policing and Society* 21.4: 395–407.

CHAPTER 13

A good day out
Applied theatre, relationality and participation

Helen Nicholson

In 1979, the socialist theatre director John McGrath delivered a series of lectures at the University of Cambridge in which he outlined his manifesto for a working-class theatre that would engage audiences in debating political issues. His vision of a popular theatre was inspired by the Marxist traditions of Brecht and Piscator, and his lecture described how his 7:84 Theatre Companies in England and Scotland performed in working men's clubs, village halls and pubs, places of entertainment that existed away from the polite constraints of bourgeois theatre. This form of theatre encouraged audience participation, and his book, *A Good Night Out* (1981), documents the dramaturgical methods he used to capture the imaginations of working-class communities using comedy, popular song and local stories that audiences recognised.

Thirty-six years later, the idea that audiences might participate in constructing their own dramatic narratives has spread to what John McGrath might have described as 'bourgeois theatre'. Contemporary theatre-makers are creating theatrical experiences that put their audiences at the heart of the process, making theatre in non-theatrical spaces that depends on the active engagement of audience members as co-producers of the dramatic event. Artistically successful companies such as Punchdrunk in the United Kingdom and Ontroerend Goed in Belgium use some of the aesthetic and dramaturgical strategies associated with applied theatre, apparently promising audiences agency and the power to make decisions that alter the action, or to negotiate their own way through a labyrinthine set of narrative possibilities. Often taking place in found spaces such as disused shopping malls, factories and warehouses, these theatrical experiences are designed to engage audiences in new forms of participation and spectatorship. This way of working has been commercially successful, perhaps particularly attracting the young, metropolitan arty crowd drawn to an immersive theatrical experience as a part of a good night out. Outside the theatre, participation has become integral to the cultural economy and to the service industries, where everything from shopping to museum visits is sold as an 'experience'. On the one hand, affective atmospheres are carefully constructed in the heritage industry as a way of encouraging visitors to imagine living in former times. On the other, consumers are seduced into brand-loyalty through shopping experiences that are conceived as good days out and marketed as part of the kind of consumer society Mauyra Wickstrom (2006) described as performative.

In the second decade of the twenty-first century, it is no longer possible to suggest that participation is in and of itself radical. Nor is it the case that tapping into local issues will produce either a collective political vision or shared social identity. Popular entertainment takes many different cultural forms, and participatory methods of theatre-making are applied to many different experiences and social imaginaries. This is not, however, art that necessarily lies outside political ambition; there is a strong trend towards making work that encourages participants to reflect on matters of social importance. The National Theatre of Wales' production *Bordergame* (2014), for example, addressed the pressing issue of illegal immigration as the focus of its interactive performance. Taking audiences on a train journey from Bristol in England to Newport in Wales, *Bordergame* challenges them to escape from the fictional perils of their lives without raising the suspicions of the Border Agency. Inspired by computer games, it is possible to play online in role as a member of the 'volunteer army of Active Citizens' who are charged with reporting any suspicion of illegal activity on the train. Infused with an enthusiasm for co-creation, this may not be conceived as a process of sharing 'political solidarity and cultural identity' with the working class that John McGrath imagined (1981: 97), but his namesake John E. McGrath, then artistic director of the National Theatre of Wales, was similarly keen to make popular, innovative and politically challenging theatre. The theatre has changed, class divisions have been troubled, and the lines between theatre that is 'applied' to community engagement and political activism and 'the theatre' have become increasingly blurred. It is perhaps not surprising that the affective turn in applied theatre and the social turn in the theatre, so elegantly described by James Thompson (2009) and Shannon Jackson (2011), coincided with the theatricalised experience economy first advocated by Pine and Gilmore in 1999 that has taken root in the twenty-first century. This is the paradox: affect captures social imaginations, and affect also sells.

My intention in this chapter is to chip away at this paradox but, rather than seeing the distinctions between activist and consumerist forms of participation as either fixed or politically paralysing, I hope to find ways to negotiate this tricky terrain. The title of this chapter invokes (and perhaps recycles) John McGrath's book, *A Good Night Out*, a phrase he used to capture the energy of his popular theatre that was linked to the radicalism of the political Left. I am interested in finding out how this history might be reconfigured or rescued for a new generation. By focusing attention on Good Days Out rather than good nights out, I am thinking about both places outside theatre buildings and the experiences of those whose late-night partying days may be over or not yet begun. To illustrate this debate, I am focusing on two very different examples of practice. Firstly, I shall discuss my experience of working creatively with an elderly woman who lives locally, and with whom I worked voluntarily as part of a network of neighbourly support. The second example, inspired by Jenny Hughes' work on poverty, reflects on the ways in which old workhouses have been reimagined as heritage sites and marketed as a good day out for schools and families. Days out can be educational as well as recreational, and I am interested in acknowledging the ways in which participatory performance practices have become embedded in the experience economy and might also be found in the intimate spaces of home. Rather than defining one as the ugly side of commercial capitalism and the other as emancipatory, I am attempting to think through how an emphasis on participatory experiences contributes to shaping the imagination and how the relationality of performance re-sites and re-situates the locus of power.

The invitation in this chapter is to find a conceptual architecture for applied theatre that both recognises its egalitarian intentions and emancipatory roots and engages with twenty-first century concerns. It represents an attempt to capture the political implications of a relational ontology for applied theatre, in which it is recognised that pathways to social agency are created not only through overthrowing structures of power but also biopolitically, in performative flows and rhythms of human and non-human interaction, and the spatial, temporal and material habits of everyday life. This way of thinking about relationality, as I hope to demonstrate, offers an opportunity to unpick entrenched patterns of thought that no longer seem appropriate to today's networked societies, and to apply theatre to new forms of artistic and political creativity, whether or not it is 'participatory' in the sense that it involves actively joining in. I remain interested in the ways in which practices are unsettled, not as a shock to thought but as a slower process of inhabitation, experienced affectively, over time.

Relational ontologies of applied theatre

Throughout the various histories of applied theatre, there has been a strong rhetorical pull towards the idea that participating in particular kinds of theatre leads to positive social outcomes that are felt and enacted outside the rehearsal space. There have been different languages used to describe this instrumentalism, each reflecting contemporary concerns; the nineteenth century social reformists regarded the arts as 'civilising' and twentieth century activists emphasised the 'humanising' effects of the arts. Ghosted by the idea that social transformation is achieved when the oppressed become 'humanised', it was taken as axiomatic that creating alternative narratives within the drama would subsequently lead to emancipation. Augusto Boal is part of this tradition and famous for developing an arsenal of games designed for 'non-actors' that served, he hoped, as a *'rehearsal* of revolution' (1979: 155, my italics). This pattern of thought has continued into the twenty-first century, where the arts are often harnessed to neoliberal ideas of self-care by accepting that cultural participation promotes well-being and self-entrepreneurship.

Contemporary debates about art and politics are often concerned to erode the ontological separation between art as an autonomous form and the heteronomy of socially engaged art. In the theatre, new aesthetic strategies and forms of performance have been developed in response to contemporary patterns of thought. Writing about the history and contemporary practices of collaboration, Claire MacDonald notes that the twenty-first century has introduced a paradigm shift in this aspect of cultural performance, in which the 'models of collective and ensemble working' that found their place in the industrial economies of the 1960s and 1970s have been replaced by a 'new and relational version of collaboration' that is responsive to the contemporary networked society (2012: 148). Although the collectivity of the ensemble aimed to challenge social hierarchies and widen artistic collaboration, MacDonald argues, it developed at a time of rigid class division and when a well-organised political Left mobilised collective resistance. Yet, as Michael Hardt and Antonio Negri suggest, in the twenty-first century, power is no longer primarily exerted institutionally through visible hierarchies, but is experienced in ways that are temporal, mobile and fluid:

> In disciplinary society, then, the relationship between power and the individual remained a static one: the disciplinary invasion of power corresponded to the resistance of the individual. By contrast, when power

becomes entirely biopolitical, the whole social body is comprised by power's machine . . . The relationship is open, qualitative and affective. (2000: 24)

The renewed interest in the affective qualities of artistic participation in applied theatre reflects this way of thinking and, I suggest, opens new questions about the relationship between theatre, social change and temporality. The twenty-first century cultural landscape is defined by a plethora of words that capture the non-linearity of biopolitical experience, vocabularies that might also respond to the post-colonial critique of Western constructions of history as progressive. Prasenjit Duara, for example, persuasively argues that many epistemological traditions in Chinese and Indian thought do not conform to Western notions of progressive and linear time, and his analysis of sustainable modernity is built on constructions of temporality that recognise that time is circular and that different temporalities co-exist (2015: 59–60). The prefixes 're' and 'co' seem to define the contemporary moment; recycling, relationality and reimagining sit alongside the practices of co-production and co-creation to suggest that the world is composed of multiple and simultaneous (his)stories, recursive and cyclical rather than dialectical and linear. The dynamics of theatre has potential to reflect this conceptualisation of temporality, and is often similarly defined by the prefix 're-', as Marvin Carlson has suggested, and recycling, re-enacting and remembering stories is part of the 'richness and density' of theatrical experience (2003: 3–4).

By focusing on a *relational* ontology of applied theatre, I am interested in considering not only the inter-relationships between participants but also the ways in which affect is transmitted and experienced biopolitically, and in relation to all forms of vital materiality, including the non-human world. It is here that the affective and temporal qualities of lived experience might become politically effective. Drawing on Gilles Deleuze and Felix Guattari's notion of assemblage thought, J.D. Dewsbury makes a persuasive case for change as an affective, situated and embodied practice as well as a cognitive process:

[C]hange is not just willed by humans but comes about equally through the materialities of the world in which we are just a part, and which, through habit, we encompass in the everyday, ever changing, assemblage of thought, intensity and matter. (2011: 152)

This emphasis on change as integral to relational bodies and everyday life invokes networks, assemblages and flows rather than structures and frameworks, made up aesthetically and contingently as memory, forgetting, imagination and perception. As such, it does not rely for its efficacy on action that is subsequent to the theatrical encounter, but acknowledges that the encounter *in itself* holds potential for new forms of relationality. Equally importantly, this way of thinking allows a more expansive and post-humanist definition of affect to take hold, in which it is understood, as Dewsbury points out, that 'agency is not discretely distributed between the human and the non-human; rather it mutually comes about in the immediate material constitution of any experiential encounter' (2012: 74). For applied theatre, sensory attentiveness to different forms of ontological encounters suggests that affective experience may prompt a disposition towards the political by recognising that human agency and non-human actants are mutually embedded. As Elspeth Probyn notes, 'affects have specific effects; it makes no sense to talk about them outside this understanding' (2010: 74).

A relational ontology of applied theatre has the effect of de-centring human agency and consequently exerts pressure on the principles of social constructivism on which many theories of the efficacy of applied theatre have been based. Social constructivism depends on the view that because social reality is made by people, changing the world involves adopting a critical distance from the 'reality' as it is collectively understood, and a process of re-shaping and restructuring its symbolic order. For social constructivists working in applied theatre, therefore, participants are invited to distance themselves from the world in order to understand and know it better. This is, of course, the central premise of the work of Brecht and Boal, whose political efficacy depended on a casual effect between theatre and social change. Cultural geographers Ben Anderson and Paul Harrison challenge this position and, taking their lead from non-representational theory, propose that social constructivism might be inverted in order to acknowledge that knowing the world comes from enactment as well as (or rather than) cognitive forms of meaning-making. Rather than seeing the world 'out there' as a 'meaningless perceptual mess in needs of (symbolic) organisation' and as an 'inert backdrop' on which human desires and hopes are projected, they advocate a phenomenological approach that recognises that all human activity is relational and embodied:

> Humans are envisioned in constant relations of modification and reciprocity with their environs, action being understood not as a one way street running from the actor to the acted upon, from the active to the passive or mind to matter, but as a *relational phenomenon* incessantly looping back and regulating itself through feedback phenomena such as proprioception,

resistance, balance, rhythm and tone; put simply, all action is inter-action. (2010: 7, my italics)

This re-situates the ambition of applied theatre. Rather than seeking to represent and re-order a (socially constructed) world, it acknowledges that life is constantly improvised and constantly in flux and that social change happens not only through challenging institutional structures of power but also through the relationality of experience, and in the unreflexive practices of everyday life, as enactment, embodiment and inhabitation.

Social change in the twenty-first century is predicated on a renewed impulse to participate; it is affective and contagious. New ideas and trends that capture the imagination can quickly spread and go viral, or get lost in the chatter of too much information. For applied theatre, the idea that social action stems from quotidian habits and embodied experience as well as cognitive deliberation enables a practical response to the ways in which biopolitical power is recognised and understood. In the examples that follow, I am interested in exploring how a relational ontology of applied theatre can reshape understanding of its efficacy and how a more expansive understanding of the social might include both human and non-human inter-activity and recognise their inter-dependence. By paying attention to how the smaller activities of everyday life accumulate over time, I hope to explore how theatre and performance might contribute to re-imagining the spaces of everyday life as part of the affective experience of a good day out.

Applied theatre at home: relationality and one-to-one performance

In the winter of 2015, my neighbour Mary was in her late eighties and preparing to leave the small rural cottage she had lived in for much of her life and move into residential care. Although she was clear that it was 'the right thing to do', she was finding the move from home to 'a home' bewildering and, without family, neighbours were rallying round to help. A relative newcomer to the village, I had been friendly with Mary whenever we met, but I was unsure what I might offer without being intrusive. One of the local farmers knew that I had worked with people living in residential care, and when I visited the farm shop she asked if I would help Mary select things that would be useful to take with her. This suggestion began a series of visits to Mary, first in her cottage and later in her new home, a recently built residential care home a couple of miles away. I was keen to give my time to people in my own local community, in part as a way of re-situating my practice-based research in a different political register; we may be globally networked, but we don't always know our neighbours. What started as a neighbourly act, however, developed over time into a kind of one-to-one performance in which Mary and I told stories, sang, baked cakes and sometimes just sat together. Informed by theories of care that value the network of relationships that exist within caring environments (Bartlett and O'Connor 2007), my work with Mary was not only moving and intensely rewarding, it opened new ways of thinking about the texture and temporality of place-based identities.

On each occasion that we met, I wanted to give house-bound Mary something of the experience of a good day out. Of course there were practical tasks to undertake, clearing shelves, moving boxes and, under her instruction, opening drawers and cupboards so that she could decide what to do with the contents. Often stoical and at times confused, Mary sorted her possessions into piles – sometimes forgetting what she'd done, and occasionally closing her eyes for 'forty winks' when things seemed to get too much for her. I shuffled things about for her a bit, but neither of us felt entirely comfortable with the intimacy of packing up a life into boxes. I felt the process needed a ritual that would not only allow Mary to remember the past and contemplate a different future but would also enable us both to feel safe enough to enjoy the present. Material objects carry complex emotional resonance, and Mary's house was full of a life-time of accumulated stuff, an evocative emotional geography. In his ethnography of a London street, Daniel Miller memorably describes objects as comforting and notes how they contribute to emotional resilience:

> [P]eople sediment possessions, lay them down as foundations, material walls mortared with memory, strong supports that come into their own when times are difficult and the people who laid them down face experiences of loss. (2008: 91)

There is fragility about objects that inspire this kind of reassurance; Sara Ahmed describes the feelings associated with 'happy objects' as contagious, but this is also temporal, relying on the embodied comfort of habit and maintained through affective social bonds with both people and places (2010: 32–35). As Mary was about to leave her cottage for good, I felt that my role was not to seek out 'happy objects' that would gloss over the emotional complexity of the moment. Rather, I felt that the encounter needed to feel creative in the here-and-now and that the process of moving house should recognise the many different emotional registers that are embedded in the material world and acknowledge how her home of nearly sixty years had shaped and archived her life.

It took time for the artistic shape of the meetings to emerge. Searching for ideas, I was drawn to the work of live artists who work in one-to-one performance, and it is here that the boundaries between applied theatre and studio-based performance are perhaps less distinct than they sometimes appear. The participatory performance strategies developed in live art are often designed to take risks and test boundaries and depend upon a solo audience member's willingness to concede to the physical proximity of the performer, sometimes intimate and confessional, sometimes a provocation. Critics of one-to-one performance suggest that it individualises experience, socially isolating audiences, as Jen Harvie suggests, in ways in which work and life become unhealthily blurred (2013: 53–54). Resituating one-to-one performance in geriatric care, however, draws attention to the demographic of the audiences for live art, many of whom are experienced cultural consumers and uninhibited enough to break the rules. Mary is no longer concerned with work–life balance, and I'm not sure that she would have been all that chuffed if I'd followed Kira O'Reilly's lead in *Home* (2009) by taking my clothes off and draping a dead pig over me, though she would have certainly known how to turn it into sausages. Yet one-to-one performance depends on relationality, and I turned to the evocative work of Adrian Howells for inspiration, and particularly to his installation *The Garden of Adrian*, first developed in collaboration with Minty Donald in 2009 at the University of Glasgow. In this participatory performance, Howells led individual audience-members through a garden designed and constructed in the Gilmorehill Theatre, taking them on an evocative sensory journey.[1] Although I knew my work with Mary would never acquire the richness of texture that Howells brought to the performance, his work enabled me to think through how the intimacy of autobiography can be invoked in a multi-sensory performance and how the experience of being outside can be brought indoors.

One of the things I learnt from reading about Howells' one-to-one performances was that they were always carefully choreographed, and the structure defined the emotional and physical boundaries for the participant. He also described the experience as a process of 'letting go' of the analytical, the self-analytical and the self-reflexive, and 'being really, really present, being in the moment, sitting with stillness or silence or whatever has been set up' (2013: 267). This approach resonated with how I hoped to work with Mary; there is a risk that all creative practice with older adults is orientated towards the past, inviting reminiscence rather than engaging in the present and imagining the future. Mary had been a gardener and lacemaker, a skilled craftswoman, and focusing on the sensory and embodied memory of craft seemed particularly appropriate when she struggled to remember details of events, and when her words became indistinct. By paying attention to the sensory and non-human world that had been such an important part of Mary's life, I hoped to find synergies between relational art and relationship-centred care. Relational art often creates intersubjective encounters between material objects and audiences, and relationship-centred care focuses on the interdependent qualities of the caring relationship between people and their environment, framing care as an intuitive and reciprocal process of exchange. This emphasis on relationality recognises that the body is a source of selfhood as well as the mind, and that, as Pia Kontos puts it, selfhood 'does not derive its agency from a cognitive form of knowledge' (2004: 837).

The turning point came one Sunday morning in mid-February. It was a crisp bright day, and the snowdrops were out in my garden and in the woods. I had noticed a small clump at the back door of Mary's cottage. Each year, she told me, they herald the 'passing of winter', and as a child she had gathered their bulbs 'in the green' from the woodland to plant in her garden. The snowdrop bulb became a metaphor for the possessions she was unable to take with her to her new home. Carefully buried and almost forgotten, snowdrops bloom almost as a surprise each year, and as we wrapped and sorted, it became evident that the changing seasons featured large in Mary's environmental imaginary. She seemed anxious that she would miss outdoor life in the rather small and antiseptic first-floor room she had been allocated in the care home. Inspired by the sensory intimacy of Howells' garden, I suggested to Mary that we might make a kind of almanac of her things, choosing objects and stories that would invoke each month of the year. Each month's collection could be gathered into a suitable receptacle, I suggested, and, as storage space was limited in her new home, each 'month' would be kept by twelve different friends who would act as guardians of her belongings and bring them to her new home at the appropriate time of year. Mary readily agreed, recognising that this was a practical way to keep rather more things that had emotional significance for her, and also providing her with a 'good excuse' to give away some of her more valued possessions as a way of saying thank you. For many older adults entering residential care, the move often involves a profound shift in identity, not only because social environments and daily routines change but also because their domestic spaces no longer reflect their life-histories. As Jenny Hockey et al. point out, the experience of living in communal spaces and cramped accommodation in residential care erodes a sense of self and makes older adults 'vulnerable to externally imposed social identities' (2007: 137). I have also found that residents' rooms often feel rather static because, unlike other homes, the arrangement of space and objects rarely changes over time or responds to different seasons. With this in mind, it felt important that Mary's transition into her new care home was relational, textural and sensory rather than inert and two-dimensional, enabling her to maintain a sense of identity and also constructing the circumstances in which she might respond positively to her new environment.

This plan gave Mary and me a renewed sense of purpose as we sorted her stuff. We started by finding suitable receptacles for each month – a suitcase for August that she had used to go on holiday, a handbag for March that had once matched her Spring outfit, a tin bucket used for gathering eggs, a pine drawer from her linen cupboard and a pair of old boots that had stomped through fields in November. With these containers lined up in the kitchen, Mary invited twelve friends to help her fill them with belongings or plants that invoked their seasonal theme, a relational process that sometimes re-storied shared memories and, at other times, offered her friends surprising new insights into her life. In her ethnographic study of older-adults, Catherine Degnen describes how 'memory talk' is often three dimensional, built on a 'web of relations' that, she observes, 'brought the past and the present together' (2012: 21). Methodologically, my role was to curate a relational space where creative conversations might happen. I became both ethnographer and practitioner, sometimes working creatively with Mary, and at other times recording her songs and stories. As well as providing an emotional connection with her friends, I hoped that the recordings would serve a practical purpose if Mary's memory faded and her speech became less distinct over time, enabling any future carers to understand a little of how she had lived. Each of the twelve collections had a different smell and texture, from the up-cycled jelly mould planted with snowdrops to the collection of souvenirs, sun-hats and holiday photographs in her August suitcase. It felt appropriate to pay attention to the temporality of seasonal change and to capture how Mary's everyday rural life was determined by it. What emerged, however, was not so much a reassertion of Mary's personal or individual identity as she left her home, but a renewed sense that her life was defined by a network of relationalities with the human and non-human world, a shifting social landscape and community that shaped her life.

On each occasion I visited house-bound Mary, I wanted to invoke some of the feelings of a good day out rather than encourage her to 'make sense' of her experiences or using her possessions primarily as prompt to reminiscence. For most people a good day out is best enjoyed as a shared experience, designed for the mutual enjoyment of everyone involved rather than for the benefit of just one person in the party. There are synergies here between relational art and relationship-centred care, where paying attention to the affective reciprocity of friendship, care and environment is integral to the experience. As Degnen also found, the identities of older people is not linear but constantly defined in relation to people and places that are both present and absent, remembered and imagined (2012: 21–22). Kwame Anthony Appiah envisions this reciprocity in terms of scale, and as a series of interlocking circles:

> It is because humans live best on a smaller scale that we should defend not just the state, but the country, the town, the street, the business, the craft, the profession ... as circles among the many circles narrower than the human horizon, that are the appropriate spheres of moral concern. (1998: 94)

My suggestion is that applied theatre has the potential to elucidate these 'spheres of moral concern', both in the aesthetic of performance and the everyday relational spaces of encounter. This vision of equality depends on understanding how human and non-human experience might be conceived as reciprocal, compassionate and mutually affirming.

A good day out and the workhouse experience

One of the central arguments in this chapter is that an affectual and relational ontology of applied theatre re-situates human agency within a wider political ecology. Cultural geographer Sarah Whatmore suggests that this form of social agency 'reopens the interval between sense and sense-making, and multiplies the sensory dimensions of acting in the world' (2006: 604). This effectively shifts the register from applying theatre to the constructing order (or meaning) on the world 'out there' to focusing attention on performative action in the here-and-now. I had learnt from Mary, as well as philosophers and political theorists, about the vital materialism of 'things', but the work also suggested new temporal configurations as the past and future became attuned to the relational present. In Chapter 2, Baz Kershaw invokes Paul Ricoeur's notion of the 'history of the present' as a way of re-imagining what he describes as 'the many shadows of *Homo Sapiens'* present day predicaments' (2016: 33). To explore this idea further, and to move from the intimate and private spaces of Mary's home to a more public and commercial setting, I turned to the museum and heritage industry, where the imaged past and the material present are recycled, re-branded and co-fabricated as part of a good day out. As Duncan Grewcock points out, the contemporary 'relational museum' is both ephemeral and material; it is 'connected, plural, distributed, multi-vocal, affective, material, embodied, experiential, political and performative' (2014: 5).

My decision to focus on the workhouse, one of the most feared and stigmatising institutions in nineteenth and twentieth century England, was in part inspired by Hughes' research on the relationship between contemporary applied theatre and the cultural pastimes approved by these nineteenth century institutions. Following my work with elderly people living in residential care, I have also become interested in the history of institutions that provided housing for society's most vulnerable citizens. Perhaps one of the most surprising aspects of this social history is that workhouses existed in the relatively recent past; as a schoolgirl in the 1970s, I can remember an elderly man called Albert who was born in the local workhouse during the First World War and lived all his life in the same institution, dying in the 1990s when it was a council-run old people's home. Each morning Albert caught the double-decker bus on which we travelled to school, always sitting near the door, muttering quietly and wearing the same brown-sacking coat tied at the waist with string. Albert's life is now, appropriately, memorialised in a stained-glass window in the church. Although I am too young to remember workhouses themselves, memories of Albert bring the past into the present, and it is this kind of personal connection with history that museums often seek to invoke. In many ways the treatment of the poor, the ill and the oldest-old reveals the values of society at their most acute, reflecting changing cultural attitudes as well as illuminating the material circumstances that shaped people's lives. Repackaging the world that Albert and his counterparts inhabited as part of a commodified heritage industry is similarly value-laden, particularly if it is accompanied by the theatricalised sensationalism that is sometimes a feature of the experience economy.

The museum and heritage industry thrives on the drama of atmospheric sites, often with costumed interpreters providing visitors with immersive experiences of historic events in highly theatricalised visitor experiences. The National Trust market their Southwell Workhouse as 'atmospheric', but it is the architecture, rather than the people, that is credited with stirring the imagination:

Walking up the paupers' path towards The Workhouse it is easy to imagine how the Victorian poor might have felt as they sought refuge here. This austere building, the most complete workhouse in existence, was built in 1824 as a place of last resort for the destitute.[2]

Costumed amateur performers capture the workhouse experience in events such as a 'Pop-up Pauper Weekend', and advice on what to pack in your 'paupers' picnic' is given on the website, suggesting that an atmospheric place, lively performance and themed picnics form the ingredients of a good day out. Much has been written about enactment and living history in museums and heritage sites, with some pointing out their pedagogic potential and others suggesting that it constitutes 'prosumerism', a blend of consumer and producer that is exploited by the cultural economy. On the one hand, as Jenny Kidd points out, participatory performance can invite visitors to become active interpreters of the past rather than passive recipients of knowledge (2010: 217). On the other, Silke Arnold-de Simine suggests, dramatised narratives of the suffering poor can create empathy which can easily become commodified and empty (2013: 122). The effects of these performative interventions on visitors experience depend, of course, on how they are constructed and delivered. But however they are staged, it is the place itself that affords its own cultural performance, and my interest here lies in the relational experience of the non-human world and its affective atmosphere rather than the costumed re-enactment of paupers' lives. As Jenny Hughes comments on her visit to Southwell Workhouse, 'I enjoyed the pop up paupers a great deal – but at times found their light-heartedness at odds with the harshness of the site itself'.[3]

I had chosen to visit Gressenhall Workhouse museum in Norfolk, a coastal county in the east of England, in part because it represents a history of the rural poor that is sometimes overlooked; it is the city that represents both edgy metropolitanism and social deprivation in the twenty-first century, whereas the countryside is often regarded as a place of cosy conservativism to which people 'escape'. Prior to my visit, I knew little about Gressenhall Workhouse itself, but I was aware that agricultural labourers were not immune to poverty and that the failed harvests of the 1770s, increasing mechanisation of farm labour and regulation of land rights left many rural people destitute. Many workers lived in tied cottages in the eighteenth and nineteenth centuries, leaving them vulnerable to wealthy landowners who could evict them at a moment's notice if they became too old or infirm to be economically productive. When I arrived at Gressenhall on a grey Sunday morning in early spring, I was immediately struck by the height of the perimeter walls, and the scale of its red-brick building. The looming walls seemed designed to intimidate, and it was instantly clear that Gressenhall was not conceived as a place of comfort on a domestic scale. As Felix Driver has observed, workhouses were disciplined and disciplinary institutions, designed not for the paupers themselves but for their management (1993: 4). Walking through a small doorway and into the courtyard, I paid my £10 entrance fee and sat down to read the potted history I had been given. Gressenhall had been built as a House of Industry in 1777, offering housing and work to labourers and their families in a relatively benign regime. The Poor Law Amendment Act of 1834 meant that it became a Union Workhouse and served a wider geographical area, and it was at this point that the high wall had been constructed around it and a more degrading and pernicious system put in place. Families were no longer allowed to live together and by 1836, men, women and children had been segregated into different wards with very little contact allowed between them. It survived as a workhouse until the repeal of the Poor Laws in 1948, becoming an old people's home until 1974, re-opening in 1976 as a museum of rural life.

When I visited Gressenhall in 2015, the buildings were being renovated, transforming from a museum of rural life to one that narrated its workhouse heritage. This change is significant, I think, in that it suggests a temporal distance from the stigmatised experience of being an inmate in the workhouse and also signifies a new interest in educating visitors about the experience of destitution. One volunteer guide told me that new exhibitions would show the dire consequences of poverty, explaining that many young visitors had little understanding of how people lived without access to social care or a free national health service. Walking round the site, the museum of rural life seemed to overlay the social meanings of the workhouse buildings, and I was struck by the cosy charm of a reconstructed village shop and post office that occupied workhouse buildings formerly used to accommodate 'jacket women' – unmarried mothers who were known by the stigmatising uniform they were compelled to wear. There was no trace of jacket women nor the vagrants who later occupied this building, and the well-stocked grocers' shelves seemed to capture a nostalgic image of comfortable community cohesion. Frederick Jameson famously argued that nostalgia turns social history into a 'stereotype or cultural fantasy' that erases the harsh realities of living in the past and, in turn, allows this idealisation of history to be exploited for commercial purposes (1991: 170). And although more recent analyses of nostalgia have pointed to its potential for social criticism, Arnold-de

Simine, amongst others, has argued persuasively that there can never be an 'authentic' representation of the past (2013. 54 67). In this instance, the erasure of the workhouse paupers seemed to confirm Jameson's view.

It was on entering the workhouse chapel that the museum's atmosphere seemed to change. The chapel was silent, and the stark wooden benches arranged in neat rows seemed to emphasise its stillness and desolation. The workhouse was organised around religion, education and labour, and I wondered how far the chapel exerted its own discipline on the paupers who were expected to worship there. The schoolroom had an obvious panopticism, with the teacher's desk raised on a platform so that he or she could keep the children under surveillance, but the chapel seemed to carry a more ambiguous set of cultural meanings. Perhaps this was social control at its most successful, with religion the opium of the masses, or perhaps a Christian faith did offer some hope to the destitute, the bereaved and the infirm. The afternoon light on that wet spring Sunday afternoon was dim, and I was alone in the chapel, without the clutter of interpretation. My shoes clattered on the wooden floor, echoing in the space that did not quite feel empty. The chapel felt marked by the lives of the paupers who had worshipped there, invoking Edward Casey's suggestion that some places have a 'power of gathering' that hold memory and experience long after the inhabitants have left (1996: 24–25). Perhaps Gay McAuley's idea of a 'memory site' is the most apt way to describe the chapel, where traces of the past are preserved, a practice that is particularly prevalent where there has been trauma (2006: 151–153). It was easy to conjure the repetitive beat of wooden clogs on the floors, the echoes of hymns once sung and the murmur of collective, obedient prayer. To me as a visitor, this was an evocative and atmospheric place, but for the paupers, a sense of self was inevitably shaped by daily humiliations and embodied habits of workhouse life, perhaps captured not through words but in their bodies, accumulating over time and constrained in ways that Foucault would have called docile.

In the old refectory, I spent some time reading compelling narratives of paupers who had refused to become institutionalised and were punished by officials, and the building became populated with names and stories. The Board of Guardians who governed Gressenhall kept meticulous records, with minutes of meetings documenting the diet, punishment and daily routines of workhouse life. Sometimes official reports delivered harsh judgments; the rebellious Harriet Kettle was described in 1863 as 'quick witted and intelligent', but her face showed 'cunning, the sort of defiance resulting from her long, continued and well-known wickedness'. But I was also struck by the compassionate tone of an inspection report

written in 1893 or 1895 that reminded me of the occupational poverty that is
not uncommon in twenty-first century care homes where elderly residents
stare blankly at a television:

> The old men were in the day room, seating on benches around the fire,
> watching it, a monotonous occupation in a dreary room. Does it never enter
> the heads of the authorities that a harsh upright seat offers little rest for old
> bones?[4]

Such archival records provide a rich resource for workhouse museums,
but the paupers' voices are still missing, their actions recorded by long-
dead officials. Reading the accounts was a creative process, filling the gaps
of an imagined past, and although new research is revealing a rich stock of
letters written by workhouse inmates,[5] I hoped that any future performative interpretations would recognise that these archival accounts capture
only whispers, fragments and glimpses of the people who once took
residence behind those high walls. Turning shards of information into
coherent dramatic narratives risks flattening the agency of place and
smothering its evocative power, and, however 'authentic' the enactment
in the museum, the paupers' words will always be interpreted by actors.
'We cannot extract a representation of the world', writes Grewcock, and
a relational museum is a practised and performative space, always
mediated (2014: 10).

For all its incompleteness – or perhaps because of it – I found my time at
Gressenhall Workhouse affecting. It afforded a form of aesthetic engagement that is perhaps closest to Jane Bennett's 'ethic of enchanted materialism' which is responsive to both nonhuman and human 'sites of vitality'
(2001: 157). Enchantment is, according to Bennett, a way of becoming
attuned to the world, inspiring an ethical sensibility that opens new
possibilities for agency. Steven Shaviro, following Deleuze, suggests that
this kind of relationality seeks to

> discover new facets of experience: to work out the notions and trace the
> relations that allow us to encounter aspects of the world – and things within
> the world – to which we have never paid attention before. (2009: 149)

This intensive relationality is neither entirely individual nor sociocultural
but, like the affective atmosphere of place, hovers somewhere in between the
ephemeral and the material, in the space between sense and sense-making.
As I left the workhouse, I noticed for the first time the long straight road that
led to its gates. The destitute must have tramped for miles to reach
Gressenhall, and it looked bleak and desolate in the rain. I shook the mud

from my shoes, but Gressenhall and the paupers' lives had entered my imagination and my memory, just as Its dust had entered my body.

Good relations and good days out

My visit to Gressingham Workhouse illuminated the present, pressing parallels with contemporary practices of care. Mary may not be judged for her morality in the same way as the paupers, but if she is fortunate enough to be offered creative activities in her care home, it is likely that she will be assessed according to 'measurable outcomes' and observed to see whether her mood or 'well-being' has improved. Perhaps social change has not come as far we might like to think, and although judged according to different criteria, the most vulnerable in society are still subject to surveillance. This returns the question to how applied theatre might retain its traditional commitment to social justice and equality, prompting again a reassessment of what it means to be good in the twenty-first century and how might that 'good' be recognised and understood in applied theatre? Or, put another way, what is the 'good' in good days out?

Each chapter in this book sheds light on that question, each looking at the prism of applied theatre from a different angle. There are recurring themes that mark the most important contemporary concerns: the social and environmental devastation; the effects of global capitalism; the erosion of local cultures and cultural memory; the treatment of the poor and vulnerable in neoliberal regimes that promote self-care and self-entrepreneurship rather than social welfare. Can theatre-making provide solutions to such weighty matters? Well, it seems unlikely, and there is, of course, no definitive answer to what constitutes a good life. But throughout this collection there is, I think, a renewed concern to take responsibility for how, as researchers, we perform knowledge. One of the shifts evident in this volume is that researchers have become less concerned with the politics of identity and more alert to the geopolitics of knowledge. Authors gathered in this book are raising pertinent and rigorous questions about where the research is situated, refiguring the politics and poetics of research practices by asking, more pressingly than ever, to consider whose interests applied theatre serves, and with whom knowledge and creative experiences are co-fabricated.

My own contribution to this political debate is to argue for reassessment of agency in a biopolitical world, where non-linear models of time and narrative are more readily integrated into contemporary cultural performance than modernist ideals of social progress as cause-

and-effect. Because biopolitical societies exert control by encouraging constant self-surveillance, there is a need for new forms of opposition and social imaginaries. My challenge to the orthodoxies of social constructivism is not intended to imply that all life pertains to a natural order, but rather, to erode patterns of binary thought that accepted the equation between social action and theatre-making developed in a different political era. A relational ontology of applied theatre has something in common with Paul Dwyer's idea of a 'slower' applied theatre, suggesting a new and affectual politics that might be understood relationally, materially and temporally, revised and revisited over time. It brings together the ephemeral, the technological, the environmental and the material, and in ways that extend beyond binary thought, enabling new affective patterns of relationality. It shares the same impulse as Spinoza's analysis of relationality, invoked by Paul Heritage and Silvia Ramos in their chapter, taking affect beyond interpersonal relationships and into a more expansive ecology of matter, flows, assemblages and bodies. Any answer to the question about what constitutes the good in a good day out is always and inevitably contingent, relational and temporal. Perhaps the most appropriate way to close this chapter and conclude this book is by revisiting the past, and recycling the wise words of John McGrath, who ends his book *A Good Night Out* by addressing an audience of Cambridge University students hoping to work in theatre:

> All I would ask is that those of you who do enter the theatre see every step as a site of serious struggle, which calls for well-informed and principled decisions. Then at least you will have created your own future. (1981: 117)

References

Ahmed, S. 2010. 'Happy objects' in Gregg, M. and Seigworth, G. (eds.) *The Affect Theory Reader*. New York: Duke University Press, pp. 29–51.

Anderson, B. and Harrison, P. (eds.) 2010. *Taking-Place: Non-Representation Theories and Geography*. Farnham: Ashgate Publishers.

Appiah, K.A. 1998. 'Cosmopolitan patriots' in Robbins, B. and Cheah, P. (eds.) *Cosmopolitics: Thinking and Feeling beyond the Nation*. Minneapolis: University of Minnesota Press, pp. 91–116.

Arnold-de Simine, S. 2013. *Mediating Memory in the Museum: Trauma, Empathy, Nostalgia*. Basingstoke: Palgrave Macmillan.

Bartlett, R. and O'Connor, D. 2007. 'From personhood to citizenship: Broadening the lens for dementia practice and research', *Journal of Aging Studies* 21: 107–118.

Bennett, J. 2001. *The Enchantment of Modern Life: Attachment, Crossings, and Ethics*. Princeton: Princeton University Press.

Boal, A. 1979. *Theatre of the Oppressed*. London: Pluto Press.

Carlson, M. 2003. *The Haunted Stage: The Theatre as Memory Machine*. Ann Arbour: University of Michigan Press.

Casey, E.S. 1996. 'How to get from space to place in a fairly short stretch of time' in Feld, S. and Basso, K. (eds.) *Senses of Place*. Santa Fe: School of American Research Press, pp. 13–52.

Degnen, C. 2012. *Ageing Selves and Everyday Life in the North of England: Years in the Making*. Manchester: Manchester University Press.

Dewsbury, J.D. 2011 'The Deleuze-Guattarian assemblage: Plastic habits'. *Area* 4: 148–153.

Dewsbury, J.D. 2012. 'Affective habit ecologies: Material dispositions and imma-nent inhabitations'. *Performance Research: On Ecology* 17.4: 74–82.

Driver, F. 1993. *Power and Pauperism: The Workhouse System, 1834–1884*. Cambridge: Cambridge University Press.

Duara, P. 2015. *The Crisis of Global Modernity: Asian Traditions and a Sustainable Future*. Cambridge: Cambridge University Press.

Grewcock, D. (ed.) 2014. *Doing Museology Differently*. London: Routledge.

Hardt, M. and Negri, A. 2000. *Empire*. Cambridge, MA: Harvard University Press.

Harvie, J. 2013. *Fair Play: Art, Performance and Neoliberalism*. Basingstoke: Palgrave Macmillan.

Heddon, D. 2016. 'The cultivation of listening: an ensemble of more-than-human participants' in Harpin, A. and Nicholson, H. (eds.) *Performance and Participation: Practices, Audiences, Politics*. London: Palgrave Macmillan.

Hockey, J., Penhale, B. and Sibley, D. 2007. 'Environments of memory: Home space, later life and grief' in Davidson, J. Bondi, L. and Smith, M. (eds.) *Emotional Geographies*. Aldershot: Ashgate Press, pp. 135–146.

Howells, A. 2013. 'The epic in the intimate' in Machon, J. (ed.) *Immersive Theatres: Intimacy and Immediacy in Contemporary Performance*. Basingstoke: Palgrave Macmillan, pp. 260–267.

Jackson, A. and Kidd, J. (eds.) 2011. *Performing Heritage: Research, Practice and Innovation in Museum Theatre and Live Interpretation*. Manchester: Manchester University Press.

Jackson, S. 2011. *Social Works: Performing Art, Supporting Publics*. London: Routledge.

Jameson, F. 1991. *Postmodernism or, the Cultural Logic of Late Capitalism*. London: Verso.

Kontos, P.C. 2004. 'Ethnographic reflections on selfhood, embodiment and Alzheimer's disease'. *Ageing and Society* 24.6: 829–849.

Kidd, J. 2010. '"The costume of openness": Heritage performance as a participatory cultural practice' in Jackson and Kidd, pp. 204–219.

MacDonald, C. 2012. 'All together now: Performance and collaboration' in Heddon, D. and Klein, J. (eds.) *Histories and Practices of Live Art*. Basingstoke: Palgrave Macmillan, pp. 148–174.

McAuley, G. 2006. *Unstable Ground: Performance and the Politics of Place*. London: Peter Lang.

McGrath, J. 1981. *A Good Night Out*. London: Nick Hern Books.

Miller, D. 2008. *The Comfort of Things*. Cambridge: Polity Press.

Probyn, E. 2010. 'Writing shame' in Gregg, M. and G. Seigworth (eds.) *The Affect Theory Reader*. New York: Duke University Press, pp. 71–90.

Shaviro, S. 2009. *Without Criteria: Kant, Whitehead, Deleuze, and Aesthetics*. Cambridge, MA: The MIT Press.

Thompson, J. 2009. *Performance Affects: Applied Theatre and the End of Effect*. Basingstoke: Palgrave Macmillan.

Whatmore, S. 2006. 'Materialist returns: Practising cultural geography in and for a more-than-human world'. *Cultural Geographies* 13: 600–609.

Wickstrom, M. 2006. *Performing Consumers: Global Capital and its Theatrical Seductions*. London: Routledge.

Notes

1 Applied theatre

1. www.liberatetate.org.uk/performances/time-piece/. Last accessed 29 July 2015.

3 A pre-history of applied theatre

1. The Band of Hope is still in operation – renamed Hope UK in 1995, it delivers drug and alcohol education to young people.

6 Performing location

1. Margaret Ames and Mike Pearson from Aberystwyth University were co-investigators on Challenging Place, working with company Cyrff Ystwyth in Aberystwyth, Wales. The website for interested practitioners/researchers is www.performingplaces.org. For the work with lighting gels explored below, see '2: Gels' at www.performingplaces.org/placepracopenotw.html. For the indoor market, see '5: Market Performance', www.performingplaces.org/place pracstudiootw.html. Last accessed 8 July 2015
2. See www.inplaceofwar.net. Last accessed 27 July 2015.
3. For the 2007 report see www.ipcc.ch/publications_and_data/ar4/syr/en/spm s4.html. For the 2014 report see www.ipcc.ch/report/ar5/wg2/. Last accessed 27 July 2015.

7 Peacebuilding performances in the aftermath of war

1. The key NGOs that I have liaised with during this research are Peace Foundation Melanesia (in particular through Br Pat Howley, Gary McPherson, Rhoda Belden, Clarence Dency and Andrew Kuiai), the Nazareth Centre for Rehabilitation (Sr Lorraine Garasu) and the Hako Women's Collective (Marilyn Taleo Havini), although other individuals – many more than I will have cause to name in this essay – have provided invaluable advice.

2. There is not the space here to offer anything like a full account of the factors leading up to the war on Bougainville and, needless to say, the history of what took place during the conflict is contested. For more details, see Braithwaite et al. (2010); Dorney (1998); Howley (2002); Sirivi and Havini (2004). On any account, the 'grizzly algebra' of the war makes for bleak reading. Estimates for the number of lives lost generally range between 5,000 and 20,000 in a population that numbered around 160,000 before the war. The discrepancies partly relate to whether or not one includes preventable deaths owing to the withdrawal of medical supplies and services during the blockade imposed by PNG. Beyond the number of deaths, there are also, of course, the unfathomable consequences of widespread torture, including rape, internal displacement and loss of livelihoods. Approximately 60,000 Bougainvilleans were forced out of their villages and a generation of young people (those upon whom the future of the Bougainville Peace Agreement increasingly rests) went without formal education for a decade.

3. I have argued elsewhere (Dwyer 2007) that Boal's 'method of theatre therapy' – the Rainbow of Desire techniques – is steeped in a similar style of psychodynamic theory to that which characterises much of the literature on trauma therapy and that there is potential for productively re-aligning these techniques within a more systemic, narrative therapy framework.

4. Native English speakers can acquire a basic knowledge of *Tok Pisin* in a matter of weeks, although to be able to speak fluently and with nuance takes considerably longer. In addition to *Tok Pisin*, there are dozens of distinct and highly complex local languages which I have not been able to learn. Many of these are Austronesian languages which provide part of the sub-stratum for *Tok Pisin* and use a similar grammar of in/exclusivity.

5. There are many variations in the way that reconciliations are carried out among the different language groups and cultures of Bougainville but useful introductions are provided by Boege and Garasu (2011), Howley (2002) and Tanis (2002). *Breaking Bows and Arrows*, the award-winning documentary film by Liz Thompson (2001), is another invaluable source.

6. Readers who are interested in the production history of *The Bougainville Photoplay Project* will find details on the website of Version 1.0, the company with which I was a dramaturg on a number of verbatim/documentary works between 2004 and 2012 (www.versiononepointzero.com/index.php/projects/t he_bougainville_photoplay_project). The *Photoplay* was directed by David Williams, with video design by Sean Bacon and technical assistance from Russell Emerson. The show was performed over sixty times between 2008 and 2011, with two three-week seasons in Sydney theatres as well as short tours to Melbourne, Brisbane, Darwin, Perth and Launceston. As well as supporting

the reconciliation in Hari, I donated my performance fees to Buka District Hospital and the Young Ambassadors for Peace project in South Bougainville.

7. The notion of 'cultural barter' is, of course, associated with Eugenio Barba, the director of Odin Teatret, although, in his usage, the emphasis is on trading in and through performance as a purely symbolic gift exchange. He does not envisage, as Pierre Bourdieu would have it, the possibility for conversion of symbolic and cultural capital into economic capital (and vice versa). The denial of this dimension of trade arguably betrays an elitist strain in Barba's formulation.

8. 'Stumble stone' is borrowed from the German term, *Stolpersteine*, which is used to describe a slightly raised cobblestone, topped by a brass nameplate, that has become a way of memorialising victims of the Holocaust.

11 Staging *Labour Rites*

1. Joel Valentin-Martinez choreographed all the dances. It was his artistic vision and use of movement and embodied interpretation that created the beauty and narrative power of the show.

12 The micro-political and the socio-structural in applied theatre with homeless youth

1. The research is part of a seven-year, multi-disciplinary Social Science and Humanities Research Council of Canada-funded National Partnership Grant, *Neighbourhood Inequality, Diversity, and Change: Trends, Processes, Consequences, and Policy Options for Canada's Large Metropolitan Areas.*

2. My deepest appreciation to my community partners Project: Humanity and Seeking Shelter (pseudonym) and also to my research assistants, Anne Wessels, Rebecca Starkman, and Dirk Rodricks, for their research instincts and their deep knowledge of theatre and youth.

3. This thinking is very consistent with our study. In their report on the 'working poor' of Toronto, Stappleton, Murphy, and Xing demonstrated how the inner suburbs of Toronto (where our youth shelter is located) are home to concentrated levels of poverty among residents who are often working multiple, precarious, low-paying jobs, and struggling to earn enough to afford their inflated rent (2012: 33).

4. See also O'Sullivan (2001), Neelands (2007), and Prentki (2012).

5. Wortley and Owusu-Bempah (2011), using self-reporting by Toronto residents, argue that black respondents are more likely to view racial profiling as a major problem in Canada than whites or Asians. Racial differences in police stop and

search experiences remain statistically significant after controlling for relevant factors.

13 A good day out

1. For a beautifully evocative analysis of Adrian Howells' work, see Heddon, D. 2016. 'The cultivation of listening: An ensemble of more-than-human participants' in A. Harpin and H. Nicholson (eds.) *Performance and Participation: Practices, Audiences, Politics.* London Palgrave Macmillan.
2. See www.nationaltrust.org.uk/workhouse-southwell. Last accessed 27 July 2015.
3. http://blog.poortheatres.manchester.ac.uk/pop-up-paupers-pathways-and-pa uper-mice-at-the-workhouse-southwell/. Last accessed 15 June 2015.
4. All citations taken from information folders at Gressenhall Workhouse, visited 29 March 2015.
5. The University of Leicester, Steven King. '"Rhetoricising poverty": A comparison of pauper narratives in Britain and Germany 1753–1930'. Funded jointly by the Arts and Humanities Research Council and the German Research Foundation.

Index

/Xam culture, 36, 193

A Fine Old English Gentlemen, song, 48
activist performance, 212, 215, 216, 218,
    221, 226
aesthetic
    aesthetic dimension of arts-based
        peacebuilding, 131
    aesthetic of talk, 10, 231, 233
    aesthetic pleasure, 183
    aesthetic strategies, 251
    aesthetics of duration, 10
affect, 216, 253
    affect and beauty, 227
    affective atmospheres, 249
    affective register, 10, 235
    affective turn, 131
AfroReggae, Brazil, 89, 90
Agamben, G., 15
agency
    human and non-human agency, 253
Ahmed, S., 255
Ames, M., 119
Amin, A., 110, 115, 122
Amit, A., 16
Anderson, B. and Harrison, P., 253
Appadurai, A., 120
Appiah, K.A., 259
Arendt, H., 197, 199, 202, 207, 208
Arnold-de Simine, S., 261, 263
Artaud, A., 98
artistic occupation, 87, 92
arts-based peacebuilding work, 129
Ashley, D., 16
Asif, S., 162
assemblage thought, 252
Assmann, J. and Czaplicka, J., 70
atmosphere
    atmospheric sites, 260
authority, 10, 193, 195
    redistributing authority, 201–204
autoethnographic performances, 233

Bailey, P., 44
Balfour, M., 134
Balkan States, 30
Band of Hope, 49–52, 54
Bangladesh, 11, 150–168
Barish, J., 45
Barnes, S., 121
Barrett, W., 48
Bartlett, R. and O'Connor, D., 255
Baxter, V., 183
Bayer, K., 180
Bennett, J., 9, 18, 264
binary thought, 266
    binary divisions, 34
    binary opposition, 136
biopolitics
    biopolitical power, 254
    biopolitical societies, 266
Blast Theory, UK, 122
Bleek and Lloyd Collection, 193
Blencowe, C., 202, 203, 204, 209
Boal, A., 21, 24, 101, 127, 251, 253
    Forum Theatre, 67, 129, 130, 134, 135, 146, 181,
        231, 232
    Theatre of the Oppressed, 120, 127, 232
Boege, V., 146
Bolton, G., 43
Bosnia
    Bosnian conflict, 179
Bourdieu, P., 71
Bradford, UK, 114
Brecht, B., 21, 33, 101, 248, 253
Breed, A., 132
Bucharest Youth Theatre, Romania, 234–235
Bundy, P., 23
Burnley, UK, 114
Butler, C., 16
Butler, J., 42
Byam, L. Dale, 23

Calvino, I., 61
Cantle, T., 115

273